INTERRACIAL AMERICA
OPPOSING VIEWPOINTS®

Other Books of Related Interest

Opposing Viewpoints Series

Adoption
American Values
America's Children
America's Cities
America's Prisons
Culture Wars
The Family in America
Gangs
Immigration
Islam
Population
Race Relations
Social Justice

Current Controversies Series

Hate Crimes
Illegal Immigration
Nationalism and Ethnic Conflict
Youth Violence

At Issue Series

Affirmative Action
Ethnic Conflict
Immigration Policy

American History Series

The Civil Rights Movement
The Civil War
Immigration
Reconstruction
Slavery

INTERRACIAL AMERICA
OPPOSING VIEWPOINTS®

David Bender & Bruno Leone, *Series Editors*

Bonnie Szumski, *Book Editor*

OPPOSING VIEWPOINTS® SERIES

Greenhaven Press, Inc., San Diego, CA

Greenhaven Press, Inc.
PO Box 289009
San Diego, CA 92198-9009

Library of Congress Cataloging-in-Publication Data

Interracial America : opposing viewpoints / Bonnie Szumski,
    book editor.
        p.   cm. — (Opposing viewpoints series)
    Includes bibliographical references and index.
    ISBN 1-56510-392-0 (pbk. : alk. paper). —
ISBN 1-56510-393-9 (lib. bdg. : alk. paper)
    1. United States—Race relations. I. Szumski, Bonnie,
1958–   . II. Series: Opposing viewpoints series (Unnumbered)
E184.A1I6   1996
305.8'00973—dc20   95-52626
                                                            CIP

"Congress shall make no law . . .
abridging the freedom of speech,
or of the press."

First Amendment to the U.S. Constitution

The basic foundation of our democracy is the First Amendment guarantee of freedom of expression. The Opposing Viewpoints Series is dedicated to the concept of this basic freedom and the idea that it is more important to practice it than to enshrine it.

Contents

Page

Why Consider Opposing Viewpoints?   9

Introduction   12

Chapter 1: Should America's Racial Differences
            Be Emphasized?
Chapter Preface   16
1. America's Cultural Heritage Is Distinctly European   17
    Russell Kirk
2. America's Cultural Heritage Is Diverse and
    Multiethnic   24
    Lillian S. Robinson
3. Ethnic and Racial Loyalties Endanger American
    Culture   31
    Gerald F. Kreyche
4. Racial and Ethnic Loyalties Are Not Dangerous   35
    Virginia I. Postrel
5. Emphasizing Racial Diversity Leads to Greater
    Understanding   40
    Judy Scales-Trent
6. Emphasizing Racial Diversity Is Counterproductive   45
    Marc Elrich
Periodical Bibliography   51

Chapter 2: Is Racism to Blame for Blacks' Lack
            of Success?
Chapter Preface   53
1. White Racism Is Not to Blame for Black Inequality   54
    Dinesh D'Souza
2. White Racism Is to Blame for Black Inequality   64
    Andrew Hacker
3. Blacks Must Recognize and Fight Oppression   72
    bell hooks
4. Blacks' Claims of Oppression by Whites Hamper
    Black Success   82
    Anne Wortham
5. Racism Prevents Blacks from Achieving Economic
    Justice   93
    Claud Anderson
6. Racism Cannot Explain Poverty Among Blacks   104
    Yehudi O. Webster
Periodical Bibliography   111

Chapter 3: Will Immigration Lead to an
      Interracial Crisis?

Chapter Preface   113

1. America's Cultural Identity Is Shaped by Continued
   Immigration   114
   Luther S. Luedtke

2. Immigration Threatens America's Cultural Identity   123
   Dwight D. Murphey

3. Immigrants Unwilling to Assimilate Will Cause
   Interracial Conflict   129
   Brent A. Nelson

4. Increasing Immigration Will Not Lead to
   Interracial Conflict   136
   Peter H. Schuck

Periodical Bibliography   141

Chapter 4: How Has Affirmative Action
      Affected Race Relations?

Chapter Preface   143

1. Affirmative Action Is Reverse Discrimination   144
   Irving Kristol

2. Discrimination in Favor of Minorities Is Necessary   149
   Eric Foner

3. Affirmative Action Combats Unintentional Racism   154
   Alec R. Levenson & Darrell L. Williams

4. Affirmative Action Aggravates Racial Tension   159
   Linda Chavez

5. Government Must Do More for Minorities Than
   Affirmative Action   165
   Seymour Martin Lipset

6. Government Should Not Be Responsible for
   Alleviating Discrimination   172
   Lilian & Oscar Handlin

Periodical Bibliography   181

Chapter 5: How Should Society Treat Interracial
      Families?

Chapter Preface   183

1. Racial Matching in Adoptions Should Be Encouraged   184
   Ruth G. McRoy

2. Racial Matching in Adoptions Is Racist and
   Discriminatory   190
   Elizabeth Bartholet

3. Children of Mixed-Race Unions Should Be Raised
   Biracially   197
      Francis Wardle
4. Children of Mixed-Race Unions Should Not Be Raised
   Biracially   204
      Hettie Jones
5. Interracial Marriage Is Identical to Same-Race
   Marriage   210
      Candy Mills
6. Interracial Marriage Cannot Be Treated Identically
   to Same-Race Marriage   216
      Jacqueline Adams
Periodical Bibliography   220

For Further Discussion   221
Organizations to Contact   224
Bibliography of Books   229
Index   232

Why Consider Opposing Viewpoints?

"The only way in which a human being can make some approach to knowing the whole of a subject is by hearing what can be said about it by persons of every variety of opinion and studying all modes in which it can be looked at by every character of mind. No wise man ever acquired his wisdom in any mode but this."

John Stuart Mill

In our media-intensive culture it is not difficult to find differing opinions. Thousands of newspapers and magazines and dozens of radio and television talk shows resound with differing points of view. The difficulty lies in deciding which opinion to agree with and which "experts" seem the most credible. The more inundated we become with differing opinions and claims, the more essential it is to hone critical reading and thinking skills to evaluate these ideas. Opposing Viewpoints books address this problem directly by presenting stimulating debates that can be used to enhance and teach these skills. The varied opinions contained in each book examine many different aspects of a single issue. While examining these conveniently edited opposing views, readers can develop critical thinking skills such as the ability to compare and contrast authors' credibility, facts, argumentation styles, use of persuasive techniques, and other stylistic tools. In short, the Opposing Viewpoints Series is an ideal way to attain the higher-level thinking and reading skills so essential in a culture of diverse and contradictory opinions.

In addition to providing a tool for critical thinking, Opposing Viewpoints books challenge readers to question their own strongly held opinions and assumptions. Most people form their opinions on the basis of upbringing, peer pressure, and personal, cultural, or professional bias. By reading carefully balanced opposing views, readers must directly confront new ideas as well as the opinions of those with whom they disagree. This is not to simplistically argue that everyone who reads opposing views will—or should—change his or her opinion. Instead, the series enhances readers' depth of understanding of their own views by encouraging confrontation with opposing ideas. Careful examination of others' views can lead to the readers' understanding of the logical inconsistencies in their own opinions, perspective on why they hold an opinion, and the consideration of the possibility that their opinion requires further evaluation.

Evaluating Other Opinions

To ensure that this type of examination occurs, Opposing Viewpoints books present all types of opinions. Prominent spokespeople on different sides of each issue as well as well-known professionals from many disciplines challenge the reader. An additional goal of the series is to provide a forum for other, less known, or even unpopular viewpoints. The opinion of an ordinary person who has had to make the decision to cut off life support from a terminally ill relative, for example, may be just as valuable and provide just as much insight as a medical ethicist's professional opinion. The editors have two additional purposes in including these less known views. One, the editors encourage readers to respect others' opinions—even when not enhanced by professional credibility. It is only by reading or listening to and objectively evaluating others' ideas that one can determine whether they are worthy of consideration. Two, the inclusion of such viewpoints encourages the important critical thinking skill of objectively evaluating an author's credentials and bias. This evaluation will illuminate an author's reasons for taking a particular stance on an issue and will aid in readers' evaluation of the author's ideas.

As series editors of the Opposing Viewpoints Series, it is our hope that these books will give readers a deeper understanding of the issues debated and an appreciation of the complexity of even seemingly simple issues when good and honest people disagree. This awareness is particularly important in a democratic society such as ours in which people enter into public debate to determine the common good. Those with whom one disagrees should not be regarded as enemies but rather as people whose views deserve careful examination and may shed light on one's own.

Thomas Jefferson once said that "difference of opinion leads to inquiry, and inquiry to truth." Jefferson, a broadly educated man, argued that "if a nation expects to be ignorant and free . . . it expects what never was and never will be." As individuals and as a nation, it is imperative that we consider the opinions of others and examine them with skill and discernment. The Opposing Viewpoints Series is intended to help readers achieve this goal.

David L. Bender & Bruno Leone,
Series Editors

Introduction

"There never was—and never will be—a single American way of life."

David Glidden,
Professor of Philosophy,
University of California at Riverside

On the morning of October 3, 1995, Americans across the country became intimately aware of the deep divisions between blacks and whites when in a Los Angeles County courtroom O.J. Simpson was found not guilty of murdering his ex-wife, Nicole, and her friend, Ron Goldman. Across the nation, news photos displayed an eerily similar reaction among blacks and whites hearing the verdict: whites appeared open-mouthed and shocked, while blacks joyfully laughed and smiled, many holding their fists thrust in the air in a sign of victory.

Many blacks interviewed believed the Simpson acquittal was a triumph. To blacks who view justice in America as elusive, the verdict represented one black man's victory over an unfair system and a racist society. As black psychiatrist William H. Grier, quoted in the *Los Angeles Times*, said, "I think it's important that every now and then we have a victory. . . . I don't know of a single black who didn't feel like standing up and cheering."

To many whites, the Simpson verdict and the reaction to it seemed unfathomable. Many could not understand how the trial had become focused on racism in the Los Angeles Police Department instead of Simpson's guilt or innocence. The way that many blacks seemed to identify with Simpson was also mystifying to many whites as Simpson had never been involved in civil rights or black issues. As commentator Mortimer Zuckerman contends, "Now many whites have joined blacks and lost confidence in the ability of jurors of the opposite color to reach an honest verdict based purely on the evidence."

Although its depth cannot be completely measured, this racial divide over the Simpson verdict seemed to bring to the forefront a reexamination of race, and of what it means to be an American. If, as reaction to the trial appeared to show, Americans of different races and ethnicities could grasp so little of each other's realities, how is it then possible to work as a nation and perform duties in the interest of the common good? Is it even possible to come to terms with the idea of a common good?

Many despair that the answer to this question is no. They see America divided by ethnic and minority interests, each group competing for public resources, government programs, and recognition. These divisions, many believe, will lead to the balkanization of America, a house divided, a crumbling of the ideas that the United States stands for: equality, liberty, and equal treatment under the law. As distinguished historian Arthur M. Schlesinger writes in *The Disuniting of America*:

> The division of society into fixed ethnicities nourishes a culture of victimization and a contagion of inflammable sensitivities. And when a vocal and visible minority pledges primary allegiance to their groups, whether ethnic, sexual, religious, or, in rare cases political, it presents a threat to the brittle bonds of national identity that hold this diverse and fractious society together.

Others, while admitting that interracial conflicts exist, believe that they are less serious. They argue that racial and ethnic groups have been at odds with one another throughout America's history: English colonists and Native Americans, western settlers and Chinese immigrants, and, today, Koreans and blacks during the Rodney King riots in 1992. Somehow, America's defenders of diversity argue, the nation has endured, even through times of such incredible racial stress as occurred during the civil rights movement of the 1960s. These defenders see the strength of the United States as larger than its individuals. It is the strength of America's institutions, especially its laws and constitutional emphasis on the individual, that can allow for differences, even racial hatred, and survive. As David Glidden, quoted at the start of this introduction, points out:

> All walks of life, creeds or colors intermingle in public commerce, only to return to private lives and exclusive associations of family, friends, religious and cultural identities. Public lives co-exist alongside private preferences and even racial prejudice. . . . Such is the American free marketplace. The open secret of its successes, when compared with far more troubled places in the world, is the presence of a common law.

> By defining every citizen as equal, the American rule of law distances itself from ethnocentricity.

The topics covered in *Interracial America: Opposing Viewpoints* are imbued with the racial and ethnic tensions that concern many Americans today. The chapters are: Should America's Racial Differences Be Emphasized? Is Racism to Blame for Blacks' Lack of Success? Will Immigration Lead to Interracial Crisis? How Has Affirmative Action Affected Race Relations? How Should Society Treat Interracial Families? Although interracial conflicts are certain to continue, this book attempts to provoke discussion, and thus, perhaps lead to deeper understanding. As Harlon L. Dalton, author of *Racial Healing: Confronting the Fear Between Blacks and Whites*, notes, "We have to understand that there is an upside to talking about race. We all know that we can be made to feel real bad, whatever color we are, when talking about race. What's harder is to recognize the advantages of that type of discussion. . . . There needs to be an understanding that everybody wins from improved race relations."

Should America's Racial Differences Be Emphasized?

Chapter Preface

In an article for the *Christian Science Monitor*, Milton Ezrati tells a story of his young daughter requesting a flag from their native land for a multicultural day at school. Ezrati explains, "Like many Americans, our background was mixed and I was not even sure of all its elements. I could not choose a single flag. Besides, we did not feel a particular link with any of our background groups." After going to school armed with an American flag and some baked goods, the daughter "returned home that day in tears. The teacher was disappointed, and the children accused her of claiming to be more American than others." Ezrati, dismayed by the emphasis on historical group identity, concludes his article by saying, "The US and its Constitution have traditionally emphasized the individual and largely ignored groups as simply agglomerations of individuals. The idea has created a remarkably open, fluid, and diverse society." Ezrati and others argue that as the United States becomes more fixated on celebrating different cultures, it loses sight of its own unique national heritage, which is the result of an assimilation of many different cultures. Thus, Ezrati concludes, the very ideas that make the United States great—its continual renewal by the addition and assimilation of different cultures into its own—are undermined by a perverse insistence on preserving differences.

While Ezrati sees a danger in the multicultural trend, others, like Michael Lind, senior editor at *Harper's Magazine*, believe it is harmless: "The assimilatory power of American vernacular culture is so great that the fears of nativists and the hopes of multiculturalists will almost certainly be confounded as today's so-called Third World immigrants become tomorrow's bland, conventional Middle Americans only incidentally named Ramirez and Wong." Lind contends that Americans are more concerned with issues such as economic opportunity than whether they can preserve a separate identity. These economic pressures almost guarantee continued national patriotism and assimilation.

Whether an emphasis on separate racial and ethnic identities is undermining America's national goals or is simply a temporary, harmless fad is debated in the following chapter.

"Whatever the racial or ethnic or national
origins of Americans, the principal features of
the culture within which they have their being
are British in origin."

America's Cultural Heritage Is Distinctly European

Russell Kirk

One of the many arguments for encouraging and appreciating
ethnic diversity in American culture is that the United States has
no single culture, but is an amalgam of many different ethnic
contributions; thus, multiculturalism is the only means of incor-
porating these many influences. In the following viewpoint,
Russell Kirk takes exception to this view, arguing that only by
recognizing and appreciating America's British heritage will the
United States avoid falling into divisive ethnic conflicts. Kirk is
the author of *America's British Culture*, from which this viewpoint
is taken, and the series editor for The Library of Conservative
Thought, a series of books by well-known conservative authors.

As you read, consider the following questions:

1. What generally happens to immigrants after they enter the
   United States, according to the author? What implications
   does this have for American culture?
2. What four cultural contributions has America received from
   Britain, according to Kirk?

"Down with Euroculture!" During the past several years, strident voices have been crying that commination in many states of the Union. The adversaries of the dominant culture in the United States demand that in American schooling, and in American life generally, Eurocentric assumptions must be supplanted by a "multiculture" emphasizing the cultural achievements of "African Americans, Asian Americans, Puerto Ricans/Latinos, and Native Americans." (This list of "minorities" is found in an official report of a task force appointed by the educational commissioner of the State of New York.) The culture of women also is incorporated in some demands for a cultural revolution in America—despite the fact that America's dominant higher culture already, in considerable part, is sustained by intelligent and conscientious women.

Of course it is true that into the culture, the British culture, of North America have entered large elements, in the nineteenth and twentieth centuries, of other major cultures, chiefly from Europe—but also, and increasingly, from China, Japan, the Levant, Mexico, Puerto Rico, and (quite recently) Korea and Indochina. But these and other cultures from abroad have been peacefully incorporated into the dominant British culture of North America. Even Mexican culture, which soon may be the biggest minority ethnic bloc in the United States, commonly is woven into the fabric of American society—after the passage of a single generation.

America Has a Single Definable British Culture

Now American society is imperfect, as is everything else here below. Yet the transplanted culture of Britain in America has been one of humankind's more successful achievements. The United States today is flooded with immigrants, lawful or unlawful, eager to enjoy the security, prosperity, freedom, and cultural opportunities of America. America's successes, substantially, have been made possible by the vigor of the British culture that most Americans now take for granted. Who, then, are the people desiring to pull down this dominant culture and set up in its place some amorphous "multiculture"?

One does not find the Vietnamese, or other Asiatics who have taken refuge in America, complaining about "cultural oppression." Most of them swiftly and intelligently adapt themselves to American culture. Most Spanish-surname Americans do not deny the merits of European civilization. Of "Native Americans," only a handful pretend to desire some sort of return to their ancestors' folkways of the eighteenth century. One hears no cultural howls of rage from Eskimo or Aleut.

In truth, the adversaries of America's dominant culture may be classified in three categories: certain militant blacks; white radicals, mostly "civil rights" zealots of yesteryear; and a mob of bored, indolent students to whom any culture but pop culture is anathema. Near the close of the twentieth century, the hardest haters of inherited high culture are to be found within the Academy—embittered ideologues, their character warped in the turbulent 'sixties, whose ambition it is to pull down whatever has long been regarded as true and noble. On nearly every campus, some of the purported guardians of culture have become the destroyers of culture. Ratlike, they gnaw at the foundations of society—quite as Karl Marx admonished intellectuals to do. At bottom, this "Down with Euroculture!" is the symptom of an intellectual disease that has been festering for a quarter of a century and longer.

Reprinted by permission of Chuck Asay and Creators Syndicate.

The malign silliness of the academic radicals' shrieks is sufficiently suggested by their complaint that most books prescribed for college reading were written by "dead white males"—as if one might alter retroactively the pigmentation and the gender of William Shakespeare or Isaac Newton. This is like endeavoring to repeal the law of gravity, or to annul all human history. (Newton is mentioned here because the denouncers of "Euroculture" declare that the scientific departments, too, must be

19

purged of racism, sexism, and the dread sin of Eurocentrism.)

Much in American education requires improvement. Indeed oppression exists in the typical curriculum; but it is the tyranny of Giant Dullness, not the despotism of White Capitalistic Exploitation. So Multiculturalists' denunciation of existing educational programs sometimes hits the mark. Yet what would the multiculturalist champions of the intellectual rights of blacks, Latinos, and American Indians bestow upon high school and college by way of substitutions? Apparently an omnium-gatherum, in American history, of incidents of oppression of minorities or of "minority" heroism, mingled with ideological denunciations of the American Republic. They would erect historical falsehoods in the interest of equality of condition; they would establish on the American campus a proletarian dictatorship of the mind. In the teaching of literature, they would efface the "Euroculture" of Plato and Aristotle, Dante and Cervantes and Shakespeare, supplanting these old fuddy-duddies with minor writers of approved "minority" affiliations, and feminist ideologues of the present century. As for English literature, or American literature in the British tradition, the radicals would chuck it all down the memory-hole—except for such "workers in the dawn" writing as might seem sufficiently denunciatory of capitalism and white supremacy.

The culture of America is but two centuries old—or little more than three centuries and a half, if we turn back to the earliest English settlements on the Atlantic shore. The culture of Britain is some sixteen centuries old, if we begin with the triumph of the Angles and the Saxons. If Americans lose that British patrimony, they must become barbarians, and on their darkling plains ignorant armies of ideologues may clash by night.

The Case for a Defense of the English-Speaking Cultures

The majority of American citizens nowadays are *not* descended from English-speaking ancestors. They are outnumbered by people descended from German-speaking stock: Germans, Austrians, and German-speakers of central Europe. And the proportion of America's population with Italian, Polish, and other European language-roots bulks large. Spanish was spoken, and often still is spoken, by the parents or the grandparents of the ethnic group most rapidly increasing in the United States—that is, Latin-Americans. Asiatic and African immigrants, fugitives most of them from the twentieth-century Time of Troubles, must acquire some proficiency in the English language, a tongue altogether unrelated to their ancestral languages.

Nevertheless, whatever the racial or ethnic or national origins of Americans, the principal features of the culture within which they have their being are British in origin. It is not possible to participate effectively in American society without acquiring

20

that English-speaking culture. For, as Thomas Sowell (some of whose ancestors were African) remarked, "Cultural features do not exist merely as badges of 'identity' to which we have some emotional attachment. They exist to meet the necessities and forward the purposes of human life."

The Danger of Emphasizing Differences

Imposed uniformity—whether of sameness or difference—cannot prepare citizens of a democracy to exercise civic and social responsibilities. So-called "multicultural" curricula are designed explicitly to entrench differences. As a form of ideological teaching, multicultural absolutism isolates us in our own skins and equates culture with racial or ethnic identity. "Resegregation," some call it. How long will it take before we move from separate approaches for black children in the name of Afrocentrism, to a quest for entirely separate schools? The glory of American public education has been its mingling of classes, genders, ethnicities, and races.

Jean Bethke Elshtain, *The Responsive Community*, Spring 1994.

In June 1991, the Social Studies Syllabus Review Committee of the state of New York issued a report embracing the notion of "multicultural education" in public schools and rejecting "previous ideals of assimilation to an Anglo-American model." This Syllabus Review Committee, under the authority of the New York State Board of Regents, approved a new "Curriculum of Inclusion" drafted by Leonard Jeffries, a radical black professor who called the existing syllabus "White Nationalism" and ethnocentric.

Professor Arthur Schlesinger, Jr. had been a member of that Syllabus Review Committee; he dissented strongly from the "multicultural" report that the Committee endorsed. His remarks on the report carry weight:

> The underlying philosophy of the report, as I read it, is that ethnicity is the defining experience for most Americans, that ethnic ties are permanent and indelible, that the division into ethnic groups establishes the basic structure of American society and that a main objective of public education should be the protection, strengthening, celebration, and perpetuation of ethnic origins and identities. Implicit in the report is the classification of all Americans according to ethnic and racial criteria.

Similar endeavors to repudiate the long-established common culture of America, rooted in many centuries of thought and experience on either side of the Atlantic, have been militant in states other than New York. Were the zealots of multiculturalism to succeed, Americans of differing ethnic origins would scarcely be able to converse together, let alone work together.

Assailants of "the Anglo-American model" for culture often seem to assume that sweeping aside America's established culture would be merely a matter of public policy, with no consequences except a different teaching in classrooms. Thomas Sowell refutes that assumption:

> Cultures exist to serve the vital practical requirements of human life—to structure a society so as to perpetuate the species, to pass on the hard-earned knowledge and experience of generations past and centuries past to the young and inexperienced, in order to spare the next generation the costly and dangerous process of learning everything all over again from scratch through trial and error—including fatal errors.

> Cultures exist so that people can know how to get food and put a roof over their heads, how to cure the sick, how to cope with the death of loved ones and how to get along with the living. Cultures are not bumper stickers. They are living, changing ways of doing all the things that have to be done in life.

Professor Schlesinger points out that America's language and political purposes and institutions are derived from Britain: "To pretend otherwise is to falsify history. To teach otherwise is to mislead our students." But he adds that "the British legacy has been modified, enriched, and reconstituted by the absorption of non-Anglo cultures and traditions as well as by the distinctive experiences of American life." Very true that is. Yet the British culture is central in certain ways; the other cultures often are peripheral.

Schlesinger concludes by asking his colleagues "to consider what kind of nation we will have if we press further down the road to cultural separatism and ethnic fragmentation, if we institutionalize the classification of our citizens by ethnic and racial criteria and if we abandon our historic commitment to an American identity. What will hold our people together then?" Amen to that!

British culture is central to American society. Should that cultural heritage be long and widely neglected, the American nation would drift toward brutishness in private life, anarchy or the mailed fist in public life.

A British Legacy

In four major fashions—folkways, if you will—the British mind and British experience, for more than a dozen generations, have shaped the American culture.

The first of these three ways is the English language and the wealth of great literature in that language. Bestriding the world, that English language should be of even greater advantage to

Americans today than it has been in the past.

The second of these ways is the rule of law, American common law and positive law being derived chiefly from English law. This body of laws gives fuller protection to the individual person than does the legal system of any other country.

The third of these ways is representative government, patterned upon British institutions that began to develop in medieval times, and patterned especially upon "the mother of parliaments," at Westminster.

The fourth of these ways is a body of *mores*, or moral habits and beliefs and conventions and customs, joined to certain intellectual disciplines. These compose an ethical heritage. According to Tocqueville, Americans' *mores* have been the cause of the success of the American Republic.

In yet other ways, the United States benefits from a British patrimony: the American economy, for instance, developed out of British experience and precedent; and American patterns of community and of family life are British in considerable part. But time being limited, we confine ourselves here to British beliefs and social institutions of which the influence upon Americans has not much diminished with the elapse of four centuries. They will be rejected by those interesting persons who demand that Swahili, rather than English, be taught in urban schools; but most Americans, today as well as yesteryear, take for granted the patterns of Anglo-American culture that I describe.

A culture is perennially in need of renewal. . . . A culture does not survive and prosper merely by being taken for granted; active defense always is required, and imaginative growth, too. Let us brighten the cultural corner where we find ourselves. For, as T.S. Eliot remarked more than four decades ago, "Culture may even be described simply as that which makes life worth living."

"We have no single national identity or belief system but rather a set of diverse and sometimes conflicting identities and beliefs."

America's Cultural Heritage Is Diverse and Multiethnic

Lillian S. Robinson

Lillian S. Robinson takes issue with the idea that the United States harks back to a single, common heritage. In the following viewpoint, she argues that American culture is a mixture of many different ethnicities and races and that these differences must be communicated and taught. Robinson is the Garvin Professor of English at Virginia Tech and the author of *Sex, Class, and Culture.*

As you read, consider the following questions:

1. Why does Robinson believe that assigning primarily white male authors in school denies her son his cultural heritage?
2. What does Robinson think anthropologists mean by culture?
3. How does the author define multiculturalism?

My son's English teacher denied Toni Morrison the Nobel Prize. Put less sensationally, what happened was that the advanced placement American literature class was told that Pearl Buck, whose work they were studying, was the only American woman to win the Nobel Prize for literature.

For those benefit-of-the-doubters who think she meant "the first," the teacher added that Saul Bellow was the last American so honored. I start with this incident because I believe it offers some common ground. For, wherever we stand on the question of cultural traditions, none of us wants America's children to be taught—quite literally, in this case—that black is white.

The story also raises some controversial questions about why Morrison's work is not part of the standard curriculum and why a teacher's selective memory blanks out Morrison, whose *Playing in the Dark* challenges the traditional canon and how we read it, while enshrining Bellow, whose preface to Allan Bloom's *The Closing of the American Mind* defends the canon and insists that it alone is worth reading.

As a parent, I feel that my son and the other white teenagers in his class are being shortchanged, denied a part of our common cultural heritage, when their assignments include William Cullen Bryant but not James Weldon Johnson, Buck but not Morrison. (Yes, they also read the major white authors—Hawthorne, Emerson, Thoreau, Whitman, Melville, Dickinson, Twain, Hemingway, Steinbeck, Miller, Porter, Welty—but not Jacobs, Dunbar, Dubois, Cullen, Hurston, Hughes, Wright, Baldwin, Hansberry, Walker—Alice or Margaret—Marshall, Gaines Naylor. And no Kingston, Tan, Yamimoto, Anaya, Cisneros, Hinojosa, Anzaldua, Silko, Momaday, Gunn Allen, either.)

Erasing Voices

As a citizen, I am concerned that a just and decent society will remain an impossible goal as long as we continue to erase the range of voices from our culture. To do so implies that only those who already have social power have anything to say about human experience and its meanings, that only they possess the imagination, insight and wit to say it well. On the global scale, I fear for a world whose cultural authorities argue that white Europeans such as Tolstoy and Proust are great writers, while black Africans like Soyinka, Ba, Ngugi, Nwapa, Achebe, Emecheta, LaGuma, Tlali, Tutuola, Head and Sembene cannot be worth reading because they are not Tolstoy but themselves.

But I am not just an outraged parent or a concerned citizen; I am a scholar and teacher who has been engaged for some 25 years in the effort to change and enrich the literary curriculum. This means I have taken the multicultural side in what members of my profession call "the culture war." We call it a war, and we talk about canons. We call one literary tradition a canon, and we make uneasy jokes about guns. For instance, there's my own title *Their Canon, Our Arsenal*, Henry Louis Gates Jr.'s *Loose Canons*, Robert Scholes's *Aiming a Canon at the Curriculum* and three pieces that play on Tennyson's "cannons to right of them, cannons to left of them." In the same martial spirit, columnist George Will compared the embattled role of Lynne Cheney, director of the National Endowment for the Humanities in the Reagan and Bush administrations, to that of her husband, who then was serving as secretary of defense.

Rooting for a Multicultural America

Blind allegiance to the myth that America is a melting pot has brought us militarism and consumerism, as well as a bland, soulless, lowest-common-denominator culture typified by identical fast food outlets and shopping malls from coast to coast. But there is another America that endures, embodying the idea that cultures can coexist side by side and even cross-pollinate. This is the America that has given us Louis Armstrong, Tennessee Williams, and Lauren Bacall as well as filet gumbo, flautas, fettuccine, and much, much more.

The battle now raging over multiculturalism is a showdown between these two cultures. As a white male, I'm selfishly rooting for the triumph of a multicultural America, a nation that celebrates diversity along with purple mountains' majesty and amber waves of grain. Perhaps Americans will be able to move into the 21st century with more sureness and pride about who we really are—and with genuine liberty and justice for all.

Jay Walljasper, *Utne Reader*, November/December 1991.

Because both sides use military language with overtones of a crusade, I think it is important to understand what is invested in this war over the canon—starting with why it is called a canon. Only recently has the term had a literary connotation. Its original use in connection with texts was biblical: The canon is the set of books that make up the Book. This inclusion has a basis in scholarship, the application of certain standards—theological, philological and historical standards—to a text.

But what of those that don't pass the tests? Many noncanonical religious stories are collected in the Apocrypha, which also has its place within Judeo-Christian tradition. The Jewish celebration of Hanukkah, based upon events narrated in the two books of Maccabees; the representation in Christian art of scenes from the books of Tobit or Judith; and poetic retellings of the story of Susanna all bear witness to the status of the Apocrypha in spiritual and imaginative life. Believers are encouraged to accept them as sacred narratives, even though they are not accepted as sacred texts. In our everyday spoken language, however, the Apocrypha doesn't come off so well. When we call a story "apocryphal," we mean it is not worthy of belief. It is inauthentic.

The term "canon" entered literary studies with a very restricted meaning—namely, all the works recognized by the appropriate authorities as being by some particular major author. So we had the "Shakespeare canon," the "Milton canon" and so on, with experts applying philological and historical standards to determine whether a given work could be attributed properly to the great man. This use of the word "canon" initially was meant as a mild, self-deprecatory academic joke, for certifying a play or poem as the authentic word of Shakespeare—even Shakespeare—is hardly the same as certifying it as the word of God.

This was the state of things some three decades ago. In those days, we also studied the body of literature that now is called "the canon" then known as the tradition, or our tradition. That definite article was very definite indeed: No other tradition need apply for consideration among the great books, for only this set bore the possessive adjective preempting questions about who we were. The shift in terminology came when some of us began challenging those underlying assumptions, in the name of literature excluded from the list of "greats," particularly the work of women and people of color.

Now, I don't know which of my professional colleagues first referred to the classics as "the canon," but use of the term has expanded with the increasing challenges to tradition and consequent demonization of the challengers, assuring that it has had no chance to become a dead metaphor. The monoculturalists' approach to literary tradition as a secular religion also helps me to understand their attitude toward the included material (the sacred texts)—as when Paul Weyrich maintains that cultural conservatives should support the Western tradition because it is "fundamentally true"—and the excluded material (the nonsacred)—which must, like an apocryphal story, be inauthentic, spurious and essentially untrue.

A Stagnant Religion

A few years back, *Time* magazine quoted my observation that traditionalists treat culture as a "stagnant secular religion." A paragraph or so further, the article mentioned another professor, who called her course on canonical American literature "White Male Writers." In both cases, quotation replaced argumentation, since it was supposed to be self-evident that our statements were absurd. Making a case in this way is a symptom of secular fundamentalism in that it assumes a community of belief, with a shared conviction that certain views are within the pale and others ridiculously outside it.

Multiculturalism makes the opposite assumption: that we have no single national identity or belief system but rather a set of diverse and sometimes conflicting identities and beliefs. Our cultural diversity is the result of a common history that we experienced differently. The painful divisions are caused by inequality and oppression, not by the cultural products that give form and voice to the pain and may help us understand one another. Everyone possesses a gender, a race and a class identity, and saying so should not be regarded as sacrilege. Identifying an author as white and male is no more pejorative than identifying another as black and female. In neither case does the label sum up the author. Rather, it provides indications of the kind of cultural experience that shaped that person's consciousness and that the literary work may be expected to take seriously.

The Persistence of Culture

The melting pot is a misleading figure of speech for America as a whole. It ignores the persistence of ethnicity. It denies the legitimacy, and value, of ancestral groups. It underestimates the strength of family, religious, ethnic, and racial constraints against intermarriage.

Arthur Mann in *Making America*, 1992.

What is offensive is the assumption that only the nonwhite or nonmale should be so identified, should be the "marked variant." When the *Texas Monthly* attacked the English department at the University of Texas, faculty members were pilloried for advocating a multicultural curriculum in literature. Why, some professors would rather teach the works of Sandra Cisneros in an American literature course than an acknowledged classic such as *The Great Gatsby*, the magazine exclaimed. Cisneros was identified as a young Chicana writer, but F. Scott Fitzgerald, author of the "classic" text, apparently possessed no social characteristics—certainly none that shaped a novel that happens to be all about sex and class at a specific moment in American history. A classic is "pure" above race, gender and class, above history.

The *Texas Monthly* felt free to dismiss Cisneros's books, *The House on Mango Street* and *Woman Hollering Creek*, which were never named in the article, as unworthy of a place in the canon or curriculum because their author is young, female and Mexican-

American. In this and similar instances, no further argument is made than the pairing of certain tainted names, female and ethnic, with those of the inferentially sex- and race-free authors of "classics." (Cisneros against Fitzgerald in Gregory Curtis's *Texas Monthly* construction, Alice Walker vs. William Shakespeare in Christopher Clausen's *Chronicle of Higher Education* rhetoric.

When the mere mention of a Cisneros or a Walker is expected to provoke hilarity or contempt, it is because those who laugh or sneer are convinced that great books cannot possibly come from such sources. The marked variant in an author's personal identity (female, black, Latina) reflects a marked variant in themes (marginal, particular, local), whereas the unmarked norm (white, male) writes about experiences that are general, human and universal. And culture is about what brings us together, not what divides us, about commonality, not about difference. Or is it?

The problem may reside in this definition, which is drawn from official culture, the civil equivalent of a state church. After all, when anthropologists speak of culture, they mean the texture and rhythm of life in a given society, all the ways human experience is organized. By contrast, monoculturalists promote a version of American culture that reflects only a piece of this larger definition, the piece accepted by those who hold economic and political power and who essentially are saying, "My identity is our identity."

In the official culture, the declaration that all men are created equal and possess certain unalienable rights looms large. Certainly, if you have to pay lip service to a civic ideal, I don't know a better one. But it is an ideal, and often it is only lip service. To behave as if this doctrine actually has been the guiding force of American life is to deny the historical realities of American experience, realities that have contributed to our actual culture, which is made up of a range of realities expressed in voices from all parts of that range.

A Rich Interchange

Multiculturalism is not about these voices speaking only to one another, but about the complex interchange that makes up the whole. Mark Twain's *Adventures of Huckleberry Finn*, a mainstay of the American canon, is a novel about race relations, about slavery and freedom, written by a white man. As Shelley Fisher Fishkin points out in *Was Huck Black?*, Twain's sense of that story and his sense of the language in which to tell it were shaped by listening to African-American voices. *Huckleberry Finn*, in turn, freed up an American voice in both black and white novelists of succeeding generations. The cultural exchange goes both ways, and no single text encompasses it all. To treat *Huckleberry Finn* as if it were a sufficient summation—of either the race issue or the way to tell an American story—and to deny students access to the voices that Twain heard is to deny them access to an area of our common culture to which Twain's masterpiece is an opening. Fishkin argues that the "diminished voice" of Jim "must not be the only African-American voice from the 19th century that is heard in the classroom."

Calling *Huckleberry Finn*'s deployment of black voices "an act of appreciation, rather than appropriation," she adds that it becomes "appropriation to delegate to that novel the entire burden of . . . engaging students in questions about black-white relations in America. Our classrooms must be as open to an appreciation of African-American voices as was Twain's imagination."

In our own day, Toni Morrison's *Beloved* is a brilliant exploration of the meanings of slavery and freedom. Morrison's telling of the story is influenced by her reading of the Bible, of slave narratives—and of Twain. Her identity as a descendant of enslaved people is written into *Beloved*, and to ignore that cultural resonance is to miss some of what it is about. But to consider either the novel or its theme to be other than central to American culture, as *Huckleberry Finn* is central to that culture, is to distort our culture. And it is only a short step from that distortion to the next one, the claim that the king of Sweden didn't give Toni Morrison that medal.

"Multiculturalism and diversity never can produce unity."

Ethnic and Racial Loyalties Endanger American Culture

Gerald F. Kreyche

Gerald F. Kreyche is professor emeritus of philosophy at DePaul University in Chicago and an editor for the national magazine *USA Today*. In the following viewpoint, Kreyche argues that true multiculturalism is, by definition, dangerous. He cites ethnic conflict throughout the world to prove his case that loyalty to one's own ethnic or racial heritage naturally leads to hatred of others. Kreyche blames the call for similar ethnic loyalty in the United States for increasing racial and ethnic tensions.

As you read, consider the following questions:

1. What movements does Kreyche cite as being the negative outgrowth of the civil rights movement?
2. What does the author ironically refer to as the "benefits" of multiculturalism?
3. What do you think of Kreyche's assertion that ethnic or racial loyalty leads to hatred? Give an example to support your argument.

However upsetting at the time, the civil rights legislation of the 1960s and its subsequent enforcement was a good and necessary thing for the nation. Americans all knew in their hearts that it was a moral imperative. Yet, what often begins as virtue, when pressed to the extreme, turns into vice. To redress past wrongs, governmental programs encouraged affirmative action. Soft-hearted liberals became soft-headed as they replaced one form of discrimination with another. Affirmative action metamorphosed into quota systems and minority preference programs, and some civil "rights" begot civil "wrongs" and now civil unrest.

Children were used as pawns in school busing programs that upset nearly everyone, yet never achieved their purpose. Welfare became a monster of society's own making, as the citizenry was reluctant to criticize the disvalues produced by this dependence. "Sensitivity" legislation was passed that made "hate" crimes a special category—hate often being confused for dislike of antithetical value systems. Academe went one step further in prohibiting free speech that was considered offensive to minorities—an affront to the First Amendment. Educational institutions also were given far from uncertain "suggestions" to enroll and graduate minorities who couldn't qualify for admission otherwise.

Police and fire departments and other public agencies have been required to overlook a lack of qualifications and hire on the basis of minority status. The use of minority firms, in preference to experienced and established ones run by whites, often resulted in shoddy work. Such charges have been expressed *sotto voce* in reference to the much-delayed new Denver International Airport and elsewhere.

Integration's Fallout

The hopeful outcome of integration only produced resentment and increased freely chosen segregation *by* minorities themselves. In academe, blacks and Hispanics wanted their own teachers, counselors, study programs, and organizations, as did women. They separated themselves in the cafeteria and dorms. Ethnic studies departments seldom were pillars of intellectual research, their very *raison d'être* being political activism.

Paradoxically, the armed forces, which liberals seem to hate, are about the only successful example of integration, although problems persist with gays and women.

Integration having failed, next came the contradictory propagandist push toward multiculturalism and diversity. Pres. Clinton says he wants his administration to look like the nation, echoing the nation's ethnic and sexual mix. It seems he wants an idealized human version of Edward Hicks' painting, "The Peaceable Kingdom," in which nature's fiercest wild animals live in complete harmony.

Interestingly enough, Americans never are told *why* multiculturalism and diversity as such are necessarily good. They simply are declared so by fiat, strongly suggesting that their good is only a political one for an administration that is teetering on the edge.

An American Example

To see the "benefits" of multiculturalism and diversity, take a hard look around the world. When Indians were America's sole inhabitants, it was a way of life for tribes to fight each other or make alliances to battle other coalitions. Crow and Blackfeet were hereditary enemies, as were Sioux and Mandan. Taking each other's scalps or using their enemies as slaves was commonplace. Even today in the Southwest, the Utes and Navajo want little or nothing to do with each other, and the Hopi and Navajo remain at odds over land disputes.

A Portent of Fascism

Let me make myself absolutely clear. The contemporary passion to classify and divide the American people is a portent of fascism both red and black. Where the communal approach rules (Yugoslavia, the Middle East, Northern Ireland, Soviet Central Asia, Hitler's Germany, Stalin's Russia) blood flows and no one is treated fairly. We, on the other hand, have fought many times for the sake of being apprehended not as classes of people but as individual souls.

Six generations ago, my forebears left Russia after the Kishinev Pogrom, left behind the weight of a thousand years, for a future that they thought sparkled and shone like a diamond, because it was fair, because the great, euphoric gift of America—its essential condition, its clarity, its purity, and its decency—was that it took them for what they were, just as God would, looking past the accidents of birth and the complications of history. I cannot imagine that we would willingly leave this behind, and I, for one, will not.

Mark Helprin, *The Wall Street Journal*, November 25, 1994.

Canada has its national unity threatened by the language and ethnic dispute between French-speaking Quebec and the English-speaking provinces. In Europe, the disintegration of Yugoslavia triggered deadly conflict among Croatians, Serbs, Bosnians, and mixed Moslem groups. (Ask the beleaguered UN troops there about the good that multiculturalism has produced.) The Czechs and the Slovaks have split into two countries because of differences. Since the dissolution of the U.S.S.R., Russia has had nothing but troubles with the Ukraine, Azerbaijan, and especially, Chechen rebels. Sporadically, Spain suffers terrorist attacks from separatist-minded Basques.

In the Middle East, Israel has all it can do to ameliorate differences among its secular, reformed, orthodox, and extreme conservative Sephardic citizens—in addition to having to deal with the issue of Palestinians working in the country. In Asia, Sri Lanka has political problems because of multicultural elements, as does India with its many different classes. One should not forget how quickly Chairman Mao Tse-tung of China changed his chaos-causing views of "Let many flowers bloom."

Africa's Conflicts

In Africa, multiculturalism can be blamed for the strife in Rwanda and Burundi, where the Tutsi and the Hutu are deadly enemies. The death toll in the struggle between these tribes has exceeded 100,000. Ethiopia remains in constant ethnic ferment.

Africa clearly hates multiculturalism and, as a consequence, it keeps producing more nation-states. It already has 52, the greatest number of any continent, and it is likely more will emerge. Eritrea, the Western Sahara, the southern Sudan, or northern Somaliland may be the next, suggests the National Geographic News Service. The Zulus well may create a new one out of South Africa.

It is readily apparent that multiculturalism and diversity never can produce unity. Yet, schools that are meant to educate the nation fail to take a critical look at what harm they are doing in pushing multiculturalism. As news services report, guidelines in New York City urge "teachers to encourage children to use their own language"—this in a school system that is home to 120 foreign tongues. The teachers there also are given a "diversity checklist" to make sure they are not promoting bias.

It is high time to begin educating the nation's youngsters, and those not so young, of the existence, reality, and meaning of an American culture. Otherwise, we must get ready to welcome chaos.

> "America is a multicultural nation. It would be a multicultural nation if every non-Caucasian vanished tomorrow."

Racial and Ethnic Loyalties Are Not Dangerous

Virginia I. Postrel

Virginia I. Postrel is the editor of *Reason* magazine, which advocates libertarianism, or the political philosophy of limited government. In the following article, Postrel argues that the United States is in no danger of falling prey to overwhelming ethnic and racial conflicts. Even though America is a nation of immigrants, she argues, individuals of various racial and ethnic groups participate in a common American culture.

As you read, consider the following questions:

1. What evidence does Postrel give for her argument that Americans cannot resist assimilation?
2. What reasons does Postrel give to prove her assertion that America is ruining its colleges?

Excerpted from Virginia I. Postrel, "Uncommon Culture." Reprinted, with permission, from the May 1993 issue of *Reason* magazine. Copyright ©1993 by the Reason Foundation, 3415 S. Sepulveda Blvd., Suite 400, Los Angeles, CA 90034.

He was a Berber from Algeria. And, like many a Washington cab driver, he had a story to tell about politics. The Algerian government had done his people wrong, had done him wrong when he was a student demonstrator standing up for Berber rights. But Americans didn't understand his struggle. "Americans won't fight for principles," he said.

Thinking of my country as the would-be world policeman and idealistic guardian of human rights, I demurred. But then he started talking about soccer riots, about how Americans didn't understand the principle behind them, the notion of standing up for your team no matter what. The notion of blind, dehumanizing, clan loyalties.

To the cab driver, "principles" weren't abstract ideals like liberty or equality. They were group allegiances. "Principles" were what set Serbs against Bosnians, Hindus against Muslims, neo-Nazis against Turks. And Americans won't fight for principles. It is one of our defining characteristics.

The cab driver was, I believe, correct. But not everyone is so sure. A lot of very smart people see the Balkans in America's future. They point to the L.A. riots and say race relations are worse than ever. They look at immigrants pouring in from Third World nations and say (on the left) that we must accommodate diverse cultures and (on the right) that we must shut the doors. They worry about a fragmenting nation—too many ethnicities, too many religions, even too many cable TV channels. They're afraid America will disappear. "Unless a common purpose binds [Americans] together, tribal hostilities will drive them apart," says liberal historian Arthur M. Schlesinger Jr., neatly encapsulating the centrist position.

"There is no American heritage," proclaims Rubén Martínez, one of L.A.'s angry young pundits, voicing the multiculturalism of the left.

Writing in *National Review*, Peter Brimelow declares that Americans, to remain a nation, must have genetic ties. "'Nation'—as suggested by its Latin root *nacere*, to be born—intrinsically implies a link by blood. A nation is like an extended family," he writes, and later, "Americans are now being urged to abandon the bonds of a common ethnicity and instead to trust entirely to ideology to hold together their state (polity). This is an extraordinary experiment, like suddenly replacing all the blood in a patient's body."

An Experiment That Works

Martínez and Brimelow are both right, in part. America has more than one heritage, and America is an extraordinary experiment. But it is an experiment that works.

And it will continue to work as long as the multiculturalists of the left and the monoculturalists of the right aren't allowed to impose their visions on America. The United States is neither the Balkans nor Little England, West. And the forces of assimilation—the forces of American culture—are as powerful as they are utterly misunderstood. . . .

"Americans Have No Principles"

The old segregationists understood the American character. They knew that if the law didn't keep people apart, common humanity would bring them together. Americans have no principles. Restaurants and hotels and railroads and department-store dressing rooms would let the races mingle—all in pursuit of the almighty dollar. Jim Crow was a bulwark against the integrating forces of commerce, education, and, above all, love. Allow the races to mingle, the segregationists said, and you'd soon have mixed-race children.

They were right. In 1970, there were 310,000 interracial marriages in the United States. In 1988, there were almost a million. "But would you want your daughter to marry one?" is now an irrelevant question. Your daughter will do as she pleases. America melts tribal ties. Jewish leaders write and preach incessantly on the evils of intermarriage. And the Jewish intermarriage rate has gone from 10 percent before 1965 to more than 50 percent since 1985—not counting ethnic non-Jews who convert. "We have lost more Jews to intermarriage than to the Holocaust," thundered a direct-mail appeal I once received.

But most American Jews—most Americans—don't think of assimilation as death. Most Americans, lacking the cab driver's principles, do not disown their children for marrying outside their kind. We teach our ninth-graders *Romeo and Juliet*. It tells them adolescent love is more important than family loyalty. It says we are all the same kind.

Americanization Is a Process

For the last quarter century, the children of the New Deal have been fighting with the children of the '60s over what it means to be an American. Shall we melt everyone down in an Eisenhower-era cultural pot and call it America? Or shall we divide up on principle and get together only to insult each other's ancestors? Shall we protect "the common culture" or champion "cultural pluralism"? On and on the battle has raged—in the schools, in the newspapers, over the airwaves.

The debate over the American character has it all wrong. Assimilation is not an evil (or a good) foisted upon unwilling, unmeltable ethnics. It does not represent a betrayal of the self, a denial of identity. And it does not require public schools. . . .

America is not a finished artifact but an irresistible process.

The assumptions of America—ambition, tolerance, social equality, the individual pursuit of happiness—do not dictate an outcome. But they produce an atmosphere, an atmosphere that permeates every institution, that undermines every group. Even the Amish lose many of their children.

Not American Enough

The truth is, we simply do not trust some ethnic minorities to be like the Irish, to be fiercely proud of their grandfather's afternoon stories and yet just as fiercely patriotic. It is expected by those who want to have it both ways that Latinos, for instance, will break the bargain and remain too Latino and not American enough. We are infinitely more troubled by Chicano studies at UCLA than we are by Celtic studies at Boston College. Perhaps our proximity to Mexico or the steady flow of immigrants across the border, or startling demographic shifts or a guilty conscience over the discrimination endured by our fathers and mothers have convinced cultural alarmists that Mexican-Americans simply cannot be trusted to keep their loyalties straight. And, so from the back of a crowded auditorium comes the plea: "Why can't we all just be Americans?"

Ruben Navarrette Jr., *Los Angeles Times*, September 20, 1995.

"For the child of immigrant parents the knowledge comes like a slap: America exists," writes Rodriguez. "America exists in the slouch of the crowd, the pacing of traffic lights, the assertions of neon, the cry of freedom overriding the nineteenth-century melodic line. Grasp the implications of American democracy in a handshake or in a stranger's Jeffersonian 'hi.' America is irresistible. Nothing to do with choosing."

Well, choice has *something* to do with it. We choose America, and we choose which America to choose.

America is a multicultural nation. It would be a multicultural nation if every non-Caucasian vanished tomorrow. New England is not the South is not California is not Utah. Understanding America, and American assimilation, has to start with that fact.

America's Subcultures

America exists quite comfortably with numerous enduring subcultures. Indeed, the greatest testimony to America's irresistibility may be the persistence of our regional cultures. Though they differ from each other less than America differs from the world, American regions have maintained distinctive cultures through centuries of changing populations. My husband's great-grandparents lived in the *shtetls* of Ukraine and Lithuania, but he is the unmistakable child of the Delaware Valley. His ancestors are William Penn and Benjamin Franklin. . . .

My friend Kris, the Indiana-born child of German parents, moved to South Carolina in the ninth grade, having spent the previous few years in France. If you met her today, the only signs of her roots would be her Catholicism and an unusual level of thrift. She drawls and flirts and cheers for Clemson football like any other child of the Carolina Piedmont. She makes the South more Southern.

As do I, by living elsewhere. In the fall of 1978 I left the religious, conservative, biracial, slow-paced culture of South Carolina for the secular, liberal, multi-ethnic, intense culture of Princeton University. Like most immigrants, I was looking for a better life in a place I only half understood. Like many immigrants, I found educational and economic opportunities greater than any in my homeland. And I assimilated—dropped most of my accent, changed my politics and my religion, stopped trying to get a tan. I did these things not because anyone foisted a common culture upon me but because they made me happy.

That is how, and why, most immigrants assimilate. Not because they hate themselves or deny their roots. Not because the government has prohibited their native tongue or forced them to swear allegiance to a new religion. Not because they've gone through the homogenizing experience of public school. Assimilation is a combination of willful self-fashioning (11 percent of the Mormons in L.A. are Latino; they didn't accidentally convert) and unconscious adaptation. I dropped most of my twang because prejudiced people, on hearing it, would think me stupid and a bigot; I replaced it with a hodge-podge of Northeastern strains, because that is where I lived. Happiness and practicality, the pursuit of personal fulfillment and financial success, preserve the common culture. A common purpose has nothing to do with it.

A Mosaic of Individuals

America won't crack up in the next 25 years because its mosaic is not the one the Balkanizing multiculturalists describe. America is a mosaic not of groups but of individuals, each of whom carries a host of cultural influences, some chosen, some inherited, some absorbed by osmosis. That mosaic is held together by the pursuit of happiness, the most powerful mortar ever conceived. Left alone, it will long endure.

"The only real question is whether America wants to teach its youth to value African American culture, Latin American culture, Native culture, Asian American culture."

Emphasizing Racial Diversity Leads to Greater Understanding

Judy Scales-Trent

Judy Scales-Trent is the author of the book *Notes of a White Black Woman*, a collection of essays on race, black women, and culture, from which the following viewpoint is taken. In it, Trent uses her background as a French teacher to argue that multicultural education will lead to a better, more understanding world. Trent believes that other cultures should be taught in school just as French and German cultures are taught—with an emphasis on language, culture, and history.

As you read, consider the following questions:

1. Why does the author spend so much time recalling her dedication to French language and culture?
2. Do you think the author's ideas on teaching African-American culture like French would work? Why or why not?

When the subject comes up, I tell people that it was "in a former life" that I was a student and teacher of French. It seems like that long ago.

And it was even longer ago than that when I started my love affair with the French language. I was probably about seven or eight, the adoring follower of my older sister, Kay, and her best friend, Jane. Jane was studying French in school. Sometimes, when the two big girls were off by themselves, I would look through Jane's schoolbooks, wistfully. I must have thought that if I could learn French, I could be like her—worldly, sophisticated, an artist—and all of fourteen!

I was lucky. Although I was always hopelessly confused by mathematics and science, I had a gift for languages. I still remember how much I enjoyed Latin I, my first language course, in junior high school. I loved it all—the declensions (Mr. Brockway waved his arms and led our chant: "hic, haec, hoc; huius—three—times . . ."), the orderliness, the thrill of decoding a sentence. When I started French in high school, I discovered I had a "good ear." I could hear and reproduce the tonal and rhythmic subtleties of a foreign language.

By then, I was hopelessly in love with all things French—music and movies, books, magazines, newspapers. As a high school student, when I went to the French bookstore in Rockefeller Center, it was as if I had arrived in the Holy Land. I mooned around the bookshelves, fingering the uncut pages of books published by Gallimard and Hachette, eavesdropping on the conversations of real French people just steps away. In my freshman year of college I took my first literature course ever— a course in French literature. In this class, I was swept away by a deepened appreciation of literature, as well as by Emma Bovary's passion for Rodolphe. I adored the tragic poetry of Baudelaire and Gérard de Nerval ("Je suis le ténébreux, le veuf, l'inconsolé . . ."). I spent one college summer studying and living with a French family in Aix-en-Provence. And because it was the 1960s, and because I was at Oberlin College, my passion for all things French was transmuted into a passion for the liberation of Algeria, which we read about in magazines from French Africa as well as in the leftist French paper *Express*.

My love affair was well rewarded. There was a certain cachet to being able to speak French, to being bilingual and bicultural, to having lived, even for a short time, in France. It was assumed that I had a certain knowledge about French culture and style, that I knew certain things about French politics and daily life.

This obsession with French language and culture was my own choice, a very personal passion. But there is no doubt that it was created and encouraged by a society that values and rewards learning other languages and learning about other cultures. My interest was also valued and rewarded by my friends and family. Relatives could introduce me to their friends, with some admiration: "Now, this is Judy. She speaks French!" It was considered quite acceptable that I knew everything about French literature and nothing about American or English literature. It was considered charming when I sometimes thought of a word in French before I could remember it in English. It was a social coup that I could not only cook "blanquette de veau à l'ancienne," but also understood the French on a restaurant menu and said it correctly for the French waiter, who would beam at my pronunciation. The lesson society taught me, then, was that being bilingual and bicultural was not only exciting but also valuable. I was well on my way to being bilingual, and this fact was applauded all around.

Ending Isolation

Most of us live very segregated lives. Many of us don't come into contact with people of a different race, except in situations which are formal—like employer-employee, where having a frank conversation is too risky. So part of the answer is to put ourselves in positions where we spend enough time with people of other races, so we know we can take those risks and come back a day later and patch things up if there's a problem. Apart from that, we have to understand that there is an upside to talking about race. We all know that we can be made to feel real bad, whatever color we are, when talking about race. What's harder is to recognize the advantages of that type of discussion. And those advantages are many. We'll take steps toward ameliorating the conditions in our inner cities. We will do our economy a world of good, and lessen the despair and sense of hopelessness that many black folk feel. There needs to be an understanding that everybody wins from improved race relations.

Harlon L. Dalton, *Los Angeles Times*, October 8, 1995.

We are lucky in this country. We don't have to cross the Atlantic or travel thousands of miles to study another rich culture. We have many right here. But the same lessons are not taught with respect to African American culture—a culture with a rich history, with important intellectual and artistic traditions. One might expect that, given the value America places on learning about other cultures, in every high school, along with the traditional four-year sequence on Euro-American culture, there would be a four-year sequence on the language, history, and literature of African Americans. One would expect that the teacher would do just what I did when I taught French to high school students. Along with presenting the substantive material, the teacher would arrange field trips, set up musical presentations, invite guest speakers, set aside special days for cooking and eating the food from this culture, create ever-changing wall displays, have students subscribe to newspapers and magazines, and organize plays and musical events for families and community. And as with French, white parents would push school principals to include these lessons as early as first grade. As with French, the high school curriculum on African America would be tested in statewide exams. As with French, white parents would be delighted if their children "slipped" for a moment, and thought that they were black; and black parents would be delighted if their children did the same. And all the children would grow up being praised and admired for being bilingual and bicultural, black and white, in America.

I suppose you're laughing by now! And why not? That is surely not the way it works. The culture of African Americans is not considered as valuable as the culture of the French. The reason is clear. Unlike the French and the Americans, these two groups, black and white, are at war. And the valuation of culture is one of the most important tools of combat. A white student who becomes bilingual and bicultural black/white is probably punished by his parents, not praised. (Can you imagine the stir it would create in her family if a white college student told her parents that she wanted to major in African American literature?) And a black student who becomes bilingual and bicultural, black/white, is often considered suspect by members of the black community who become anxious if white America is engaged too deeply. (This is a true story: The black students at a predominantly white college formally voted Heather "out of the race" after she joined the school's debating team.)

We must do better than this. And an important way to start is to take control of the business of definition and valuation.

For years, I accepted the definition of others. I believed that, as a white black American, both inside and out of both black and white communities, my life was a prime example of what sociologists call "marginal"—someone who is on the margin of two major groups but a member of neither. This is clearly not a joyous place to be. But I have decided not to reinforce this view of me by accepting it. I prefer a more positive definition. And I think that if you turn the word "marginal" over, you find the word "bilingual"—and at the same time you emphasize inclusion and richness rather than exclusion and isolation. So I have decided to hark back to the great American lesson that it is valuable, and a great advantage, to be bilingual and bicultural. It is better to see and hear the world in stereophonic wide wraparound sound, than in mono. If one has been placed in the middle of everything that is going on, why not enjoy it? And I do. I am as moved by Schubert's Trout Quartet as I am by the songs of Sweet Honey in the Rock. I weep when I hear a choir sing "Precious Lord, Take My Hand," and I am filled with joy when I hear Puccini's "Messa di Gloria." I embrace all the treasures these two cultures offer me. Why choose less, when one could have more? And why cheat our children out of all this richness?

The truth is that it is easy to be bicultural and bilingual. And the truth is that this is easy to teach, and we teach it in school all the time. There is really no great need for new course material or workshops or planning sessions on diversity. This is old stuff. Schools have been teaching students to value other cultures and learn other languages for hundreds, probably thousands, of years. The only real question is whether America wants to teach its youth to value African American culture, Latin American culture, Native culture, Asian American culture. Does America want all its children so bilingual and bicultural that they have access to the deep richness of these cultures? Do we want our children to be so steeped in these cultures that a black child might slip and ask her mother to pass the "papas" instead of the "potatoes"? That an Asian American girl might get frustrated because she can't figure out how to corn-row her hair? That a little white boy might say to his mother, who has just picked him up from a party at a black classmate's house, "Mom, did you feel funny being the only white person there?"

We don't have to glorify the borders and the margins. We can all be bilingual and bicultural in many different ways. And it is a rich, rich way to be in the world.

"Many students see their diversity not as a source of strength, but as an indicator of their likely future failure."

Emphasizing Racial Diversity Is Counterproductive

Marc Elrich

Marc Elrich, a teacher and member of the Takoma Park City Council in Maryland, uses his teaching experiences to prove that a curriculum to celebrate diversity and racial differences will not change racial attitudes. In the following viewpoint, Elrich argues that as long as minorities face the everyday realities of poverty, crime, and economic hopelessness, celebrating diversity with such activities as Black History Month will ring hollow.

As you read, consider the following questions:

1. The author talks about his students believing themselves to be "bad." What point is he trying to make about the way his students think about themselves?
2. Why does Elrich believe that emphasizing racial differences leads to cynicism, fear, and jealousy?
3. Elrich talks about reaching an ideal goal in education, "to offer our children genuine knowledge and insight." Although he does not say exactly how this should be achieved, he hints at some ideas. What are some of the ways you think Elrich's goals could be achieved?

Marc Elrich, "Divided by Diversity: Why My Students Don't Buy Black History Month," *Washington Post National Weekly Edition*, February 21–27, 1994. Reprinted by permission of the author.

Everyone loves diversity and we talk about it as a source of strength. But I'm not sure that this is how our students see it. My encounters as an elementary school teacher in culturally diverse classrooms in Montgomery County, Md., have left me feeling that many students see their diversity not as a source of strength, but as an indicator of their likely future failure.

In 1994, I taught a sixth grade class of 29 students, of whom all but two were black or Hispanic, and all but three received free lunch (an indicator of low socioeconomic status). Most of the class read at a fourth grade level or lower and more than a third of the class posed serious behavior problems. They were by far my hardest class of the day. Numerous discussions with the students indicated that many of them saw no value in education and would argue against the premise that success in school had any connection to success in their lives. The majority of these students had low self-esteem and low expectations. They had, at the ages of 10 or 11, already effectively opted out of the educational system.

In trying to deal with their seeming acceptance of bad outcomes in their lives, I decided to show a film based on a Langston Hughes story about a young black boy who attempts to steal the purse of an elderly black woman. He fails and the woman takes him into her home, where she proceeds to apply generous amounts of love and understanding to his wounds. Love is a powerful medicine and we learn that all of us have it within to be better people. Nice message. I was not at all prepared for my class's response. I turned on the lights and asked if anyone wanted to share their reactions to the film. An "A" student, who is black, raised his hand and said "You knew something bad was going to happen when it started. As soon as you see a black boy you know he's gonna do something bad."

Me: "Just because he's black, he's bad?"

Student: "Everybody knows that black people are bad. That's the way we are."

I was becoming a little horrified, both at the answer and that it would be coming from him, of all students. I also counted on the class to rebuke him. To provoke a class response, I restated his proposition that "Black people are bad" and asked who agreed with that. Twenty-four of 29 hands went up.

Maybe I was misunderstanding the use of "bad." "Do you mean 'cool' or 'tough' or 'hot'? Or do you mean bad as in 'not good' or 'evil'?," I asked. One of the best female students in the class assured me she meant the latter, as did everyone else.

Bad People

In her view, and in the view of most of my class, black people are determined inherently, genetically, naturally, to be bad peo-

46

ple. To my students it wasn't a matter of choice, or upbringing, but simply a racial attribute. They had no doubt in this, nor was this their sole racial stereotype. As the discussion continued a disturbing picture of their self-image emerged. All of the following comments received a near consensus in the class.

- Blacks are poor and stay poor because they're dumber than whites (and Asians).
- Black people don't like to work hard.
- Black people have to be bad so they can fight and defend themselves from other blacks.
- As students, they see their badness as natural. They don't mean any disrespect to me personally: It's "just how we are."

Reprinted by permission: Tribune Media Services.

- They don't need to work hard because it won't matter in the end.
- Black men make women pregnant and leave.
- Black boys expect to die young and unnaturally.
- White people are smart and have money.
- Asians are smart and make money.
- Hispanics are more like blacks than whites. They can't be white so they try to be black.
- Hispanics are poor and don't try hard because, like blacks,

they know it doesn't matter. They will be like blacks because when you're poor you have to be bad to survive.

- Black kids who do their school work and behave want to be white. White kids who do poorly or dress cool want to be blacks. Hispanic kids want to be black because they aren't smart (like whites).

My students had developed a bipolar view of the world with whiteness and goodness at one pole and darkness and badness at the other. The Caribbean-born author Franz Fanon wrote about this phenomenon 40 years ago in "Black Skin, White Masks." He focused on how oppressed people internalize the loathing of the oppressor (the colonizer) and on how people who are told that they are despised learn to despise themselves. In Montgomery County, in the '90s, this is not supposed to happen. When everything we do is an effort to show we value diversity, how do these bleak stereotypes persist? . . .

The students talked about life. In their world, hard work does not equal success. Hard work means that parents are gone and children take care of children. The people who have the material goods that reflect the good life often come with guns and drugs. Wimps die young and live in fear. Tough guys die young but are proud. Rodney King was the only current event that they had even a glimmer of knowledge about. In their world there were no doctors, scientists or lawyers, only people who understand the hard reality of what they will be. They accept their fate and their place.

Good at Being Bad

Within their paradigm these young people don't lack for pride. In fact, they are quite proud of what they are. They were good at being bad; some were excellent at it. The badder they were, the greater their social status. They made a game of it and sometimes competed quite intensely to be recognized for it. They had found a way to deal with success—on their own terms.

I felt simultaneously paralyzed and enlightened by this experience. I kept the discussion going for three class periods until it seemed to die a natural death, though we returned to it from time to time, often at the prompting of the class. For the rest of the year, despite being trapped in the 6th grade curriculum of Ancient Mediterranean Civilizations, I ventured out into their world with discussions of slavery, racism and class.

They asked why a white guy was talking about bad things that white people did. I told them about how we, white people, lived historically and how we haven't had much to say about what we learned and how the world was shaped. I also told them that I wanted them to see that the world into which they were born was not of their making and not their fault, or the fault of their

48

race and that, in fact, the world is constantly remade by what we do and that they could have a chance to make it different, if they would work at it. And I acknowledged that, yes, I was privileged, but I wasn't particularly interested in maintaining my privileged status. Some of them thought I was cool. Some of them thought I was crazy, but, in all of this, they were thinking and that was good.

I came to understand their behaviors differently. As prisoners of badness, they had no options. Their acting poorly wasn't anything personal, it just happened. When the impulse came to do something wrong, thinking about controlling it (they assumed) would be unnatural—it would be "white." I slowly, and painfully, shifted my responses from focusing on their irritating behavior, to pushing them to consider options. My class atmosphere never became what I wanted it to be, but it did get better.

Fooling Children

I gave a lot of thought to what we do in school. The thoughts and words of my students made a mockery of our celebrations. Esteem building is fine, but it is in no way sufficient. Black History Month is well-intentioned, but it isn't likely to fool children who aren't naive. History needs to be inclusive, but it needs to be natural so that children come to see that there's nothing strange or odd about black people. I have begun to fear that singling out groups for special attention does more to foster fear, suspicion, jealousy and cynicism, than it does to promote understanding, empathy and community.

All students need to deal with real history early on. They need to see the connection of history to poverty: that the road out of slavery was paved, for the most part, with horrible intentions and that poverty is the logical outcome of how black Americans were treated in the 120-odd years since the end of slavery. These children have to learn that the picture of black America that stares at them from TV screens, movie houses, newspapers and their own street-corners is not a true picture of their race nor a product of their race.

We should be deeply concerned because children form their impressions early on and they sense the dissonance between the reality of life and the pretty pictures offered in school. If we're concerned with our children genuinely valuing diversity and with all our children developing high self-esteem, then we have to offer our children genuine knowledge and insight into the world in which they live. I don't think we do.

We have tried to pass, in barely three decades, from social attitudes that held that blacks were subhuman to celebrating our multicultural roots. We act as if 300 years of racism had affected neither blacks nor whites. Yet just 32 years ago, I sat in a

49

Montgomery County public school classroom, participating in a serious, sincere discussion of whether blacks were human beings (and thus deserving of rights) or a lower species (who could and should be denied them). The arguments I heard were not invented by my friends but rather were passed on to them by parents, schools and churches as part of a body of socially accepted knowledge.

The same process is at work today. To too many whites, the central unspoken question of race has become "What's wrong with them?" while to too many blacks it's "What's wrong with us?" Whites routinely compare blacks to other ethnic groups as if the intolerance shown to the Irish, to the southern and eastern Europeans, to Asians or Native Americans was somehow comparable to the hatred and dehumanization of blacks. Anyone who insists that racism is the central issue risks scorn as an extremist, a naif or a "guilty liberal."

White Guilt

But ultimately, the question is not one of guilt or responsibility. Whites living today are not guilty of the crimes of the past but they are—we are—responsible for the conditions of the present. We bear an obligation to change the things that we can, not because we whites, individually or collectively, did something to cause them, but because not changing is to perpetuate an affront to the human condition.

In the face of this challenge, we in the schools stress the happy themes of self-esteem and diversity. We teach about good black kings of ancient Africa (as if any king could be a "good" king), modern inventors and contemporary scholars. We bring in authentic black writers and scientists. We have a party and praise our diversity. The children know better. They go home and into the real world. They carry the secret of racism inside them, harboring questions and doubts about themselves and others. We try to convince them that school has some bearing on their lives and that it can change their sense of what is possible. And they respond, as one of my sixth-graders did, "What do you mean grow up? I'm a man now," or (as another told me) "I ain't going to live to be no 25, so what do you know?" Without real answers or real knowledge (certainly not the garbage spewing from the TV), their doubts and questions will grow to facts and fears. We offer them a way out and they, thinking it a trap or a trick, may well decide that the prison they know is safer. They may come to our parties, but only because it's a place to eat. They will probably wonder about what it is we are celebrating. They won't believe us when we tell them. Too bad. Too late?

Periodical Bibliography

The following articles have been selected to supplement the diverse views presented in this chapter. Addresses are provided for periodicals not indexed in the *Readers' Guide to Periodical Literature*, the *Alternative Press Index*, or the *Social Sciences Index*.

Carl N. Degler "In Search of the Un-hyphenated American," *Kettering Review*, Summer 1992. Available from 259 Regency Ridge, Dayton, OH 45459.

Gerald Early "Their Malcolm, My Problem: On the Abuses of Afrocentrism and Black Anger," *Harper's Magazine*, December 1992.

Jean Bethke Elshtain "Democracy and the Politics of Difference," *Responsive Community*, Spring 1994. Available from 2020 Pennsylvania Ave. NW, Suite 282, Washington, DC 20052.

John Gray "The Virtues of Toleration," *National Review*, October 5, 1992.

Mark Helprin "Diversity Is Not a Virtue," *Wall Street Journal*, November 25, 1994.

Joel Kotkin "The Difference Principle: Can Ethnic Identity and Individual Freedom Coexist?" *Reason*, February 1993.

Gerald F. Kreyche "The Age of Disrespect: The U.S.'s Uncivil War," *USA Today*, September 1995.

James Kurth "The Clash in Western Society: Toward a New World Order," *Current*, January 1995.

John Leo "It's the Culture, Stupid," *U.S. News & World Report*, November 21, 1994.

Glenn C. Loury "Individualism Before Multiculturalism," *Public Interest*, Fall 1995.

Orlando Patterson "The Paradox of Integration," *New Republic*, November 6, 1995.

Llewellyn H. Rockwell Jr. "To Repair the Culture, Free the Market," *Freeman*, March 1994.

Benjamin Schwarz "The Diversity Myth: America's Leading Export," *Atlantic Monthly*, May 1995.

Shelby Steele "Rise of the 'New Segregation,'" *USA Today*, March 1993.

Is Racism to Blame for Blacks' Lack of Success?

Chapter Preface

It is apparent that blacks in America have progressed since the 1960s. According to a recent survey conducted by the *New York Times*, "The number of black lawyers, doctors and engineers has risen sharply; the earnings of a growing contingent of government workers, pharmacists, mathematicians, designers, engineers and others approaches or even surpasses that of comparable whites, and this group now accounts for a higher proportion of blacks in their chosen professions than their proportion in the general population."

Yet, other statistics reveal that blacks still remain unequal to whites. According to the same survey: "The proportion of poorest blacks has also grown. . . . Blacks, overall, still lag far behind whites in income—earning about $63 for every $100 a white household earns—and they lag even farther behind in accumulated wealth." Blacks also suffer higher rates of imprisonment, illegitimacy, and poor, single-parent households.

The cause of these social and economic discrepancies between blacks and whites leads to much discussion. Are blacks themselves responsible for the lack of progress, or is racism to blame? If blacks themselves are responsible, as people like Dinesh D'Souza argue in the following chapter, then it is blacks themselves who must change. Gregory Howard Williams, author of *Life on the Color Line*, describes being brought up in the worst kind of segregation and poverty in Virginia in the 1950s, then concludes that his success has more to do with upbringing than society: "I . . . realize that my five degrees and more than 20 years in higher education didn't make me Dean of the Ohio State University College of Law. It was the belief of a woman with an eighth grade education [who raised him] that I deserved a chance, and her willingness to share everything she had to make that a reality."

If, on the other hand, blacks' continual lagging behind whites is society's fault, and racism prevents blacks' attainment of equality, then perhaps government must pursue policies that can enable blacks to achieve an equal piece of the American dream. Douglas S. Massey and Nancy A. Denton argue in *American Apartheid: Segregation and the Making of the Underclass* that persistent segregation is proof that blacks have a more difficult time entering the world of economic opportunity: "It seems to us amazing that people [are] even debating whether race [is] declining in importance when levels of residential segregation [are] so high and so structured along racial lines." The following chapter offers viewpoints from some of the most authoritative authors examining these controversial issues.

"*Racism itself becomes a scapegoat: It is blamed for problems it has little or nothing to do with, such as blacks performing poorly on math tests.*"

White Racism Is Not to Blame for Black Inequality

Dinesh D'Souza

Dinesh D'Souza is John M. Olin fellow at the American Enterprise Institute, a conservative think tank, and the author of *The End of Racism*, from which the following viewpoint is adapted. In it, D'Souza argues that lack of equality between blacks and whites is due to pathologies that are pervasive in black culture. The only way for blacks to attack their problems, D'Souza contends, is to admit that their culture encourages many of them, including lack of education, marital and family breakdown, and criminal activity. D'Souza argues that current attitudes diminish blacks' capacity to achieve any kind of economic or political success.

As you read, consider the following questions:

1. What evidence does D'Souza give to support his point that blacks are perpetrators of their own demise?
2. What is the black "oppositional culture" that the author explains?

Excerpted from "Black America's Moment of Truth" by Dinesh D'Souza, *American Spectator*, October 1995. Reprinted by permission of the author.

The last few decades have witnessed nothing less than a breakdown of civilization within the African-American community. Vital institutions such as the small business, the church, and the family are now greatly weakened; in some areas, they are on the verge of collapsing altogether. And the symptoms of systemic decline are both numerous and ominous—extremely high rates of criminal activity, the normalization of illegitimacy, a preponderance of single-parent families, high levels of drug and alcohol addiction, a parasitic reliance on government provision, hostility to academic achievement, and a scarcity of independent enterprises. The next generation of young blacks is especially vulnerable. "We are in danger of becoming superfluous people in this society," says African-American scholar Anthony Walton. "We are not essential or even integral to the economy." Marian Wright Edelman of the Children's Defense Fund puts it more bluntly: "We have a black child crisis worse than any since slavery."

This crisis did not exist a generation ago. In 1960, 78 percent of all black families were headed by married couples; today that figure is less than 40 percent. In the 1950s black crime rates, while higher than those for whites, were vastly lower than they are today. These figures suggest that the dire circumstances of the black community are not the result of genes or racism. The black gene pool has not changed substantially since mid-century, and racism then was far worse. The main problem facing African Americans is that they have developed a culture that represents an adaptation to past circumstances, but one that is now, in crucial respects, dysfunctional and pathological. . . .

Black Culture

For all their regional and economic diversity, blacks in America do share a culture, one that emerged out of the crucible of racism and oppression. Blacks who came from diverse tribes, speaking different languages and practicing varied ways of life, forged a distinct African-American identity in the new country—an identity that was solidified under segregation, when blacks were involuntarily united by the one-drop rule. Although black culture contains elements of Southern rural culture, modern urban culture, and lower-class culture, it has fused these elements into a distinct amalgam. . . .

Blacks in America seem to have developed what some scholars term an "oppositional culture" which is based on a comprehensive rejection of the white man's worldview. African-American psychiatrist Alvin Poussaint articulates a view popular among African-American leaders: "For blacks to mindlessly strive to be like the white middle class in a white racist, capitalist, exploitative society is without question detrimental to the cause of black people." . . .

Today, that oppositional culture has become an obstacle that prevents blacks from taking advantage of rights and opportunities that have multiplied in a new social environment. Even many middle-class and upper-middle-class blacks routinely permit blackness to be defined by the underclass. Middle-class behavior by African Americans is seen as inauthentic, while lower-class behavior is seen as genuinely black—a reversal of what W.E.B. Du Bois had in mind with his Talented Tenth. While most immigrant groups tend to look to their most successful citizens for emulation and self-definition, on many issues the moral tone in the black community is set from below. The underclass exercises such a powerful influence in shaping black cultural norms because this group is perceived as the most oppositional of all: It is remote from, and organized in resistance to, white middle-class standards. . . .

Racism as an Excuse

The first dysfunctional aspect of black culture is racial paranoia—a reflexive tendency to blame racism for every failure, even those that are intensely personal. For society as a whole, promiscuous charges of racism are dangerous because they undermine the credibility of the charge and make it more difficult to identify actual racists. For blacks, the risk of exaggerated charges is that they divert attention from the possibilities of the present and the future. Excessive charges of racism set up a battle with an adversary that sometimes does not exist. Consequently, blacks are in a struggle that they always lose. Racism itself becomes a scapegoat: It is blamed for problems it has little or nothing to do with, such as blacks performing poorly on math tests.

The displacement of personal or group problems onto the bugaboo of racism inspires a frenetic assault on society at large. But since racism is not the problem, the assault proves futile. The problem endures, and the frustration mounts. Racism remains the culprit, now accused of having taken an even subtler and more insidious shape. . . .

The Rage of the Privileged Class

A second dysfunctional aspect of black culture, a feature mainly of middle-class African-American life, is a rage that threatens to erupt in an orgy of destruction or self-destruction. When middle-class blacks found their opportunities severely restricted under segregation, black rage was either submerged or nonexistent. But now that middle-class blacks find themselves on the receiving end of racial preferences and government set-asides, many are beside themselves with anger. "I do not believe that we can restore and expand the freedoms that our lives require," June

Jordan writes, "until we embrace the justice of our rage."

This rage is not so difficult to comprehend. It represents post–affirmative action angst, the frustration of pursuing unearned privileges and then bristling when they do not bring something that has to be earned—the respect of one's peers. Moreover, black rage arises out of the recognition that, even as middle-class activists deplore the pathologies of the underclass, by moving out of inner-city neighborhoods they have sometimes contributed to those pathologies, and are dependent on their continuation for the race-based privileges they enjoy.

Limits of White Responsibility

In *The Harder We Run*, published back in 1982 when I was considered something of a young radical, I asserted that "race is still the most important idea in America," meaning of course that racist actions do affect the life chances of young black people. And I still believe that. But I no longer believe that all of the ills that affect black people are caused by whites, either white individuals or white institutions. We cause a considerable amount of the difficulty ourselves and only we can resolve that proportion. For example, it is both sobering and horrendous to consider that in 1991, ninety-three percent of black murder victims were slain by other blacks. . . .

We must have the power and the parity, but I am convinced that before we can achieve true progress we must also have something that I would call a sense of personal responsibility. We must take responsibility for our own lives and insist that we expect the same thing of the young people who look to us for guidance and inspiration. We must insist that we will use every weapon at our command, and invent others if need be, to remove obstacles that are in the way of young people. But we must tell them as well that we expect of them a commitment to moral and ethical standards, a commitment to hard work and to understanding that unless one exerts some effort one achieves nothing, and a commitment to family and community as their part in securing their own future and in enhancing the advancement of humanity.

William H. Harris, speech before the National Bar Association, January 26, 1993.

The effect of this molten frustration is what William Grier and Price Cobbs, in their book *Black Rage*, term "a posture close to paranoid thinking and mental disorder." In *Living with Racism*, Joe Feagin and Melvin Sikes document the state of mind that seems to paralyze many middle-class blacks. The book is intended to spotlight white racism; instead, it provides illuminating insight into some blacks' precarious grip on reality:

57

On a scale of one to ten, my level of anger is a ten. Mine has had time to grow over the years more and more until I now feel that my grasp on handling myself is tenuous. I think that now I would strike out to the point of killing, and not think about it. I really wouldn't care. . . .

It is hard to imagine whites feeling secure working with such persons: Surely such inflamed ethnic sensitivities are not what companies have in mind when they extol the diversity of work environments. Yet if these individuals are cranks, they are in respectable company. Leading African-American writers and scholars seem to share their persecution complex and its attendant rage. . . .

Government as the Big House

Another destructive stance that seems deeply ingrained in African Americans, especially those in the middle class, is a heavy dependence on government, accompanied by the belief that public programs are the way to solve virtually all social problems. . . .

Meanwhile, blacks have done very poorly in the one area that is a rapid source of jobs and social mobility for other groups: small business. According to U.S. government data, in 1987 blacks, who make up 12 percent of the population, owned about 420,000 businesses in America, with receipts of $19 billion. Asians, who make up 3 percent of the population, owned 350,000 businesses with receipts of $33 billion. African Americans currently start and run less than 3 percent of the nation's businesses, and take in less than 1 percent of the nation's gross receipts. Black enterprise is so fragile that a large portion of its receipts come from the government; many black businesses would collapse instantly if they were taken off government contracting preferences and set-asides. Only about 4 percent of African-American spending each year goes to black-owned enterprises.

The black cultural orientation toward government solutions is understandable; while many whites have traditionally viewed the state as a potential threat to personal liberty and opportunity, government has been the leading protector and guarantor of black rights and freedom. It was federal intervention in the 1860s that freed the slaves. The basic right of blacks to equal protection of the laws was recognized in the Fourteenth Amendment to the Constitution, which was somewhat incongruous with the rest of the document in that it was passed to expand federal power. In the twentieth century, black leaders found themselves compelled to turn to the federal government to combat state-sanctioned segregation and private discrimination. Government was recruited as an ally out of necessity, not preference. . . .

Perhaps the most serious of African-American pathologies . . . is the normalization of illegitimacy as a way of life. Nearly 70 percent of young black children born in the United States today are illegitimate, compared with 22 percent of white children. Almost 95 percent of black teen mothers are unmarried, compared with 55 percent of their white peers. Illegitimacy and single-parent households are not exclusive characteristics of the black underclass: College-educated African-American women have children outside of marriage at a rate about seven to eight times higher than college-educated white women. The result is what sociologist Andrew Cherlin terms an "almost complete separation of marriage and childbearing among African Americans."

Sacrificing Black Lives

Racialists hold to the doctrine that "authentic" blacks must view themselves as objects of mistreatment by whites and share in a collective consciousness of that mistreatment with other blacks. Believers of this creed have shaped the broad public discussion of racial affairs in America for decades; they have also policed, and therefore stifled, black communal discourse. They have argued, in effect, that the fellow feeling amongst blacks, engendered by our common experience of racism, should serve as the basis for our personal identities. Only if whites fully acknowledge their racist culpability, the racialists insist, can the black condition improve. In this they have been monumentally, tragically wrong. They have sacrificed, on an altar of racial protest, the unlimited potential of countless black lives. These are strong statements, but I regard them as commensurate with the crimes. . . .

Ironically, to the extent that we individual blacks see ourselves primarily through a racial lens, we sacrifice several possibilities for the kind of personal development that would ultimately further our collective racial interests. For, if we continue to labor under a self-definition derived from the outlook of our putative oppressor and confined to the contingent facts of our oppression, we shall never be truly free men and women.

Glenn Loury, *The Public Interest*, Fall 1995.

Whites, too, have a problem with illegitimacy, but the white norm still remains the two-parent household. It is dangerous to euphemize the problem of broken families, because it is connected with a range of other social pathologies. According to the Centers for Disease Control, the AIDS rate among African Americans is about three times higher than that of the U.S. population overall, and more than 50 percent of children with AIDS are black. Part of the reason for this is the common practice of poor black women exchanging sex for drugs. African-American scholar

Robert Hampton writes that "sexual abuse, physical child abuse, and family violence are arguably among the most serious social problems in the black community." Richard Majors reports that wife abuse is four times more common among blacks than among whites, and that black men kill their wives at a higher rate than any other ethnic group. . . .

High black illegitimacy rates cannot be blamed on slavery or segregation. For much of the twentieth century, sociologist Sidney Kronus reports, "The personal standards of conduct and behavior of the black middle class were modeled after the prevailing norms of the middle-class white community which stressed responsibility and the leading of the respectable life." After remaining relatively stable for the first half of this century, the black illegitimacy rate seems to have reached a critical mass during the 1960s and has exploded since then. . . .

Yet despite the scandalous pain generated by illegitimacy in the underclass, leading African-American intellectuals abstain from criticizing, and go so far as to revel in, what they describe as another alternative lifestyle. Radio commentator Julianne Malveaux is appalled that anyone would question the lifestyle of welfare mothers who live off taxpayers or seek to impose work requirements on them; she insists that "being on welfare is hard work." And Nobel Prize–winner Toni Morrison proposes an abandonment of societal restraints and a return to the elemental urges of nature. "The little nuclear family is a paradigm that just doesn't work," she writes. "Why we are hanging onto it, I don't know. I don't think a female running a house is a problem. . . . What is this business that you have to finish school at 18? The body is ready to have babies. Nature wants it done then."

The Big Lie

While mainstream black leaders refuse to criticize African-American pathologies or to seek internal reform, the scholars and activists of the civil rights establishment offer only what may be termed excuse theory—an extensive literature offering literally hundreds of reasons why external constraints make it impossible for blacks to succeed. For William Julius Wilson, black pathologies are the product, not cause, of a lack of jobs: In Wilson's view, blacks just happened to arrive in the cities around the time that unskilled jobs were leaving. Douglas Massey and Nancy Denton argue that residential separation accounts for the formation and persistence of the underclass. Bernard Boxill even argues that black pathologies should be classed as a cultural injury which entitles African Americans to further subsidies from the government.

One problem with this approach is that by emphasizing how poverty and deprivation cause crime and other pathologies, excuse theorists cannot explain why the majority of poor people remain law abiding. Another problem is that by focusing almost entirely on the cause of pathologies, excuse theorists offer no coherent vision of what to do about them. Since external factors are always to blame, these activists cannot do better than propose societal remedies such as redoubled federal funding, more social engineering, or a renewed campaign to root out white racism. In some cases government programs may help, yet none of them show any prospect of reducing the pathologies themselves. The reason for the moral paralysis of mainstream black intellectuals is that their relativist framework makes it impossible to identify black pathology without placing the onus for it on society at large.

Civil Rights as Industry

Blacks as a group stand at a historic junction. Very few people in the civil rights leadership recognize this: Convinced that racism of a hundred varieties stands between African Americans and success, most of the activists are ready to battle once again with this seemingly elusive and invincible foe. Yet the agenda of securing legal rights for blacks has now been accomplished, and there is no reason for blacks to increase the temperature of accusations of racism. Historically whites have used racism to serve powerful entrenched interests, but what interests does racism serve now? Most whites have no economic stake in the ghetto. They have absolutely nothing to gain from oppressing poor blacks. Indeed the only concern that whites seem to have about the underclass is its potential for crime and its reliance on the public purse.

By contrast, the civil rights industry now has a vested interest in the persistence of the ghetto, because the miseries of poor blacks are the best advertisement for continuing programs of racial preferences and set-asides. No one is more committed to the status quo, and more likely to resist its demise, than those professional blacks whose livelihoods depend on maintaining a large and resentful African-American coalition. Publicly inconsolable about the fact that racism continues, these activists seem privately terrified that it has abated. Formerly a beacon of moral argument and social responsibility, the civil rights leadership has lost much of its moral credibility, and has a fair representation of charlatans who exploit the sufferings of the underclass to collect research grants, minority scholarships, racial preferences, and other subsidies for themselves.

The supreme challenge faced by African Americans is the one that Booker T. Washington outlined almost a century ago: the mission of building the civilizational resources of a people whose culture is frequently unsuited to the requirements of the modern world. Sadly, the habits that were needed to resist racist oppression or secure legal rights are not the ones needed to exercise personal freedom or achieve success today. As urged by black reformers, both conservative and liberal, the task ahead is one of rebuilding broken families, developing educational and job skills, fostering black entrepreneurship, and curbing the epidemic of violence in the inner cities.

Government can help, mainly by doing no harm. Undoubtedly the state has the responsibility of providing police protection in the inner city, and of ceasing to subsidize illegitimacy and provide incentives for socially destructive behavior. Other policies, such as vouchers for school choice and enterprise zones to boost urban investment, may also prove beneficial. Yet in a free society, the government necessarily has a limited role in shaping the private lives of citizens. Consequently the government is not in a good position to reform the socialization practices of African Americans, and the primary responsibility for cultural restoration must lie with the black community itself. "When we finally achieve the right of full participation in American life," Ralph Ellison wrote, "what we make of it will depend upon our sense of cultural values, and our creative use of freedom, not upon our racial identification."

Moving Toward the End of Racism

We can sympathize with the magnitude of the project facing African Americans. In order to succeed, they must rid themselves of aspects of their past that have become aspects of themselves. The most telling refutation of racism, as Frederick Douglass once said about slavery, "is the presence of an industrious, enterprising, thrifty and intelligent free black population." For many black scholars and activists, such proposals are anathema because they seem to involve ideological sellout to the white man and thus are viewed as not authentically black. . . .

Instead, African Americans should take genuine pride in their collective moral achievement in this country's history. Blacks as a group have made a vital contribution to the expansion of the franchise of liberty and opportunity in America. Through their struggle over two centuries, blacks have helped to make the principles of the American founding a legal reality not just for themselves but also for other groups. As W.E.B. Du Bois put it, "There are no truer exponents of the pure human spirit of the Declaration of Independence than the American Negroes."

Yet rejection in this country produced what Du Bois termed a "double consciousness," so that blacks experience a kind of schizophrenia between their racial and American identities. Only now, for the first time in history, is it possible for African Americans to transcend this inner polarization and become truly modern, unhyphenated Americans. Black success and social acceptance now are both tied to rebuilding the African-American community. If blacks can achieve such a cultural renaissance, they will forever dispel rumors of inferiority and bring America to the promised land that has eluded the nation for so long—a destination that we can call the end of racism.

"White America still prefers its black people to be performers who divert them as athletes and musicians and comedians."

White Racism Is to Blame for Black Inequality

Andrew Hacker

Andrew Hacker teaches political science at Queens College in New York City. His writings include studies in political philosophy, statistical research, books, and published articles in various magazines, including *Time, Newsweek, Harper's Magazine,* the *Atlantic Monthly,* and the *New York Review of Books*. In the following viewpoint, excerpted from his book *Two Nations: Black and White, Separate, Hostile, Unequal,* Hacker argues that blacks are systematically discriminated against by whites, then doubly victimized when whites argue that black culture is to blame for black inequality.

As you read, consider the following questions:

1. How do whites dictate the level of integration, according to Hacker?
2. How are black problems defined by whites and why are these definitions inaccurate, according to Hacker?

Most white Americans will say that, all things considered, things aren't so bad for black people in the United States. Of course, they will grant that many problems remain. Still, whites feel there has been steady improvement, bringing blacks closer to parity, especially when compared with conditions in the past. Some have even been heard to muse that it's better to be black, since affirmative action policies make it a disadvantage to be white.

What white people seldom stop to ask is how they may benefit from belonging to their race. Nor is this surprising. People who can see do not regard their vision as a gift for which they should offer thanks. It may also be replied that having a white skin does not immunize a person from misfortune or failure. Yet even for those who fall to the bottom, being white has a worth. . . .

Of course, no one who is white can understand what it is like to be black in America. Still, were they to spend time in a black body, here are some of the things they would learn.

In the eyes of white Americans, being black encapsulates your identity. No other racial or national origin is seen as having so pervasive a personality or character. Even if you write a book on Euclidean algorithms or Renaissance sculpture, you will still be described as a "black author." Although you are a native American, with a longer lineage than most, you will never be accorded full membership in the nation or society. More than that, you early learn that this nation feels no need or desire for your physical presence. (Indeed, your people are no longer in demand as cheap labor.) You sense that most white citizens would heave a sigh of relief were you simply to disappear. . . .

Creating an Identity

To a far greater degree than for immigrants from other lands, it rests on you to create your own identity. But it is still not easy to follow the counsel of Zora Neale Hurston: "Be as black as you want to be." For one thing, that choice is not always left to you. By citizenship and birth, you may count as an American, yet you find yourself agreeing with August Wilson when he says "We're a different people." Why else can you refer to your people as "folks" and "family," to one another as "sisters" and "brothers," in ways whites never can? . . .

You find yourself granting that there are more black faces in places where they were never seen before. Within living memory, your people were barred from major league teams; now they command the highest salaries in most professional sports. In the movies, your people had to settle for roles as servants or buffoons. Now at least some of them are cast as physicians, business executives, and police officials. But are things truly different? When everything is added up, white America still prefers its black people to be performers who divert them as athletes and musicians and comedians.

Yet where you yourself are concerned, you sense that in mainstream occupations, your prospects are quite limited. In most areas of employment, even after playing by the rules, you find yourself hitting a not-so-invisible ceiling. You wonder if you are simply corporate wallpaper, a protective coloration they find it prudent to display. You begin to suspect that a "qualification" you will always lack is white pigmentation. . . .

Black Problems

You and your people have problems, far more than your share. And it is not as if you are ignorant of them, or wish to sweep them under a rug. But how to frame your opinions is not an easy matter. For example, what should you say about black crime or addiction or out-of-wedlock pregnancies? Of course, you have much to say on these and other topics, and you certainly express your ideas when you are among your own people. And you can be critical—very critical—of a lot of behavior you agree has become common among blacks.

However, the white world also asks that black people conduct these discussions in public. In particular, they want to hear you condemn black figures they regard as outrageous or irresponsible. This cannot help but annoy you. For one thing, you have never asked for white advice. Yet whites seem to feel that you stand in need of their tutelage, as if you lack the insight to understand your own interests. Moreover, it makes sense for members of a minority to stand together, especially since so many whites delight in magnifying differences among blacks. Your people have had a long history of being divided and conquered. At the same time, you have no desire to be held responsible for what every person of your color thinks or does. You cannot count how many times you have been asked to atone for some utterances of Louis Farrakhan, or simply to assert that he does not speak for you. You want to retort that you will choose your own causes and laments. Like other Americans, you have no obligation to follow agendas set by others.

As it happens, black Americans can and do disagree on racial matters, not to mention a host of other issues. Thus a survey conducted in 1990 found that 78 percent of those polled said they preferred to think of themselves as "black," and another 20 percent chose "African-American," while the remaining 2 percent stayed with "Negro." Another study by a team of black social scientists found that less than a quarter of the blacks they polled felt that black parents should give their children African names. Indeed, on a wide range of matters, there is no fixed, let alone official, black position. Yet it is amazing how often white people ask you to tell them how "black people" think about some individual or issue. . . .

You may, by a combination of brains and luck and perseverance, make it into the middle class. And like all middle-class Americans, you will want to enjoy the comforts and pleasures that come with that status. One downside is that you will find many white people asking why you aren't doing more to help members of your race whom you have supposedly left behind. There is even the suggestion that, by moving to a safer or more spacious area, you have callously deserted your own people.

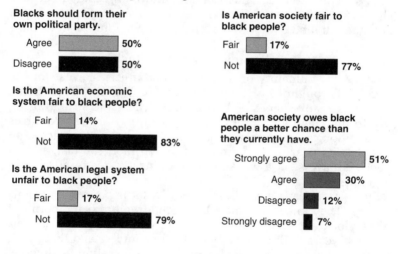

Black Disillusionment with Politics

A 1994 poll finds a high percentage of blacks in favor of abandoning past goals of integration into mainstream American society to pursue a separatist political agenda.

Blacks should form their own political party.

Agree 50%
Disagree 50%

Is the American economic system fair to black people?

Fair 14%
Not 83%

Is the American legal system unfair to black people?

Fair 17%
Not 79%

Is American society fair to black people?

Fair 17%
Not 77%

American society owes black people a better chance than they currently have.

Strongly agree 51%
Agree 30%
Disagree 12%
Strongly disagree 7%

Source: University of Chicago.

Yet hardly ever do middle-class whites reflect on the fact that they, too, have moved to better neighborhoods, usually far from poorer and less equable persons of their own race or ethnic origins. There is little evidence that middle-class whites are prepared to give much of themselves in aid of fellow whites who have fallen on misfortune. Indeed, the majority of white Americans have chosen to live in sequestered suburbs, where they are insulated from the nation's losers and failures.

Compounding these expectations, you find yourself continually subjected to comparisons with other minorities or even members of your own race. For example, you are informed that blacks who have emigrated from the Caribbean earn higher incomes than those born in the United States. Here the message seems to be that color by itself is not an insurmountable barrier. Most stinging of all are contrasts with recent immigrants. You hear people just off the boat (or, nowadays, a plane) extolled for building businesses and becoming productive citizens. Which is another way of asking why you haven't matched their achievements, considering how long your people have been here.

Moreover, immigrants are praised for being willing to start at the bottom. The fact that so many of them manage to find jobs is taken as evidence that the economy still has ample opportunities for employment. You want to reply that you are not an immigrant, but as much a citizen as any white person born here. Perhaps you can't match the mathematical skills of a teenager from Korea, but then neither can most white kids at suburban high schools. You feel much like a child being chided because she has not done as well as a precocious sister. However, you are an adult, and do not find such scolding helpful or welcome.

Family Breakdown and Racism

No law of humanity or nature posits a precise format for the family. Throughout history and even in our day, households have had many shapes and structures. The same strictures apply to marriage and parental relationships. All this requires some emphasis, given concerns expressed about "the black family" and its presumed disintegration. In fact, the last several decades have seen a weakening of domestic ties in all classes and races.

Black Americans are fully aware of what is happening in this sphere. They know that most black children are being born out of wedlock and that these youngsters will spend most of their growing years with a single parent. They understand that a majority of their marriages will dissolve in separation or divorce, and that many black men and women will never marry at all. Black Americans also realize that tensions between men and women sometimes bear a violence and bitterness that can take an awful toll.

If you are black, you soon learn it is safest to make peace with reality: to acknowledge that the conditions of your time can undercut dreams of enduring romance and "happily ever after." This is especially true if you are a black woman, since you may find yourself spending many of your years without a man in your life. Of course, you will survive and adapt, as your people always have. Central in this effort will be joining and sustaining a community of women—another form of a family—on whom you can rely for love and strength and support.

If you are a black woman, you can expect to live five fewer years than your white counterpart. Among men, the gap is seven years. Indeed, a man living in New York's Harlem is less likely to reach sixty-five than is a resident of Bangladesh. Black men have a three times greater chance of dying of AIDS, and outnumber whites as murder victims by a factor of seven. According to studies, you get less sleep, are more likely to be overweight, and to develop hypertension. This is not simply due to poverty. Your shorter and more painful life results, in considerable measure, from the anxieties that come with being black in America.

Social Evil of Racism

The tragedy . . . is that even when articulate, intelligent black men manage to rise above the temptations and traps of "the ghetto," they are often subject to continuing forms of social fear, sexual jealousy, and obnoxious racism. More pointedly, in the 1960s, during a crucial stage in the development of black pride and self-esteem, highly educated, deeply conscientious black men were gunned down in cold blood. This phenomenon finds paradigmatic expression in the deaths of Medgar Evers, Malcolm X, and Martin Luther King, Jr. These events of public death are structured deep in the psyches of surviving black men, and the ways in which these horrible spectacles of racial catastrophe represent and implicitly sanction lesser forms of social evil against black men remains hurtful to black America.

Michael Eric Dyson, *Reflecting Black*, 1993.

If you are a black young man, life can be an interlude with an early demise. Black youths do what they must to survive in a hostile world, with the prospect of violence and death on its battlefields. Attitudes can turn fatalistic, even suicidal: gladiators without even the cheers of an audience.

When white people hear the cry, "the police are coming!" for them it almost always means, "help is on the way." Black citizens cannot make the same assumption. If you have been the victim of a crime, you cannot presume that the police will actually show up; or, if they do, that they will take much note of your losses or suffering. You sense police officials feel that blacks should accept being robbed or raped as one of life's everyday risks. It seems to you obvious that more detectives are assigned to a case when a white person is murdered.

If you are black and young and a man, the arrival of the police does not usually signify help, but something very different. If you are a teenager simply socializing with some friends, the police may order you to disperse and get off the streets. They may turn on a searchlight, order you against a wall. Then comes the command to spread your legs and empty out your pockets, and stand splayed there while they call in your identity over their radio. You may be a college student and sing in a church choir, but that will not overcome the police presumption that you have probably done something they can arrest you for.

If you find yourself caught up in the system, it will seem like alien terrain. Usually your judge and prosecutor will be white, as will most members of the jury, as well as your attorney. In short, your fate will be decided by a white world.

This may help to explain why you have so many harsh words for the police, even though you want and need their protection more than white people do. . . .

Has It Changed?

As you look back on the way this nation has treated your people, you wonder how so many have managed to persevere amid so much adversity. About slavery, of course, too much cannot be said. Yet even within living memory, there were beaches and parks—in the North as well as in the South—where black Americans simply could not set foot. Segregation meant separation without even a pretense of equal facilities. In Southern communities that had only a single public library or swimming pool, black residents and taxpayers could never borrow a book or go for a swim. Indeed, black youths were even forbidden to stroll past the pool, lest they catch a glimpse of white girls in their bathing costumes.

How did they endure the endless insults and humiliations? Grown people being called by their first names, having to avert their eyes when addressed by white people, even being expected to step off a sidewalk when whites walked by. Overarching it all was the terror, with white police and prosecutors and judges possessing all but total power over black lives. Not to mention the lynchings by white mobs, with victims even chosen at random, to remind all blacks of what could happen to them if they did not remain compliant and submissive.

You wonder how much that has changed. Suppose, for example, you find yourself having to drive across the country, stopping at gasoline stations and restaurants and motels. As you travel across the heart of white America, you can never be sure of how you will be received. While the odds are that you will reach your destination alive, you cannot be so sure that you will not be stopped by the police or spend a night in a cell. So you would be well advised to keep to the speed limit, and not exceed it by a single mile. Of course, white people are pulled over by state troopers; but how often are their cars searched? Or if a motel clerk cannot "find" your reservation, is it because she has now seen you in person? And are all the toilet facilities at this service station really out of order?

The day-to-day aggravations and humiliations add up bit by bitter bit. To take a depressingly familiar example, you stroll into a shop to look at the merchandise, and it soon becomes clear that the clerks are keeping a watchful eye on you. Too quickly, one of them comes over to inquire what it is you might want, and then remains conspicuously close as you continue your search. It also seems that they take an unusually long time verifying your credit card. And then you and a black friend enter a restaurant, and find yourselves greeted warily, with what is obviously a more anxious reception than that given to white guests. Yes, you will be served, and your table will not necessarily be next to the kitchen. Still, you sense that they would rather you had chosen some other eating place. Or has this sort of thing happened so often that you are growing paranoid?

So there is the sheer strain of living in a white world, the rage that you must suppress almost every day. No wonder black Americans, especially black men, suffer so much from hypertension. (If ever an illness had social causes, this is certainly one.) To be black in America means reining in your opinions and emotions as no whites ever have to do. Not to mention the forced and false smiles you are expected to contrive, to assure white Americans that you harbor no grievances against them.

Lasting Solutions?

Along with the tension and the strain and the rage, there come those moments of despair. At times, the conclusion seems all but self-evident that white America has no desire for your presence or any need for your people. Can this nation have an unstated strategy for annihilating your people? How else, you ask yourself, can one explain the incidence of death and debilitation from drugs and disease; the incarceration of a whole generation of your men; the consignment of millions of women and children to half-lives of poverty and dependency? Each of these debilities has its causes; indeed, analyzing them has become a minor industry. Yet with so much about these conditions that is so closely related to race, they say something about the larger society that has allowed them to happen.

This is not to say that white officials sit in secret rooms, plotting the genocide of black America. You understand as well as anyone that politics and history seldom operate that way. Nor do you think of yourself as unduly suspicious. Still, you cannot rid yourself of some lingering mistrust. Just as your people were once made to serve silently as slaves, could it be that if white America begins to conclude that you are becoming too much trouble, it will find itself contemplating more lasting solutions?

71

3 VIEWPOINT

---

*"Racial integration translated into assimilation
ultimately serves to reinforce and maintain white
supremacy."*

Blacks Must
Recognize and
Fight Oppression

bell hooks

bell hooks is Distinguished Professor of English at City College
in New York. She is a widely published commentator on race
relations. In the following viewpoint, excerpted from her book
Killing Rage: Ending Racism, hooks takes issue with those people
who argue that blacks must assimilate, even imitate, whites to
succeed in America. She argues vehemently that this approach
constitutes submission to a systematic white oppression of
blacks and should not be tolerated. Blacks must continually re-
define their identity in terms of their race in order to succeed as
a group, she concludes.

As you read, consider the following questions:

1. What evidence does hooks give to prove her case that white
   supremacy is pervasive?
2. How does assimilation serve to keep whites in a superior
   position, according to hooks?
3. What is the author's advice to white people who want to help
   blacks?

bell hooks, "Overcoming White Supremacy: A Comment," in *Killing Rage* (New York: Holt,
1995), originally appeared in *Talking Back: Thinking Feminist, Thinking Black* by bell hooks
(Boston: South End Press, 1989). Reprinted by permission of South End Press.

Black people in the United States share with black people in South Africa and with people of color globally both the pain of white supremacist oppression and exploitation and the pain that comes from resistance and struggle. The first pain wounds us, the second pain helps heal our wounds. It often troubles me that black people in the United States have not risen en masse to declare solidarity with our black sisters and brothers in South Africa. Perhaps one day soon—say, Martin Luther King's birthday—we will enter the streets at a certain hour, wherever we are, to stand for a moment, naming and affirming the primacy of black liberation.

As I write, I try to remember when the word "racism" ceased to be the term which best expressed for me exploitation of black people and other people of color in this society and when I began to understand that the most useful term was "white supremacy." It was certainly a necessary term when confronted with the liberal attitudes of white women active in feminist movement who were unlike their racist ancestors—white women in the early women's rights movement who did not wish to be caught dead in fellowship with black women. In fact, these women often requested and longed for the presence of black women. Yet when present, what we saw was that they wished to exercise control over our bodies and thoughts as their racist ancestors had—that this need to exercise power over us expressed how much they had internalized the values and attitudes of white supremacy.

It may have been this contact or contact with fellow white English professors who want very much to have "a" black person in "their" department as long as that person thinks and acts like them, shares their values and beliefs, is in no way different, that first compelled me to use the term "white supremacy" to identify the ideology that most determines how white people in this society (irrespective of their political leanings to the right or left) perceive and relate to black people and other people of color. It is the very small but highly visible liberal movement away from the perpetuation of overtly racist discrimination, exploitation, and oppression of black people which often masks how all-pervasive white supremacy is in this society, both as ideology and as behavior. When liberal whites fail to understand how they can and/or do embody white supremacist values and beliefs even though they may not embrace racism as prejudice or domination (especially domination that involves coercive control), they cannot recognize the ways their actions support and affirm the very structure of racist domination and oppression that they profess to wish to see eradicated.

Likewise, "white supremacy" is a much more useful term for understanding the complicity of people of color in upholding and maintaining racial hierarchies that do not involve force (i.e., slavery, apartheid) than the term "internalized racism"—a term most often used to suggest that black people have absorbed negative feelings and attitudes about blackness held by white people. The term "white supremacy" enables us to recognize not only that black people are socialized to embody the values and attitudes of white supremacy, but that we can exercise "white supremacist control" over other black people. This is important, for unlike the term "uncle tom," which carried with it the recognition of complicity and internalized racism, a new terminology must accurately name the way we as black people directly exercise power over one another when we perpetuate white supremacist beliefs. Speaking about changing perspectives on black identity, writer Toni Morrison said in a recent interview: "Now people choose their identities. Now people choose to be Black." At this historical moment, when a few black people no longer experience the racial apartheid and brutal racism that still determine the lot of many black people, it is easier for that few to ally themselves politically with the dominant racist white group.

The Dangers of Assimilation

Assimilation is the strategy that has provided social legitimation for this shift in allegiance. It is a strategy deeply rooted in the ideology of white supremacy and its advocates urge black people to negate blackness, to imitate racist white people so as to better absorb their values, their way of life. Ironically, many changes in social policy and social attitudes that were once seen as ways to end racial domination have served to reinforce and perpetuate white supremacy. This is especially true of social policy that has encouraged and promoted racial integration. Given the continued force of racism, racial integration translated into assimilation ultimately serves to reinforce and maintain white supremacy. Without an ongoing active movement to end white supremacy, without ongoing black liberation struggle, no social environment can exist in the United States that truly supports integration. When black people enter social contexts that remain unchanged, unaltered, in no way stripped of the framework of white supremacy, we are pressured to assimilate. We are rewarded for assimilation. Black people working or socializing in predominantly white settings whose very structures are informed by the principles of white supremacy who dare to affirm blackness, love of black culture and identity, do so at great risk. We must continually challenge, protest, resist while working to leave no gaps in our defense that will allow us to be crushed. This is especially true in work settings where we risk being fired or not receiving deserved promotions. Resisting the pressure to assimilate is a part of our struggle to end white supremacy.

When I talk with audiences around the United States about feminist issues of race and gender, my use of the term "white supremacy" always sparks a reaction, usually of a critical or hostile nature. Individual white people and even some non-whites insist that this is not a white supremacist society, that racism is not nearly the problem it used to be (it is downright frightening to hear people argue vehemently that the problem of racism has been solved), that there has been change. While it is true that the nature of racist oppression and exploitation has changed as slavery has ended and the apartheid structure of Jim Crow has legally changed, white supremacy continues to shape perspectives on reality and to inform the social status of black people and all people of color. Nowhere is this more evident than in university settings. And often it is the liberal folks in those settings who are unwilling to acknowledge this truth.

Perils of Integration

Some black intellectuals believe that the nation's integrationist philosophy itself caused the demise of healthy black communities—the very types of communities that the black middle class is trying to form today. "The effort to integrate destroyed many viable black communities," says the Iowa City *Press-Citizen's* Joe Brown. "We fell too much into integration rather than desegregation. Desegregation simply removed the barriers that allowed one to move wherever he wanted to move. Integration means forcing people—some kind of orchestrated effort to mix people together."

Elena Neuman, *Insight on the News*, June 6, 1994.

Recently in a conversation with a white male lawyer at his home where I was a guest, he informed me that someone had commented to him that children are learning very little history these days in school, that the attempt to be all-inclusive, to talk about Native Americans, blacks, women, etc. has led to a fragmented focus on particular representative individuals with no larger historical framework. I responded to this comment by suggesting that it has been easier for white people to practice this inclusion rather than change the larger framework; that it is easier to change the focus from Christopher Columbus, the important white man who "discovered" America, to Sitting Bull or Harriet Tubman, than it is to cease telling a distorted version of U.S. history which upholds white supremacy. Really teaching history in a new way would require abandoning the old myths informed by white supremacy like the notion that Columbus discovered America. It would mean talking about imperialism, colonization, about the Africans who came here before Columbus (see Ivan Van Sertima's *They Came Before Columbus*). It would mean talking about genocide, about the white colonizers' exploitation and betrayal of Native Americans; about ways the legal and governmental structures of this society from the Constitution on supported and upheld slavery, apartheid (see Derrick Bell's *And We Are Not Saved*). This history can be taught only when the perspectives of teachers are no longer shaped by white supremacy. Our conversation is one of many examples that reveal the way black people and white people can socialize in a friendly manner, be racially integrated, while deeply ingrained notions of white supremacy remain intact. Incidents like this make it necessary for concerned folks, for righteous white people, to begin to fully explore the way white supremacy determines how they see the world, even as their actions are not informed by the type of racial prejudice that promotes overt discrimination and separation.

Significantly, "assimilation" was a term that began to be more commonly used after the revolts against white supremacy in the late 1960s and early 1970s. The intense, passionate rebellion against racism and white supremacy of this period was crucial because it created a context for politicization, for education for critical consciousness, one in which black people could begin to confront the extent of our complicity, our internalization of white supremacy, and begin the process of self-recovery and collective renewal. Describing this effort in his work *The Search for a Common Ground*, black theologian Howard Thurman commented:

> "Black is Beautiful" became not merely a phrase—it was a stance, a total attitude, a metaphysics. In very positive and exciting terms it began undermining the idea that had developed over so many years into a central aspect of white mythology: that black is ugly, black is evil, black is demonic. In so doing it fundamentally attacked the front line of the defense of the myth of white supremacy and superiority.

Economic Reasons

Clearly, assimilation as a social policy upholding white supremacy was strategically an important counterdefense, one that would serve to deflect the call for radical transformation of black consciousness. Suddenly the terms for success (that is, getting a job, acquiring the means to provide materially for oneself and one's family) were redefined. It was not enough for black people to enter institutions of higher education and acquire the necessary skills to effectively compete for jobs previously occupied solely by whites; the demand was that blacks become "honorary whites," that black people assimilate to succeed.

The force that gave the social policy of assimilation power to influence and change the direction of black liberation struggle was economic. Economic distress created a climate wherein militancy—overt resistance to white supremacy and racism (which included the presentation of self in a manner that suggests black pride)—was no longer deemed a viable survival strategy. Natural hairstyles, African dress, etc. were discarded as signs of militancy that might keep one from getting ahead. A similar regressive, reactionary move was taking place among young white radicals, many of whom had been fiercely engaged in Left politics, who suddenly began to seek reincorporation into the liberal and conservative mainstream. Again the force behind their reentry into the system was economic. On a very basic level, changes in the cost of housing (as in the great apartment one had in 1965 for $100 a month cost $400 by 1975) had a frightening impact on college-educated young people of all ethnicities who thought they were committed to transforming society, but who were unable to face living without choice, without the means to escape, who feared living in poverty. Coupled with economic forces exerting pressure, many radicals despaired of the possibility that this white supremacist capitalist patriarchy could really be changed.

The End of White Radicalism

Tragically, many radical whites who had been allies in the black liberation struggle began to question whether the struggle to end racism was really that significant, or to suggest that the struggle was over, as they moved into their new liberal positions. Radical white youth who had worked in civil rights struggles, protested the war in Vietnam, and even denounced U.S. imperialism could not reconstruct their ties to prevailing systems of domination without creating a new layer of false consciousness—the assertion that racism was no longer pervasive, that race was no longer an important issue. Similarly, critiques of capitalism, especially those that urged individuals to try and live differently within the framework of capitalism, were also relegated to the back burner as people "discovered" that it was important to have class privilege so that one could better help the exploited.

It is no wonder that black radicals met these betrayals with despair and hopelessness. What had all the contemporary struggle to resist racism really achieved? What did it mean to have this period of radical questioning of white supremacy, of black is beautiful, only to witness a few years later the successful mass production by white corporations of hair care products to straighten black hair? What did it mean to witness the assault on black culture by capitalist forces which stress the production on all fronts of an image, a cultural product that can "cross over"—that is, that can speak more directly to the concerns, to

the popular imagination of white consumers, while still attract-
ing the dollars of black consumers? And what does it mean in
1987 when television viewers watch a morning talk show on
black beauty, where black women suggest that these trends are
only related to personal preferences and have no relation to
racism; when viewers witness a privileged white male, Phil
Donahue, shaking his head and trying to persuade the audience
to acknowledge the reality of racism and its impact on black
people? Or what does it mean when many black people say that
what they like most about the Bill Cosby show is that there is
little emphasis on blackness, that they are "just people"? And
again to hear reported on national news that little black children prefer playing with white dolls rather than black dolls? All
these popular narratives remind us that "we are not yet saved,"
that white supremacy prevails, that the racist oppression and
exploitation which daily assaults the bodies and spirits of black
people in South Africa assaults black people here.

Advice to White Folks

What can I say to decent white people? I think the best answer is
what so many whites invariably preach to us—self-help. In a moment of deep weariness, Thurgood Marshall once said to the
great black psychologist Kenneth Clark, "I'm so tired of trying to
save white folks' souls." Thurgood said that about forty years ago.

We can't save white folks' souls. Only they can do that. The best
have to save the rest—but to succeed, they have to work at it every day. They can start . . . at the dinner table. Parents need to
work on their children, to weed out all the racism that is so normal in our society. They have to work to get their school boards
to teach students the truth about American history, not to nurture
black self-esteem or white guilt, but to give our children a rich
and true understanding of our nation. And they have to re-teach
themselves that the "government" is our common enterprise, set
up to undertake large efforts that we believe are in the best interest of us all.

Roger Wilkins, *Mother Jones*, November/December 1992.

Years ago when I was a high school student experiencing
racial desegregation, there was a current of resistance and militancy that was so fierce. It swept over and through our bodies
as we—black students—stood, pressed against the red brick
walls, watching the National Guard with their guns, waiting for
those moments when we would enter, when we would break
through racism, waiting for the moments of change—of victory.

And now even within myself I find that spirit of militancy grow-ing faint; all too often it is assaulted by feelings of despair and powerlessness. I find that I must work to nourish it, to keep it strong. Feelings of despair and powerlessness are intensified by all the images of black self-hate that indicate that those militant 1960s did not have sustained radical impact—that the politiciza-tion and transformation of black consciousness did not become an ongoing revolutionary practice in black life. This causes such frustration and despair because it means that we must return to this basic agenda, that we must renew efforts at politicization, that we must go over old ground. Perhaps what is more dis-heartening is the fear that the seeds, though planted again, will never survive, will never grow strong. Right now it is anger and rage (see Audre Lorde's "The Uses of Anger" in *Sister Outsider*) at the continued racial genocide that rekindles within me that spirit of militancy.

Like so many radical black folks who work in university set-tings, I often feel very isolated. Often we work in environments predominantly peopled by white folks (some of whom are well-meaning and concerned) who are not committed to working to end white supremacy, or who are unsure about what that com-mitment means. Certainly the feminist movement has been one of the places where there has been renewed interest in challeng-ing and resisting racism. There too it has been easier for white women to confront racism as overt exploitation and domination, or as personal prejudice, than to confront the encompassing and profound reality of white supremacy.

What White People Can Do

In talking about race and gender recently, the question most often asked by white women has to do with white women's re-sponse to black women or women of color insisting that they are not willing to teach them about their racism—to show the way. They want to know: What should a white person do who is attempting to resist racism? It is problematic to assert that black people and other people of color who are sincerely committed to struggling against white supremacy should be unwilling to help or teach white people. Challenging black folks in the nine-teenth century, Frederick Douglass made the crucial point that "power accedes nothing without demand." For the racially op-pressed to demand of white people, of black people, of all peo-ple that we eradicate white supremacy, that those who benefit materially by exercising white supremacist power, either ac-tively or passively, willingly give up that privilege in response to that demand, and then to refuse to show the way, is to under-mine our own cause. We must show the way. There must exist a paradigm, a practical model for social change that includes an understanding of ways to transform consciousness that are linked to efforts to transform structures.

A Need for Continued Change

Fundamentally, it is our collective responsibility as radical black people and people of color, and as white people, to construct models for social change. To abdicate that responsibility, to suggest that change is just something an individual can do on his or her own or in isolation with other racist white people, is utterly misleading. If as a black person I say to a white person who shows a willingness to commit herself or himself to the struggle to end white supremacy that I refuse to affirm or help in that endeavor, it is a gesture that undermines my commitment to that struggle. Many black people have essentially responded in this way because we do not want to do the work for white people, and most importantly we cannot do the work, yet this often seems to be what is asked of us. Rejecting the work does not mean that we cannot and do not show the way by our actions, by the information we share. Those white people who want to continue the dominant-subordinate relationship so endemic to racist exploitation by insisting that we "serve" them— that we do the work of challenging and changing their consciousness—are acting in bad faith. In his work *Pedagogy in Progress: The Letters to Guinea-Bissau*, Paulo Freire reminds us:

> Authentic help means that all who are involved help each other mutually, growing together in the common effort to understand the reality which they seek to transform.

It is our collective responsibility as people of color and as white people who are committed to ending white supremacy to help one another. It is our collective responsibility to educate for critical consciousness. If I commit myself politically to black liberation struggle, to the struggle to end white supremacy, I am not making a commitment to working only for and with black people; I must engage in struggle with all willing comrades to strengthen our awareness and our resistance. (See *The Autobiography of Malcolm X* and *The Last Year of Malcolm X—The Evolution of a Revolutionary* by George Breitman.) Malcolm X is an important role model for those of us who wish to transform our consciousness for he was engaged in ongoing critical self-reflection, in changing both his words and his deeds. In thinking about black response to white people, about what they can do to end racism, I am reminded of that memorable example when Malcolm X expressed regret about an incident with a white female college student who asked him what she could do and he told her: "nothing." He later saw that there was much that she could have done. For each of us, it is work to educate ourselves to understand the nature of white supremacy with a critical consciousness. Black people are not born into this world with innate understanding of racism and white supremacy. (See John Hodge, ed., *Cultural Bases of Racism and Group Oppression*.)

In recent years, particularly among women active in feminist movement, much effort to confront racism has focused on individual prejudice. While it is important that individuals work to transform their consciousness, striving to be antiracist, it is important for us to remember that the struggle to end white supremacy is a struggle to change a system, a structure. Hodge emphasizes in his book "the problem of racism is not prejudice but domination." For our efforts to end white supremacy to be truly effective, individual struggle to change consciousness must be fundamentally linked to collective effort to transform those structures that reinforce and perpetuate white supremacy.

"It's silly, and worse, for black men and women, wearing designer suits, living in elegant homes, working at important . . . careers to pretend that we are hardly better off than a sharecropper in the rural south."

Blacks' Claims of Oppression by Whites Hamper Black Success

Anne Wortham

Anne Wortham is an associate professor of sociology at Illinois State University. In the following viewpoint, Wortham argues that an insistence by many blacks that white oppression keeps them in a victimlike state is counterproductive. Numerous blacks have succeeded in white society, and acknowledging and celebrating this fact would do much to help all blacks, Wortham concludes.

As you read, consider the following questions:

1. How has a belief in the American Dream contributed to blacks' belief in their victimhood, according to Wortham?
2. How did President Johnson's social programs aggravate social problems, according to the author?
3. Why does Wortham believe that even well-off blacks wish to maintain a victim status?

Anne Wortham, "Victimhood Versus Individual Responsibility," *Lincoln Review*, Winter 1993-94. Reprinted by permission. Endnotes in the original article have not been included.

Much of black history has been characterized by efforts to redress the injustice of racial subordination. However, since the mid-1950s, there has existed within the black community a concerted effort by individuals and groups to transform their victimization into a political advantage—to institutionalize it as a cultural symbol of moral and political status—by presenting themselves in terms of the self-as-victim image. They are by no means alone in this. Their campaign has been joined by a number of other groups that have captured categories of victimhood. Aaron Wildavsky identifies some of the groups and their transformations to victimhood as follows:

> American women have gone from being the freest women in the world to being victims of male chauvinism. The elderly have exchanged their reputation for wisdom for a designation of "disadvantaged." Youth receives preferred treatment at Democratic party conventions. Entire regions seek official designation as "underprivileged," as if it were a badge of honor. American blacks, chicanos, Native Americans, and other ethnic minorities are now considered "Third World" peoples as if they lived in a regime controlled by foreigners.

This article will examine the nature of the self-as-victim image and its opposition to individual liberty and individual responsibility. Particular attention will be given to black victimhood. Since this is a critical examination of victimhood, it is necessary to stress at the outset that it is not an attempt either to deny the victimization of disadvantaged groups or to diminish it. My aim is to draw the lines of distinction between *actual* victims and *symbolic* victims, and to illustrate how the beliefs and attitudes of the latter, which I refer to as *the stance of victimhood* or the *self-as-victim image*, are a threat to the values that are necessary for the relief of those who are disadvantaged.

The Nature of Victimhood

A victim is a person who suffers from a destructive or injurious action or agency; he may be deceived or cheated, sacrificed or regarded as sacrificed. Some definitions note that one may be a victim of one's own emotions or ignorance. But we usually think of people as victims of another person's action or of some impersonal, external agency or force beyond one's control such as natural catastrophes, accidents, physical handicaps or illness, psychological or physical abuse, or political and social injustice.

Unlike actual victimization, the stance of victimhood is a technique of self-presentation and impression management that involves the symbolic elaboration of actual victim status. Since symbolic elaboration is a quality of conceptualization and not of concrete reality, one need not be an actual victim to make a claim to victim status. Whether he has actually experienced injustice or not, the symbolic victim presents himself as the embodiment of all the real or imagined suffering of his membership group as a whole. He asks us to ignore the fact that he is not an actual victim and, instead, treat him *as if* he were a victim.

Victimhood or the self-as-victim requires that one speak in "the voice of the victim." It calls for a "posture of accusatory public testimony" that is intransigent and unceasing. As Judith Eaton points out, its approach to social problems "carries with it certain attitudes that produce difficulty for any sense of shared vision, values, or beliefs: denial of personal responsibility, insistence on society's full responsibility for any personal problem one may have, a lack of commitment to resolution of the problems that created the [alleged] victimhood status, a need to continue to feel oppressed or have enemies, and a tendency to moral bullying."

The subjective context of symbolic victimhood is the expectation of actual equality of resources, which involves the idealization of the principle of equality. Although symbolic victimhood is maintained by appealing to the ideals of justice and equality, it is distinguished not by a quest for justice, but by the quest for guilt. The quest for justice involves the expectation that injustice and the conflicts it provokes are *resolvable*; the quest for guilt assumes the *unresolvability* of injustice. For the stance taken by the symbolic victim, to paraphrase Christopher Lasch, is that the master sex, or master race, or master culture can never understand its victims, "though it might perhaps begin to understand the extent of its own crimes." It is by arousing guilt that the symbolic victim is able to acquire power. This is the reason, observes historian C. Vann Woodward, that American public life has become "the seller's market for guilt." Indeed, it is for this reason, says Richard Sennett, that "the moral status of the victim has never been greater or more dangerous than it is now."

The self-as-victim has been cultivated and given viability in the context of the transformation of the American Dream. The American Dream originated during the American Enlightenment as the dream of man's perfectibility. However, by the 1950s the American Dream had been replaced by the dream of society's perfectibility, which was to be achieved by social engineering. The dream of society's perfectibility depended on welfare liberalism's belief that for every problem there is a solution and its confidence that the United States has both the material resources and the intelligence to eliminate social problems.

But the dream and the confidence that drove it proved to be

unrealistic. During the 1960s the failure to achieve societal perfectibility led to a "crisis of the American creed." Many groups blamed the failure not on the flawed assumptions of the ideal and attempts to transform them into practical reality, but on the institutions and national character of the country. It became respectable to take a highly critical view of America and its role in the world. The self-image of America as the vanguard of progress and democracy, and the embodiment of human aspirations for a better future was attacked with unprecedented vigor by Black nationalists, leaders of the New Left, countercultural gurus, self-awareness therapists, radical feminists, and ecologists. C. Vann Woodward has called this attack on American culture and denial of its virtues a "quest for guilt."

It was in this soil of the crisis of the American creed that the self-as-victim image took root, grew and came to fruition. The fertilizer was what Nathan Glazer describes as liberalism's "tendency to blame society and the political system for social problems; [its] self-induced guilt for not having earlier recognized and acted on injustices, inequalities, and deprivations; and [its] sense of complacent moral superiority to forbears who did not recognize these problems or act on them at all." The self-as-victim image now thrives in a cultural environment in which "no one is considered a winner in American history," writes Aaron Wildavsky. "Nor are there any self-declared winners today. On all sides there is gloom; each side claims it is losing."

In this atmosphere, "Anything and everything may serve as the rallying point for a new pressure group today, provided it is someone's *weakness*," writes Ayn Rand. "Weakness of any sort—intellectual, moral, financial or numerical—is today's standard of value, criterion of rights and claim to privileges."

Welfare liberalism's role in the maintenance of symbolic victimhood is anchored in the demand for equality and its accompanying revolution of rising expectations. Since that equality is never realized, claims of victimhood have escalated as the demand for equality has increased. During the 1960s and 1970s, improvements in certain programs were frustrated by the rising expectations that were themselves reinforced by the proposals of new policies which promised more than could be delivered. When the promises were inadequately realized, the higher level of expectation which they engendered were met by new policies which also failed to realize their promises in the face of higher expectations.

There is no way to eliminate the discrepancy between expectations and actual improvements in life chances. No amount of success would be sufficient to end the demand for more. For, as Nathan Glazer notes, "rising expectations continually enlarge the sea of felt and perceived misery, whatever happens to it in actuality." And since there is no point at which misery is finally eliminated, and no point at which the demand for equality comes to an end, people become ever more sensitive to smaller and smaller degrees of inequality. In order to claim more, individuals and groups at all class levels seize on inequalities as evidence of mistreatment.

As with all statuses, the claim to victim status must be honored by others in order to have any meaningful impact on social relations, especially power relations. One of the most significant endorsements came from President Johnson in his commencement address at Howard University in 1965:

> You do not take a person who, for years, has been hobbled by chains and liberate him, bring him up to the starting line of a race and then say, "You are free to compete with all the others" and still justly believe that you have been completely fair. Thus it is not enough just to open the gates of opportunity. All our citizens must have the ability to walk through those gates. . . . We seek not just freedom but opportunity. We seek not just legal equality but human ability, not just equality as a right and a theory but equality as a fact and equality as a result.

Johnson's advocacy of equality of result legitimated the assumption that historic injustice justifies special treatment even when that treatment is itself just another form of injustice. By the end of the sixties it was clear to all that in the welfare state one could get more attention—and power—by being a victim than he could being a nonvictim.

Once conferred, victim status is a very durable and highly valuable possession. It not only confers power, but also protects the individual from being discredited, doubted, contradicted, devalued, mistreated, or embarrassed. It enables people to elicit compensation without taking responsibility for their actions. As Wildavsky notes, the triumph of egalitarianism, which fuels victim politics, is that government subsidizes victim categories, and pays people to fit into them. All the symbolic victim needs to do is claim that something or someone is responsible for his unfortunate situation and that he is powerless (through no fault of his own) to reverse his misfortune. Then, in the name of justice and with the force of law, sympathizers rush to relieve him and punish his alleged victimizers.

The Role of Social Problems Theory

Symbolic victimhood has also received legitimation from social scientific studies of social problems that find fault with the social system in behalf of the powerless. Their definitions of social problems as the consequence of unethical, illegal and destructive actions of powerful individuals, groups and institutions in American society give credence to the point of view of the subordinate group in some hierarchical relationship. Out of social problems research has emerged enduring symbolic representations that make a long list of pathologies and deficiencies associated with victimhood.

One such representation is the pathological image of the black family: that it was destroyed or undermined by slavery; that its deterioration explains the disorganized and pathological characteristics of the modern black family. Despite falsifications of

these hypotheses, the black family continues to be seen in negative terms. Another source of victimhood reinforcement is the
symbolic definition of blacks as historically objects of discrimination whose self-esteem therefore requires the assurance of
equal treatment in many types of situations, preferential treatment in others, and societal support for self-concepts that emphasize affirmation rather than negation of blackness.

Positive Self-Acceptance

Positive self-acceptance is the characteristic that gives you the
ability to be yourself, to embrace who you are, and to bring forward to a work setting your natural strengths. This characteristic
provides an internal gyroscope that allows successful blacks to
function in varying situations without getting emotionally or psychologically lost.

Successful blacks also operate from a position of racial strength.
They are not trying to escape or play down either their socioeconomic background or their culture and history, nor are they trying to be or become someone who is not black. They not only accept the positive and constructive aspects of African-American
heritage but integrate them into their professional lives. The offices of successful blacks, for instance, are often adorned by
black artwork, books by black authors, or black music playing in
the background. Such seemingly innocuous trappings are the critical cultural reference points that frequently help keep successful
blacks emotionally centered and clear about who they are, regardless of where they are.

There is a great deal of personal power inherent in positive self-
acceptance: the power comes from being psychologically grounded,
in understanding that what you bring to a corporate setting has
value and worth. Blacks who have a positive sense of their own
value and worth are much less likely to be disoriented by the vicis-
situdes of corporate cultures or the vagaries of corporate politick-
ing. They are most likely to succeed because they know they can.

Craig K. Polite, *Children of the Dream*, 1992.

Increasingly the pathology and deficit models have been chal-
lenged; however, not because these models misrepresent the circumstances and value orientations of millions of blacks, but in
order to substitute the deficit hypothesis with the view that
what are taken for deficits are actually cultural differences.
Stanley Eitzen's statement on the subject is a typical rejection of
the deficit hypothesis, known also as the "blaming-the-victim"
or cultural deprivation approach to social problems.

> Cultural deprivation is a loaded ethnocentric term applied by members of the majority to the culture of the minority group. It implies that the culture of the group in question is not only inferior but also deficient. The concept itself is patently false, because no culture can be inferior to another, it can only be different.

Cultural relativists who take this position argue that difference means deficit only if it is weighed against the standards of the dominant society. In their view, when an attribute that is viewed as cultural deprivation (nonstandard English, for example) is seen in terms of the context in which the individual is socialized and spends his or her time, it may in fact be an asset that is as adequate as what is found in the dominant culture, or even superior to it. In other words, difference is no longer considered to be deficiency.

Arguments that equate difference with deficiency are certainly fallacious, but it is equally fallacious to equate difference with adequacy. Depending on the context, an attribute may be different because it is deficient, or because it is adequate. However, the difference-is-not-deficiency argument does not recognize a universal standard by which the deficiency and adequacy can be distinguished. Rather, it asserts that deficiencies should be accorded the same merit as that granted to the prevailing standards of adequacy. This approach effectively not only evades the criteria that distinguish deficiency from adequacy; it establishes deficiency itself as the standard of value. The consequence is a double standard by which the morally praiseworthy is defined not in terms of a person's ability but in terms of his handicaps; not in terms of his achievements but in terms of his suffering; not in terms of his own individual capacity to surmount problems like racial discrimination but in terms of the collective oppression suffered by his ancestors.

The Case of Black Victimhood

As the civil rights movement of the 1960s shifted its strategy from principled protest to pragmatic politics, which involved the acquisition of material gains such as housing, welfare, and health care, black leaders imputed the disadvantaged circumstances of the black underclass and lower-income groups to the entire black community. The effect was to disguise the achievements of individual blacks and the advancement and expansion of the black middle class that had been under way long before Rosa Parks refused to go to the back of the bus. But the claim to victim status has been a significant characteristic of each stage of black activism. It legitimated the integration movement's politics of redemption as articulated by Martin Luther King, Jr. It was also present in the black power movement's politics of retribution and the black identification movement's politics of exclusion and racial solidarity. Today, it finds expression in the politics of sensitivity, compensation and remediation.

The stance of black victimhood entails an assessment of the changes in the problems and status of Blacks as compared with each other and with more advantaged groups. The perspective I call the *deprivation orientation* is consistent with the stance of black victimhood. It dismisses the changes in race relations and the socioeconomic mobility of blacks as "the illusion of inclusion." Black gains are seen as only symbolic in relation to white Americans; blacks are urged not to be dissuaded by arguments that they are making progress. Such pessimistic assessments of black progress are most often offered by people whose own lives and careers are falsifications of those assessments. One of the ironies of black victimhood is its appeal to people who have already made significant progress toward assimilation. Such upwardly mobile ethnics, says John Higham, are already strongly enough positioned to imagine that permanent minority status might be advantageous.

Black journalist William Raspberry has been one of the few observers of the black community to criticize the laments of black deprivation proponents. "It has become the new orthodoxy for black Americans—particularly those doing pretty well—to deny that anything has changed for the better," writes Raspberry. He views such denials as being motivated by the fear that an admission of progress "will take white America off the hook, reduce guilt, and preclude further advances." There is also the persistent feeling that the fragile prosperity of middle class blacks might blow away with ill economic winds, as well as their uncertainty of their status either in the white community or the black community.

Despite the risks of upward mobility and anxieties over status, Raspberry concludes that "it's time for blacks of accomplishment and influence to stop poor-mouthing in the name of black solidarity. It's silly, and worse, for black men and women, wearing designer suits, living in elegant homes, working at important and prestigious and lucrative careers to pretend that we are hardly better off than a sharecropper in the rural south. The sharecropper knows better, and so do we."

Raspberry is not alone in these sentiments. Many other blacks feel the same way. During his tenure as chairman of the Equal Employment Opportunity Commission, Supreme Court Justice Clarence Thomas told an audience with much indignation: "I'm tired of blacks being thought of only as poor people, people on welfare, people who are unemployed. That's the only way the Jesse Jacksons and the other black leaders talk about black people. To them we're all a monolith. Well, they are not talking for the 80 or 90 percent of black people in this country who have never been on welfare or in jail."

As I have indicated, it is no accident that this trend emerged as the rights of black individuals were legally recognized, and at a time when blacks were benefiting from increased social mobility and an expansion of socioeconomic opportunities. Since the indices of black progress plainly show the disparity in the advances of middle-class and lower-class blacks, what purpose does it serve to emphasize the plight of the lower class as the *sine qua non* of the problems and status of the entire black community when it is evident to everyone that this is not the case? What function does the denial of black improvement have for its proponents?

As the upward mobility of middle-class blacks increases in the socioeconomic realm, they lose the claim to what John M. Cuddihy calls "the charisma of a continuing victim status" in the cultural realm. The *fact* of their progress, however measured, threatens to dispossess them of the psychic and material benefits of victim status.

Clearly, the denial of progress disguises black success, and enables proponents of victimhood to justify their claim to the privileges of official victim status. It also enables middle-class service deliverers, spokesmen, and patrons to use the suffering of the unfortunate as a pretext for their own drive for power. For, as the quest for privileges and security under welfare-state capitalism has increasingly depended on the organized power, it has become more advantageous to present oneself as a *permanent* member of the deprived.

Abuses of Suffering

Of all of the consequences of the campaign of victimhood, the most significant is its threat to the legitimacy of the very ideas that identify the nation. During the 1960s moderate civil rights activists took the view articulated by Gunnar Myrdal that all that was needed to improve the lot of blacks was for white Americans to change their minds, to put into practice the ideals they believed in. However, as the spoils of victimhood have mounted, the view has emerged that the ideals themselves must be changed. Principles such as the primacy of individual rights, equality before the law, private enterprise, and free market capitalism are, according to writers like Derrick Bell, but abstractions that "lead to legal results that harm blacks and perpetuate their inferior status." Whites who defend such ideas are of course racists, whether they know it or not. Blacks who do so are like "those slaves willing to mimic the masters' views, carry out orders, and by their presence provide a perverse legitimacy to the oppression they aided and approved."

Other negative consequences of black victimhood stem from what Richard Sennett identifies as abuses brought about by the ennobling of suffering. "Sympathy is extended to the victim for his condition, not as a person; thus, if he improves his material circumstances or is mobile upwardly socially, then he loses his moral claims and is considered 'a traitor to his class.'" Several writers have focused on this consequence of the idea of the ennobled victim in different contexts. Peter Berger sees it as a theme in the anti-liberal and "demodernizing impulse" that emphasizes concrete "group rights" rather than individual rights. When group rights are given primacy over individual rights, says Berger, "individual success and aspiration are increasingly condemned as a betrayal of the collective effort."

In a different, but related, context, economist George Reisman reaches the same conclusion in his analysis of how the doctrine of altruism, as well as "the repressive conditions imposed on blacks by the mixed economy," have stifled the progress of blacks. The doctrine of altruism, which requires a person to place others above himself and regards self-sacrifice as the highest virtue, writes Reisman, "takes the view that those who struggle heroically and do succeed, are not to be given any moral credit; on the contrary, they are often denounced as 'Uncle Toms,' who have accepted self-interest as their goal rather than self-sacrifice for the needy. This is hardly the sort of philosophy that would inspire the effort and struggle required to get out of the slums."

Another abuse of the idea of the ennobled sufferer, says Sennett, is the notion that "no person is morally legitimate unless he or she is suffering." The sources of legitimacy through suffering are ultimately to be found in an injury inflicted by someone else or by "the environment." This leads to the devaluation of achievement, and, as mentioned earlier, the tendency of "champions" of the oppressed to use the suffering of the unfortunate as a pretext for their own drives for power. Sennett points out that the sin of viewing suffering as the condition of moral legitimacy is also committed by people who take "the oppressed as 'models,' as people who are 'really' dealing with life, people more solid and substantial than oneself. It is psychological cannibalism."

Most of all, argues Sennett, the ennobling of victims means that "in ordinary middle-class life we are forced constantly to go in search of some injury, some affliction, in order to justify even the contemplation of questions of justice, right, and entitlement in our lives."

Nothing could be more devastating to the nation that is the refuge for the victimized of the world than to permit itself to become not the haven of those yearning to breathe free, but the therapeutic sink hole of those yearning to be relieved of the risks and responsibility of liberty.

*"Blacks are too socially and economically
handicapped to effectively compete in an
integrated society with advantaged racial and
ethnic groups or other protected minorities, such
as women and the disabled."*

Racism Prevents Blacks from Achieving Economic Justice

Claud Anderson

Claud Anderson is a businessman, educator, political strategist, and researcher. He was appointed by former president Jimmy Carter to serve as assistant secretary to the U.S. Department of Commerce. He is currently establishing a national research institute called the Harvest Institute, a think tank for social and economic reform of black America. In the following viewpoint, excerpted from his book *Black Labor, White Wealth: The Search for Power and Economic Justice*, Anderson argues that blacks cannot succeed by following the models forged by immigrants or by the route of self-help.

As you read, consider the following questions:

1. Why does Anderson argue that it is important to look at the economic issues of blacks as issues of race?
2. Why is it impossible for blacks to assimilate into the economy, according to the author?

Excerpted from *Black Labor, White Wealth: The Search for Power and Economic Justice* by Claud Anderson (Edgewood, MD: Duncan & Duncan, 1994); © 1994 by Claud Anderson, Ed.D. Reprinted with permission of the publisher.

During the last three decades, it has become "politically correct" to dump blacks and their racial problems into broad categories such as ethnic issues, special interest and minority groups. It is also popular now to view the grievances of all groups as equal in all respects. Placing blacks into an aggregation of dissimilar groups and equating their circumstance with other minorities is little more than political sleight-of-hand, an illusion of equality in a so-called color-blind American society.

America is far from being color-blind and equality exists only in the minds of those who pretend that inequality is equality. It is disingenuous to equate black Americans' conditions with any other ethnic, religious or so-called disadvantaged minority. Blacks have a unique history in this country in that their status was predetermined by the dominant society's national public policy on the use of black Americans.

Grouping blacks with lesser aggrieved groups, in effect, mutes and obscures the legitimate grievances of blacks, while veiling the moral, legal, and financial responsibility the dominant society has to correct the suffering of 36 million black Americans. Declarations that the country is now color-blind are misstatements that resolve nothing. The color-blind myth simply maintains the status quo, thereby keeping blacks noncompetitive and marginal. If four centuries of slavery and Jim Crowism have taught blacks anything about race relations, it is that as long as people can see, color will be a factor. . . .

Too Handicapped

Whenever blacks attempt to change their circumstances by demanding assistance from the various levels of government, whites predictably ask the question: "Why can't blacks be self-sufficient like the Jews, Italians or other ethnic groups and help themselves, rather than going to the government for assistance?" Some blacks, those who lack competitive skills and income opportunities, ask government and white society for public assistance because they prefer public aid to stealing what they need. Most blacks are demanding compensation or reparations from the government for the centuries of expropriated labor and the legacies of slavery and Jim Crowism that continue to place European whites, Hispanics and Asians over them.

Blacks are too socially and economically handicapped to effectively compete in an integrated society with advantaged racial and ethnic groups or other protected minorities, such as women and the disabled. . . .

Black Americans cannot emulate European, Asian and Hispanic ethnics, because social barriers have never permitted blacks to access the assimilation process, which is reserved for non-black ethnics. How can marginally existing blacks walk an ethnic path towards self-improvement when they are not treated like an ethnic group? And, even if they were so treated, both the government and the majority society would continue to allow an unending flow of new ethnic immigrants to preempt blacks in the assimilation process. How fair is it to ask blacks to emulate other groups when nearly 100 percent of blacks' ancestors were in America before nearly 100 percent of the ancestors of today's Jewish, Italian, German, French, Japanese, Chinese, Irish and Hispanics?

©Mike Keefe. Reprinted with permission.

Yet, these more recently arrived ethnic groups have been assimilated and blacks have not. It was white society's willingness to offer assimilation to everybody but blacks that has placed the greatest burden on blacks and forced them to now seek alternative routes, outside of mainstream white society, to gain economic and political power. Had dominant society had any real intentions of assimilating blacks, it would have done so before it assimilated the other groups. Or, at worst, white society would have assimilated blacks immediately after the Civil War, when blacks were first freed.

In addition, it is not possible for blacks to emulate immigrant groups, because those groups have always had options to help them rise from one social class to another after they arrived in America. Immigrants were never burdened with the experiences or the legacy of slavery and Jim Crowism. They came to America with hope and a belief that the situation here would be better than in their country of origin. Centuries of immigrants have entered this nation believing that it was the land of unlimited opportunity, where a person was free to achieve and go as high as his skill and God-given talents would take him.

As Asians and Hispanics find places in the economy, they are allowed to move upward on social and occupational ladders, says historian Andrew Hacker, in his book, *Two Nations: Black and White, Separate, Hostile, Unequal*. Blacks have had no such options. Sixteen generations of blacks have been denied such a reality. Blacks continue to dream of integration as they spend their time and resources fighting for basic civil rights and the first-class citizenship that every ethnic immigrant has when he enters this nation.

On the other hand, ethnic immigrants and other minorities have directly profited from the marginal success of the black Civil Rights Movement that opened doors in the areas of employment, academics, and housing. The black movement, in its various efforts to establish affirmative action, eliminate discrimination and seek economic parity, has drawn most of the fire from a disapproving, reluctant white society. When forced to make a civil rights accommodation, whites have hired women, Asian and Hispanic ethnics and the handicapped, ahead of blacks. These other groups have achieved significant advances over the past two decades, piggybacking on the civil rights legislation blacks fought long and hard to win. Blacks' socioeconomic push was effectively neutralized when they became "minorities."

The definition of minority continues to expand and to become more amorphous. Today, almost everyone is a minority in some way. Anything that applies to every group has no real meaning for any group. However, the term minority holds major political advantage for those who wish to maintain a status quo. Blacks are further undermined when included in a minority category because none of the other so-called minorities were statutorily deprived by the government of their humanity or their right to enjoy the fruits of their own labor.

Blacks: Immigrants or Not?

Historians often refer to American Indians as the nation's only indigenous or non-immigrant population group. This notion is false. If American Indians are America's only non-immigrants, then that would make blacks immigrants, which they are not. The ancestors of American Indians migrated to North America across the Bering Straits from Asia. Black Americans did not immigrate to America. They were transported to America against their will. Inherent in the term immigrant is the element of choice in the selection of a new home in a new nation.

Many ethnic immigrants come to America fully equipped with

the economic know-how and business acumen that they developed in their home countries. As required by U.S. immigration policies, many are well educated and have professional trades. They have business experience and access to products and industries in their mother country around which they can build businesses in this country. They have boundless hope and competitive motivation to succeed in this land of opportunity.

The Times Remain the Same

Blacks have not achieved racial equality in any area of American life. And they are overrepresented on every negative variable except suicide, itself a mixed blessing since black suicide rates are highest among its young people in contrast to white suicide rates weighted toward its oldest members. And the direction of change in the U.S. has made some conditions worse than in the era before the civil rights movement. In 1950 the black unemployment rate was double that of whites: in 1990 it was triple. Housing and school segregation are worse outside the South in 1990 than in 1950. The inequality of wealth is greater in 1990 than in 1950, when most people earned money from wages. In the 1990s, people earn money, in larger numbers, from stocks, bonds, property, leveraged buyouts, etc. The percent of intact black families vis-à-vis white families was much higher in 1950 than in 1990, as was the lower number of black children born in wedlock. The times they are changing but things remain the same.

Robert Staples, *Lure and Loathing*, 1993.

Their business contacts and products may be related to importing ethnic foods, arts and craft products, or exporting American products to their home countries. Most black businessmen have limited business experience and few cultural products to market. For the most part, they do not have family, friends or other natural business contacts in Africa. European, Asian and Hispanic immigrants come here with contacts in their countries of origin, which they often use for commercializing their culture into business opportunities in America.

Few legal immigrants in modern times have come to America impoverished. Many are people of material and social substance at home, particularly those that came as political refugees, forced to leave behind businesses and careers when sudden crisis hit. Even if they are forced to start over, they are equipped to do so. Many enjoyed assistance from the U.S. Government through legislated refugee programs for groups such as the Cubans, Vietnamese, Cambodians, Hungarians and Koreans. Others received assistance and aid from the Central Intelligence

Agency (CIA) and the U.S. State Department when they arrived.

The immigration process encourages ethnics to develop and control their communities. While blacks are seeking to build their businesses around the integration process, ethnic immigrants are more nationalistic in their practices. They do not buy into the melting pot myth. Understanding the principles of the way this country's economy works, they seek to create specialized niche economies around their culture within the larger framework of the national economy. Immigrants are not opposed to venturing into other racial or ethnic communities to take advantage of wealth building opportunities. But, they keep their own community relatively closed to outsiders.

This is true in the Little Italys, China Towns and Little Havanas in this country. In Miami, Florida, for example, Cubans control the number of non-Cuban businesses going into their communities of Little Havana and Hialeah. Unlike blacks, ethnic immigrants practice a business home rule that says, "I got my neighborhood. Now I will get yours." They demonstrated their home rule philosophy and influence in 1992 when Cuban residents boldly blocked Iranian businessmen from opening stores in their communities, solely because the entering business owners were not Cuban.

As the major business owners in black neighborhoods in the Miami area, Cubans own most of the bars, liquor stores, grocery stores, automobile parts stores, banks and gas stations in black neighborhoods. Cuban business owners take capital out of black neighborhoods, but will not allow non-Cuban businesses to set up and take capital out of their communities. Clearly they understand the power dynamics of group economics. Blacks do not. . . .

Blacks Lack a Sense of Unity

Another reason that blacks cannot emulate ethnics is their lack of group unity or sense of community. Racial integration, black peoples' long standing objective, is the antithesis of group togetherness. Integration fragments blacks into even smaller groups and scatters them among the majority white society. This scattering has destroyed the cohesion of black communities.

Upper and middle class blacks live in small enclaves, as powerless minorities, among white majorities all across the nation. They are isolated, without a bond to their racial roots and typically see themselves as disunited, weakened people. Although it raises a great deal of emotional conflict, successfully integrated blacks invariably find comfort and security in being white in most respects except color. There are few emotional bridges back into the black communities, so they identify with and support the power and material resources of the white communities.

Government and dominant white society have historically rewarded blacks who identified with the larger white community and placed their welfare above that of the black community. For selling out their own community, blacks were often rewarded with special positions, money, or meritorious manumission.

There has been no similar legal or reward system to encourage members of Asian or Hispanic groups to turn against members of their own race. Contrarily, they have received rewards for maintaining a strong sense of community and ethnic identity. Cultural unity and community cohesiveness have been the key to their survival. They came with extended families intact. They came with the freedom to send back for loved ones they had left behind.

They engaged in trade, moving goods and currency back and forth. They were generally free to practice their cultures in this country, guard their traditions, school their children in their own languages, practice their respective religions, and in every other way, live as free citizens. Not one of those freedoms was historically available to blacks, certainly not during slavery.

Ethnic immigrants have good reasons to have a completely different frame of reference about America than do blacks. Ethnics enjoy the support—economic, social and otherwise—of the dominant white society. The government has been a great deliverer of jobs, wealth and relocation assistance to ethnic immigrants, to which the recent North American Free Trade Agreement (NAFTA) with Mexico will attest.

Contrary to the moral of the Horatio Alger story, that every individual and group should pull themselves up by their own boot straps, immigrants have historically received governmental assistance. In the Southwest, illegal immigrants from Mexico, who never paid taxes, have no difficulty securing welfare, social security benefits, education, or medical care. More than 50 percent of the babies born in some hospitals in Southern California in 1993 were born to illegal Mexican aliens.

Free access to public services and benefits without having to pay centuries of dues shapes the way immigrants see America. Ethnics do not view discrimination in the same way black people do. An immigrant may be more willing than blacks to sweep the streets and polish door knobs, because he would have little reason not to believe that his future will be better, if not for himself, then for his children. Blacks have no such optimism. They have spent centuries sweeping, walking and living on the streets and they realize that a brighter future for themselves and their children is questionable.

Skin Color

Skin color is the single most important factor that prevents blacks from emulating ethnic immigrants, because it defines their role, status, and limits their access to resources. The skin color and physical attributes of non-black ethnic immigrants is much closer to that of whites. White ethnics and Asians are more acceptable to the dominant white society than are blacks.

The long history of American race relations seems to point to one fact; that blacks' high visibility has made them a convenient target for many of the social conflicts and insecurities of each white ethnic group that has reached these shores. Ethnic immigrants learn early, and one of the last things they forget, is to avoid contact with America's black pariah. Other groups can blend in or assimilate into the dominant culture. Blacks' skin color does not permit them to blend. . . .

The Ethics of Hard Work

It is common to hear Japanese, Chinese and Germans being cited as model hard workers. Before blacks became obsolete as common labor in the 1960s, they were the models for doing the hardest, dirtiest, most dangerous and backbreaking work. Ironically, conservatives and government are suggesting that emulating these recent immigrants and their hard work is the cure for blacks' protracted poverty and high unemployment.

Recommending more hard work for a race of ex-slaves is similar to curing an alcoholic by suggesting that the drunk do more drinking. Having never been compensated for centuries of past labor is the bigger part of the problem, not whether black people are willing to work hard.

If blacks were unwilling to work hard, it would be understandable after 400 years of no pay to low pay. Which ethnic immigrants in America have worked harder than the black slaves? Certainly the Japanese, Chinese, and Germans did not work harder in America than black slaves. If the Japanese, Chinese and the Germans were the hardest workers, would it not have made more sense for colonial white society to have enslaved the Japanese, Chinese, or Germans, rather than blacks who were allegedly lazy and unwilling to work? Why would supposedly bright businessmen spend 250 years traveling half way around the world to kidnap 35 to 50 million innocent, but lazy blacks, then knowingly bring them to America to do work that other ethnic groups could do better?

Even in instances where these ethnic groups worked hard, they did it with the consciousness of paid free men. The indentured servants from India, the Chinese coolies, though they were mistreated, were still free and paid for their labor. They had the option to quit and return home to their homelands any time they so desired. The sweatshops in New York City were reprehensible, but the Chinese workers were free and paid. They were not property. No one owned, beat, or killed them and their families for not working.

The Japanese are often held up as labor models for blacks, but blacks were never treated as well as the Japanese, even though blacks fought with the American military troops against the Japanese in World War II. If blacks had been treated as well as the Japanese, perhaps then, they too could be held up as great respecters of hard work.

The United States government paid $20,000 in reparations to each Japanese American who was forced to live in internment camps during the four years of World War II. For their three to four years of internment, the Japanese Americans were compensated nearly 42 years later. Not only did the United States government award reparations to each relocated Japanese, it gave the Japanese community a national apology.

Granted, the reparations, made after years of court battles, and after most of those entitled to them were already dead, can in no way compensate for what was lost. Still, it was a debt acknowledged and paid. Blacks, on the other hand, after four centuries of lost humanity, life and wealth, have received nothing. . . .

Blacks and Ethnic Immigrants Compete for Resources

A continuing flow of immigrants, decade after decade, from 1607 to the present day, came believing that America abounded with freedom and wealth. Common sense dictates that had they anticipated they would face the kind of life most black people face, immigration would have ceased immediately after the first boatload arrived. The flow of immigrants never ceased, because they were never treated like blacks.

As a matter of fact, ethnic and racial immigrants historically have been a wedge between whites and blacks, giving whites an alternative to interacting with blacks. Each time in history, either before or after a war, when the American economy was expanding and could have offered material economic benefits to blacks, a new influx of immigrants or refugees arrived, to fill the void and "further exiled blacks from fruitful participation in the national life," according to historian Dan Lacy.

A major myth is that there has been competition between blacks and ethnic groups. There has been no such competition. European ethnics simply bumped blacks from whatever they were interested in getting, because they were higher in the order of social preference. After they finished competing for jobs, housing or union control, blacks then applied for anything that was available. If racial customs did not exclude blacks, they optimistically waited until jobs or housing were passed down through the ethnic hierarchy, extending from English down to Jewish.

As competition for resources increases and blacks become

more frustrated, conflicts for power, resources or even basic rights are developing between blacks and all ethnic and racial groups who rank higher than blacks in the order of preference. If blacks' marginal level of subsistence does not improve, they will become the common denominator in every social clash. Since the 1980s, blacks have clashed with Arabs in Cleveland and Detroit. In the early 1990s, New York and Boston were outraged over the slaying of blacks by Jews and ethnic whites. Violent confrontations between blacks and Koreans, Vietnamese, Laotian, and Cambodian merchants have arisen across the country in cities like Philadelphia, Washington, D.C. and Los Angeles.

The continuous conflicts in Miami between blacks and Cubans have ignited four major riots since 1973. In some instances, blacks were angered by a single offensive act. At other times, the riot was a response to what blacks perceived as a pattern of offensive acts. Centuries of unjust racial subordination to immigrants has generated a smoldering tension between blacks and those who came to the community from foreign nations higher in the preference order than blacks.

Today there is little cooperation, political or otherwise, between blacks and minority groups. For the most part, ethnic minorities do not support black causes. They have been getting a free ride at black peoples' expense on civil rights and minority programs. As members of loosely formed political "coalitions," they are mostly quiet while blacks agitate; but they are quick to stake their claim on affirmative action benefits won by blacks.

From Los Angeles, California to Miami, Florida, conflicts arise between blacks and ethnic groups as they seek their share of power and wealth in the mainstream beyond the shadow of blacks. In the 1990 mayoral election in Chicago, Hispanic leaders leapfrogged between white and black factions, offering support wherever there seemed to be the most to gain for their Hispanic communities. . . .

Conclusion

Blacks are not immigrants and cannot emulate them. Their circumstances spring from different experiences and options. Blacks have been a part of this country from its inception. They have never received recognition or benefits commensurate with their labor and wealth contributions to the development of this now rich and powerful nation. The difference in the treatment accorded Asian, Hispanic and European ethnics makes it quite clear that contributions of hard, uncompensated labor, patriotism and cultural gifts have little to do with who is permitted to assimilate and enjoy the fruits of American society.

Dominant society remains insensitive and ignorant of the great insult to injury it has committed by allowing a string of immigrants across the centuries to receive the first-class citizenship status that has been denied black Americans, who have served as builders, laborers and military veterans. Blacks are insulted when members of ethnic and racial groups come to America from countries that were formerly U.S. enemies. Indians, Asians, Hispanics and nearly every conceivable European ethnic group has engaged in some form of declared war against Americans. Blacks are the only racial or ethnic group that has fought in every major conflict on the side of white America.

The insults are further compounded when white society provides new immigrants refugee aid and family assistance, while begrudging it to blacks. More insults are added on as whites then label the newcomers "minorities," accord them equal claims to the country's affirmative action programs; sell them homes in neighborhoods where blacks remain excluded; make business loans to them that are denied to blacks, and praise them for their strong sense of cultural unity—the same unity that white society fears and seeks to destroy when exhibited by blacks.

> *"Low income is a consequence of a multiplicity of socioeconomic conditions. . . . 'Black poverty' is a metaphor, and a misnomer and, if taken literally, a case of premature racial labeling."*

Racism Cannot Explain Poverty Among Blacks

Yehudi O. Webster

In the following viewpoint, excerpted from his book *The Racialization of America*, Yehudi O. Webster argues that blaming racism for black poverty limits the discussion of the causes of poverty. Webster argues that many black issues are unnecessarily racialized—if researchers would look for color-blind solutions, rather than first looking at race, true, meaningful debate could result that would benefit all the races. At the forefront of the critical thinking movement, Webster teaches in the department of pan-African studies at the University of California at Los Angeles.

As you read, consider the following questions:

1. Webster argues that blacks and whites cannot be analyzed as categories. Why not?
2. Why does the author contend that studies attributing poverty to race are problematic?

Blacks and whites are not viable analytical categories. Indeed, any remark about the black experience may be considered controversial, or objectionable. For example: "Blacks have their own culture." One response could be: "It is racist to suggest that blacks, despite almost four centuries of residency, are not fully Americanized." If the contrary is voiced—"blacks do not have their own culture"—the reaction could be: "To deny the uniqueness of the black experience is racist." Studies of racial and ethnic relations are replete with accusations and counteraccusations of ignoring some facet of racial experiences, some empirical data, some subjective element, or some political imperative, and the development of more empirical studies of racial situations, without offering a logical justification of "racial." This is the state of the debate in meritocratic, liberal, radical, and antiracist writings. Each camp maintains "the black experience" as an object of study, without recognizing that the object of study itself is a phantom. Thus, proponents and opponents have to be politically classified and vilified. In the mist of mutual recriminations, it is rarely recognized that the suffering in the inner city is prolonged by these squabbles. Both policymakers and the public must stand immobilized by the repetition of elements of racial, ethnic, and class analyses that are, in turn, traceable to differences within social scientific traditions. . . .

Beyond Racial-Cultural Referents

In racial studies, the term *culture* is rarely explicitly stipulated. Indeed, lack of attention to key concepts is a striking feature of discussions of racial and ethnic relations. Nonetheless, conclusive discussions of racial and ethnic relations must be based on consistent definitions of culture. This ground rule is not meant to split hairs. Conceptual clarity and consistency would provide a clear answer to questions such as: What is the relationship between racial and ethnic classifications? How valid is the reference to culture to explain racial and racial-ethnic relations, and to construct racial-ethnic comparisons given the admission of various subcultures within a given culture? A case can be made that contemporary social sciences have inherited ambiguous and confusing legacies of race and culture. Proponents of the meritocratic, liberal, radical, and fundamentalist perspectives do not consider an implicit possibility that racial classification might itself be a cultural input that affects structural conditions. It is conceivable that explanatory references to race and constant studies of blacks as *a problem* produce a problem personality, a self-doubting self-image. It follows, then, that an effective approach to black socioeconomic rehabilitation would be an abandoning of racial classification. Black liberation demands the negation of blackness. This is, indeed, a paradox of Hegelian proportions.

Racial-ethnic comparisons necessarily retain the collective classifications white, African American, Asian Pacific American, and Hispanic. These classifications may be useful for census enumerators. They fail, however, to do justice to the economic, cultural, and educational differences within each of these populations. However, given the definitional elusiveness of these categories as statistical blocs, each aggregate racial fact has a counterfactual. For example, it has been suggested that black educational achievements are lower because of their comparatively inferior genetic endowments. However, some whites remain remarkably unassimilated into the mainstream. Some perform worse than Asian Americans on IQ tests and Scholastic Aptitude Tests (SATs). If these whites are genetically inferior to other whites, "poor" genes are not racially distributed and references to black genetic endowments fail as an explanation of their patterns of underachievement and overachievement.

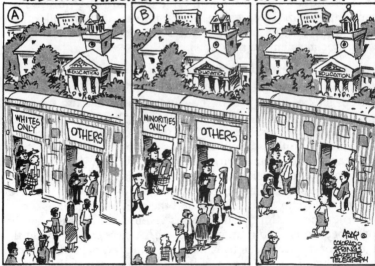

Reprinted by permission of Chuck Asay and Creators Syndicate.

Pierre L. Van den Berghe has charged that studies of race relations lack comparative focus. However, particular racial achievements are necessarily studied in relation to others. Studies of race relations are intrinsically comparative. So-called black achievements are, by definition, constructed in relation to white or other achievements. These comparisons pursue but cannot deliver conclusive arguments about the attributes of whites or nonwhites. For example, the comparison between African-American and Asian-American achievements can be said to be odious on the grounds that these immigrants had entirely different starting points and faced different levels of opposition and political climates. This discussion necessarily leads into studies of changing economic conditions, the time scales of continental patterns of migration and adaptation, processes of industrialization, regional socioeconomic variations, educational policies, past public policies, cultural attributes, and group motivation. Each of these factors can be further decomposed and mutually counterposed. Hence, the investigation of racial and ethnic inequalities opens a Pandora's box of discussions of free will and determinism, idealism and materialism, and the use of the past to explain a present that defines the nature of the past. Whatever the outcome, more philosophically sensitive social studies are needed. Their first task would be to examine the logical structure of racial and ethnic classifications.

Constant discoveries of differentiations within racial and ethnic groups question the analytical usefulness of the terms blacks, whites, Asian Americans, Native Americans, non-whites, WASPs, white ethnics, new ethnics, and the black underclass. In other words, theories of race and ethnicity do not provide viable classifications of social relations. Any reference to a black situation can be controverted with the question: Which blacks? Evidence of racism as a formative force in black deprivation can be slighted by drawing attention to the complicity of some Africans in enslavement, or the victim's responsibility for ending his or her victimization. It follows that there can be no end to the disputes over the causes of the differential rates of success between racial and ethnic groups.

These strictures apply especially to the idea of black poverty, which represents a racial description of certain economic conditions. This description obscures the controversy surrounding the concept of poverty itself. . . .

The Poor

The notion of the "poor" merely traps social studies within relations of distribution, and the racial description of the poor necessarily runs into analytic difficulties because it hints at both distributive-organizational *and* racial causes. What is the cause of black poverty? Black genes, argues the naturalist. Capitalism and racism, suggests the radical and Marxist political economist. But the question no one asks is: Has poverty been conceptually identified such that it can be racially described?

107

Even more contentious is the claim that blacks are overrepresented among the poor, that is to say, there is a racial surplus of poverty. Given the general condition of poverty, some persons classified as blacks must be expected to be poor. However, according to official and unofficial quantifications, while approximately 13 to 20 percent of the population is poor, fully 30 percent of the black population experiences this condition. The term black poverty, then, can only refer to a surplus of persons classified as blacks who are in poverty. It is this surplus—between 10 to 17 percent of the black poor—that is to be explained. The racial description can be omitted.

In radical political economic writings, it is claimed that the racial surplus of poverty is an effect of racism/capitalism. However, the racial nature of the surplus may be said to be only one of many ways of classifying the poor. The surplus could be categorized sexually, generationally, educationally, or regionally. A preponderance of young, uneducated, unskilled, single female parents and rural residents of "poor" Southern states pulls down the so-called black median income, just as surely as the residence of the majority of Asian Americans in Hawaii, New York, and California inflates the Asian-American median income. Any population that has a preponderance of persons in the eighteen-to-twenty-four-year age bracket, resides in low-income regions, and depends predominantly on a collapsing system of public education is bound to have a greater number of persons in the low-income category. The racial classification implies racial causation, but low income is a consequence of a multiplicity of socioeconomic conditions.

Blacks and Poverty

"Black poverty" is a metaphor, and a misnomer and, if taken literally, a case of premature racial labeling. What are the common attributes of the black poor, other than their skin color, hair type, and facial form? In any case, some of the black poor are poorer, or less rich, than others. They are stratified by other attributes such as age, regional origin, gender, educational level, and work experience. Because these attributes may be significant in the generation of low income, these persons should not be all lumped together as the "black poor," unless it can be demonstrated that their blackness is somehow responsible for their poverty. This signals a return to either black genes or white racism.

The toleration of the regressive nature of racial studies reflects a divestment of philosophy from social sciences, a disregard for logical rules, and a commitment to empirical means of proof. Philosophically sensitive social research would recognize that racial comparative statistics on consumption and employment/

unemployment do not depict a racial reality. Rather, they are the data produced by the racial theory. A racial comparative count of the unemployed that demonstrates an overrepresentation of black workers implies that the disparity has been racially produced. Hence, racial solutions must be advanced. However, because an infinite number of institutional, cultural, systemic, and historical processes may be said to affect human experiences, no racial solution can be considered optimum. The multiplicity of solutions to racial problems, then, is not accidental.

Abandon Race Distinctions

Studies of race relations survive because people are convinced that they reflect the real world. However, this conviction perpetuates so-called racial problems, because once the realness of race is endorsed, studies of racial problems become plagued with inconclusive disputes and interpretations of data and experiences. Therefore, discussions of solutions to racial problems are necessarily replete with cyclical references to political, economic, cultural, and biological factors. For example, economic and educational deprivation in American society is analyzed racially and, as a result, benignly neglected. Any proposed cause of this "racial" condition is susceptible to an eternal doubting. Are whites racist, or is it that blacks themselves are at fault? Blaming the victim! Blame the victimizer. Social scientists have only blamed races. The goal should be to abandon them.

Yehudi O. Webster, *The Racialization of America*, 1992.

On the other hand, racial solutions are impossible to implement. For example, a racial analysis of the labor market discovers a surplus of black unemployment. Even the most extreme solution to the racial disparity—removing white workers and giving their positions to black workers—must consider the comparative qualifications, skills, and education of white and black workers. Thus, it will not be white workers as such who will be removed but specific categories of workers. If the racial surplus of unemployment comprises unskilled workers, then, ameliorative policies should be directed to the structure of the demand for and supply of labor. An economic analysis of the labor market finds a surplus of unemployment among unskilled, uneducated, and untrained workers. This surplus is explained in terms of wage rates, human capital endowment, and the rigors of capitalist exploitation. The racial features of the unemployed population must be deemed irrelevant. If they are to be considered significant, then, why not other features, such as gender, generational, regional, and cultural attributes?

The omnipresent possibility of discovering other human attributes or social factors explains the competitive explanations of racial unemployment as well as the objections to racial explanations and solutions. Unemployment has a variety of descriptions and causations—structural, frictional, seasonal, and cyclical. A consideration of the literature on unemployment could have avoided its racial classification. With this racial classification come racial solutions that can be neither consistent nor effective. . . .

Group Identity

The allocation of persons to groups results in individual successes and failures being presented as group phenomena. A person defined as black, Italian, Native American, or Asian "makes it" and is held up as a racial or ethnic symbol. His or her success, however, could have been unrelated to racial genes or group culture. Racial and ethnic classifications simply force group evaluations of all social phenomena. On the other hand, America's legal and moral framework derives from the emphasis on individual-natural rights that formed the philosophical basis of the Enlightenment and the American Revolution. The Revolution, however, was not supplemented by educational policies designed to generate respect for reason and individual rights. Certain groups—for example, women, Indians, and Negroes—were to be kept in their natural places. Educational inputs were designed to serve that purpose. The end result is that neither whites nor nonwhites are educated in a humanistic sense. . . .

Given education's neglect of philosophy and critical thinking, the contradictions in racial and ethnic studies escape recognition and critical scrutiny. Some scholars advocate market, that is, individualist-meritocratic, solutions to racial and ethnic (group!) problems. Others propose multiculturalism, which will lead to an intensification of racial and ethnic consciousness. All such solutions fail. The image of racial and ethnic inequalities is generated by racial and ethnic consciousness and remedies in the first place. Public policies that address racial and ethnic issues are bound to conserve racial and ethnic problems. Non-recognition of this contradiction suggests that what is lacking is respect for logical and consequential reasoning. In this sense, America's dilemma is not moral but educational. It cannot be resolved until public policies concentrate on what the founding fathers ignored—the quality of education necessary to foster logical reasoning about racial and ethnic classifications.

Periodical Bibliography

The following articles have been selected to supplement the diverse views presented in this chapter. Addresses are provided for periodicals not indexed in the *Readers' Guide to Periodical Literature*, the *Alternative Press Index*, or the *Social Sciences Index*.

A. Magazine	"The Asian American Dream?" Fall 1993. Available from Metro East, 270 Lafayette St., Suite 404, New York, NY 10012.
American Prospect	"Still an American Dilemma," special issue on racism, Summer 1992.
John F. Budd Jr.	"Ambition Is Not a Right," *Vital Speeches of the Day*, April 15, 1995.
Ellis Cose	"Blinded by Color," *Newsweek*, September 25, 1995.
Dinesh D'Souza	"Is Racism a Western Idea?" *American Scholar*, Autumn 1995.
Dinesh D'Souza	"Prudent Discrimination: The Myth of the Racist Cabbie," *National Review*, October 1995.
Dinesh D'Souza	"We the Slaveowners," *Policy Review*, Fall 1995.
Gerald Early	"Understanding Afrocentrism: Why Blacks Dream of a World Without Whites," *Civilization*, July/August 1995.
Peter Erickson	"Seeing White," *Transition*, Fall 1995.
Family Therapy Networker	"The Black Middle Class: Challenging the Limits of the American Dream," special issue, July/August 1993.
Andrew Hacker	"The Myths of Racial Division," *New Republic*, March 23, 1992.
John Leo	"Separatism Won't Solve Anything," *U.S. News & World Report*, April 19, 1993.
Manning Marable	"History and Black Consciousness: The Political Culture of Black America," *Monthly Review*, July/August 1995.
Holly Sklar	"The Upperclass and Mothers N the Hood," *Z Magazine*, March 1993.
Joshua Solomon	"Reliving *Black Like Me*: My Journey into the Heart of Race-Conscious America," *Interrace*, February/March 1995. Available from PO Box 12048, Atlanta, GA 30355.

Will Immigration Lead to an Interracial Crisis?

Chapter Preface

Much of the discussion around immigration in America centers on a topic that dates back to the first colonists: Are immigrants loyal to the United States, or do they remain loyal to their nation of birth, so much so that they undermine the goals, values, and national identity of the United States?

Many nations in the world never need to answer this question. In most European countries, for example, dual citizenship is simply not allowed, and those not born in these nations cannot become citizens. In fact, the United States remains unique in its readiness to accept and grant citizenship to immigrants of every nationality, religion, and ethnic heritage. But this universal acceptance does not eliminate the suspicion among many that immigrants will resist becoming Americans and cling to the ethnic and racial identity of their birth.

This fear has intensified with a national trend to emphasize and tolerate diverse cultures. Schools, especially, in order to foster acceptance of other cultures, have attempted to change curricula to emphasize diversity. Debates over how much emphasis should be placed on American history have led to discussions of whether children should study the Magna Carta or the Mongol Empire, for example. Americans who object to these trends are also concerned about the presence of ethnic communities where little English is spoken. America's tolerance of these small cities within cities have led some to make dire predictions of an America hopelessly divided.

To many immigrants, these discussions seem overly intellectual and irrelevant to their daily lives. As Pablo, an immigrant from Mexico, says, "Here, a person has chances and choices. You can go to school. You can learn to be a mechanic. You can learn to be a teacher. You can have a business. You can do so much." To Pablo and other immigrants, opportunity is synonymous with the United States, and if getting it requires assimilation, they are ready to assimilate. Yet other facts about Pablo, such as his rudimentary English skills, and the Latino barrio in which he lives, are worrisome to those who believe immigrants are eroding a sense of American identity and culture.

Whether immigrants threaten American identity and unity is debated in the following chapter.

"America has assimilated and set its seal on an extraordinary diversity of peoples."

America's Cultural Identity Is Shaped by Continued Immigration

Luther S. Luedtke

Luther S. Luedtke is the director of graduate studies in English and American literature at the University of Southern California. In the following viewpoint, Luedtke argues that the increasing numbers of immigrants from the Third World pose no danger to American identity. In fact, he contends, the assimilation of immigrants is one of the most successful of America's experiments.

As you read, consider the following questions:

1. Why does Luedtke start his viewpoint with the quotes from George Santayana and Erik H. Erikson? How do they support his premise?
2. What point does the author make about American citizenship? How is it unique?
3. What is the foundation of American identity, according to Luedtke?

I speak of the American in the singular, as if there were not millions of them, north and south, east and west, of both sexes, of all ages, and of various races, professions, and religions. Of course the one American I speak of is mythical; but to speak in parables is inevitable in such a subject, and it is perhaps as well to do so frankly. . . . As it happens, the symbolic American can be made largely adequate to the facts; because, if there are immense differences between individual Americans . . . yet there is a great uniformity in their environment, customs, temper, and thoughts. They have all been uprooted from their several soils and ancestries and plunged together into one vortex, whirling irresistibly in a space otherwise quite empty. To be an American is of itself almost a moral condition, an education, and a career.

—George Santayana,
Character and Opinion in the United States (1920)

It is a commonplace to state that whatever one may come to consider a truly American trait can be shown to have its equally characteristic opposite. This, one suspects, is true of all "national characters," or (as I would prefer to call them) national identities—so true, in fact, that one may begin rather than end with the proposition that a nation's identity is derived from the ways in which history has, as it were, counterpointed certain opposite personalities; the ways in which it lifts this counterpoint to a unique style of civilization, or lets it disintegrate into mere contradiction.

—Erik H. Erikson, *Childhood and Society* (1950)

For the past decade and a half the American people have been enmeshed in rituals of reflection about their character, purpose, and destiny. At the close of the "American century" a series of occasions has arisen for soul-searching and prophecy. The bicentennial of the Declaration of Independence in 1976 soon gave way to anniversary celebrations of the new nation (1983), the Constitution (1987), and ratification of the Bill of Rights (1991). The quincentennial of Columbus's first voyage, in 1992, has pushed American memory further backward through its frontier, Enlightenment, and Puritan heritages to Old World designs and indigenous New World cultures.

Among these opportunities for national stocktaking, the bicentennial of the U.S. Census in 1990 holds a distinguished place. While the constitutional government of the United States is relatively unchanged after two hundred years, the composition of the American people has evolved dramatically since the first census in 1790 counted a population of 3.9 million persons with its midpoint twenty-three miles east of Baltimore. Centennials are often occasions for unbridled celebration; bicentennials tend to be more sober affairs. Up to the census of 1890, immigration

115

had not changed fundamentally the Northern European, Protestant consensus of the United States—although the director of the 1890 census declared the frontier officially "closed" because of pervasive settlement in the western territories, and this *fin de siècle* act provoked Frederick Jackson Turner to write his seminal essay "The Significance of the Frontier in American History." Even the most farsighted census-taker in 1890 could not have projected the fourfold increase of our population over the past hundred years, or its extraordinary diversity, or the fact that now a mere five million Americans farm our lands.

In September 1990 the National Park Service and a coalition of corporate and private benefactors completed a $156 million restoration of Ellis Island, the largest amount ever spent restoring an American shrine. Half of the structure is dedicated to a Museum of Immigration. Since 40 percent of Americans today are descended from immigrants who passed before the Statue of Liberty and through the gates of Ellis Island, the potent symbol seems worth the cost.

Citizenship and National Identity

Immigration to the United States is so commonplace as to be scarcely newsworthy anymore. An article headlined "6,000 Line up for U.S. Citizen Oath" got only a picture and three short columns in an interior section of the *Los Angeles Times* on 29 June 1984. The immigrants gathered at the Shrine Auditorium to swear allegiance to their new nation and pick up citizenship documents. The largest number, nearly a thousand, had come from the Philippines. They were followed closely by groups from Mexico (890) and Vietnam (704). There were 110 from Lebanon, 126 from the United Kingdom, 62 from Israel, and a few from Lithuania, Zimbabwe, and Tanzania. In the auditorium foyer, where League of Women Voters members handed out voter registration forms, one new citizen asked Rosemary Fitzpatrick if she was a Democrat or a Republican. "I want to do it right," the man said. Fitzpatrick explained that he would have to make up his own mind.

This event, so routine and inevitable, holds the keys to a process by which American character has been formed for over two hundred years. It typifies the American experience in at least three ways.

First is the continual ingathering of races and peoples—driven or drawn by religious, political, and economic forces—that have chosen to make the United States their home. Whether perceived through the now somewhat tarnished metaphor of the melting pot or through ethnic pluralism, America has assimilated and set its seal on an extraordinary diversity of peoples. Struggling to define the essence of the new land at the time of the American Revolution, the French immigrant J. Hector St. John de Crèvecoeur posed the classic question of American nationality in his *Letters from an American Farmer* (1782):

> What then is the American, this new man? He is either an European, or the descendant of an European, hence that strange mixture of blood, which you will find in no other country. I could point out to you a family whose grandfather was an Englishman, whose wife was Dutch, whose son married a French woman, and whose present four sons have now four wives of different nations. *He* is an American, who leaving behind him all his ancient prejudices and manners, receives new ones from the new mode of life he has embraced, the new government he obeys, and the new rank he holds. He becomes an American by being received in the broad lap of our great *Alma Mater*. Here individuals of all nations are melted into a new race of men, whose labours and prosperity will one day cause great changes in the world.

American Citizenship

After two hundred years the sources and genres of the "new race of men" have expanded far beyond Europe, but the process of uprooting, transplantation, adaptation, and renewal continues.

Although the massive waves of migration that added some 37 million foreign-born to the population from the 1820s to the 1920s are unlikely to recur in the same scale, during the last two decades the United States has become a haven for millions of economic and political refugees and advantage seekers, principally from Latin America and Asia. The nation is growing by some 6,300 persons daily, of which 2,000 are immigrants. During the 1980s 2.1 million of the newcomers became naturalized citizens, a 50 percent increase from the previous decade. Results of the 1990 census have indicated a total national population of 248.7 million. Thirty million (12 percent) of these were black, 22.4 million (9 percent) Hispanic, almost 2 million (.8 percent) Native American, and 7.3 million (2.9 percent) Asian or Pacific Islanders. To speak of these as minority populations is misleading, for the nation has no clear ethnic majority. The largest identifiable ethnic group, that of British ancestry, accounted for only 15 percent of the population at the 1980 census, as compared to 13 percent of German ancestry, and 8 percent Irish. The United States already has the fifth-largest Spanish-speaking population in the world, and it is assumed that Hispanics soon will be the largest single ethnic group in the United States. In the county of Los Angeles—the "new Ellis Island"—non-Hispanic whites comprise only 40.8 percent of the population; Hispanics provide 37.8 percent, non-Hispanic blacks 10.5 percent, and Asians and Pacific Islanders 10.8 percent. As the population of California as a whole grew 26.1 percent during the 1980s, the number of

Diverse Groups Share Core Beliefs

In a 1991 poll taken by the National Opinion Research Center, people were asked the following question: Some people say that people get ahead by their own hard work; others say that lucky breaks or help from other people are more important. Which do you think is most important?

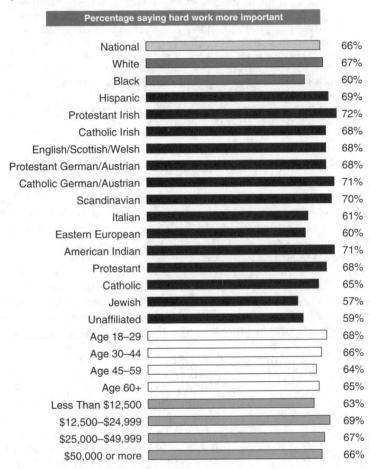

Percentage saying hard work more important

National	66%
White	67%
Black	60%
Hispanic	69%
Protestant Irish	72%
Catholic Irish	68%
English/Scottish/Welsh	68%
Protestant German/Austrian	68%
Catholic German/Austrian	71%
Scandinavian	70%
Italian	61%
Eastern European	60%
American Indian	71%
Protestant	68%
Catholic	65%
Jewish	57%
Unaffiliated	59%
Age 18–29	68%
Age 30–44	66%
Age 45–59	64%
Age 60+	65%
Less Than $12,500	63%
$12,500–$24,999	69%
$25,000–$49,999	67%
$50,000 or more	66%

Source: Gallup Organization, May 23–26, 1991.

whites increased by only 13.8 percent and blacks by 21.4 percent, while the number of persons of Hispanic origin climbed 69.2 percent and Asians and Pacific Islanders 127 percent (on top of a 140 percent increase during the 1970s). The heartland city of Fresno experienced a phenomenal 626 percent increase in its Asian population, and its Hispanic population more than doubled. A similar phenomenon is occurring from Texas and New Mexico to Missouri, Illinois, and New York.

A second key to the national experience that can be read from the *Los Angeles Times* report concerns the intentionality of American citizenship. The modern concept of citizenship derives from the American and French revolutions, which repudiated rule by monarchy and over time established the right of the individual to choose his or her own citizenship. Following the adoption of the Fourteenth Amendment to the Constitution in 1868, Congress formally declared the right of the citizen to change allegiance at will. Citizenship in the United States is conferred not indelibly by blood or culture, but by birth within the Union or by free choice. It is a matter of both covenant and achievement.

The persons taken into citizenship at the ceremony in Los Angeles had satisfied residence requirements, been found morally fit, passed simple literacy requirements, and demonstrated a basic understanding of the U.S. Constitution. Each had declared, "on oath, that I absolutely and entirely renounce and abjure all allegiance and fidelity to any foreign prince, potentate, state, or sovereignty of whom or which I have heretofore been a subject or citizen; that I will support and defend the Constitution and laws of the United States against all enemies, foreign and domestic; that I will bear true faith and allegiance to the same . . . so help me God." The majority of Americans will never attend citizenship training classes or pass through the ritual of citizenship so self-consciously as the quarter million immigrants who are "naturalized" each year, but the civics instruction and pledges of allegiance that suffuse our educational system and public observances habituate Americans to consider their citizenship a personal obligation.

A Common Legacy

The third key is closely related to the second, namely, the ideological core of the American commitment. In undertaking to "support and defend the Constitution and laws of the United States," the new Americans gave their allegiance to a national polity rooted in concepts of justice, equality, the unalienable rights of the individual, and government by and for the people. "Natural and subconscious forces have generally contributed to the process of a nation's coming into being more than free human decisions," noted Hans Kohn. "Not so with the Anglo-Americans. They established themselves as a nation without the support of any of those elements that are generally supposed to constitute a separate nation"—such as common descent, a common religion, a historically defined territory, cultural uniqueness, or a distinctive language, law, or literature. The mixed origins of the American colonists, the newness of their culture, and their constant mobility precluded any such organic solidarity. The tie that united the colonies, and at the same time separated them from all other nations, was founded "on an idea which singled out the new nation among the nations of the earth."

The Idea of America

This idea, expressed in the Constitution and the Bill of Rights, has continued to define what it means to be an American. The English tradition of liberty flourished in North America unhampered by feudalism or monarchy, encouraged by favorable geography and abundant natural resources. In a trenchant and prophetic discourse called *Barbarian Sentiments: How the American Century Ends* (1989), which appeared just before the reunification of Germany and the latest ethnic schisms in Yugoslavia, William Pfaff recently wrote: "The fate of the American, unlike that of the European, is inevitably a political fate. In this, the United States is unique. . . . The nation today rests upon a political compact or treaty among people of increasingly diverse origin and religious belief, or lack of belief, but who have in common a political vocabulary and constitutional system: and it is that which justifies the national existence. . . . If that Constitution should be abrogated, or if the political system that it established should fail or be overturned, then there would be no point to the United States." Walt Whitman was in essential agreement when he called attention in his *Democratic Vistas* (1871) to John Stuart Mill's essay *On Liberty* (1859) and to the two constituents Mill demanded "for a truly grand nationality—1st, a large variety of character—and 2nd, full play for human nature to expand itself in numberless and even conflicting directions." But he went beyond social covenant by then declaring: "The true nationality of the States, the genuine union, when we come to a mortal crisis, is, and is to be, after all, neither the written law, nor (as is generally supposed) either self-interest, or common pecuniary or material objects—but the fervid and tremendous Idea, melting everything else with resistless heat, and solving all lesser and definite distinctions in vast, indefinite, spiritual, emotional power."

Merely to remind ourselves of its ideological core, of course, hardly does justice to the colorful skein of American life today or the complex and manifold ways in which the American nation has evolved. Skeptics, indeed, will ask whether it is not futile to seek commonality among a population so large and ethnically diverse as that of the United States, spread across fifty states, six time zones, and tens of thousands of local communities, with neither a centralized educational system nor a ministry of culture. Since the 1960s scholars, journalists, and community leaders often have been more eager to feature the neglected experience of particular races, classes, and genders in the United States than to look for unity. While the public has celebrated a succession of national anniversaries, our cultural politics have moved from mainstream to margin, from hegemony to deconstruction. Yet there is no intrinsic reason why focuses on individual, group, and nation cannot be both synoptic and synchronic.

American Traits

Whether Americans perceive themselves as more diverse or more alike depends chiefly on point of view and one's purpose in posing the question. Weighing the relative diversities or unity of the United States in the 1880s, Lord James Bryce remarked: "Scotchmen and Irishmen are more unlike Englishmen, the native of Normandy more unlike the native of Provence, the Pomeranian more unlike the Wurtemberger, the Piedmontese more unlike the Neapolitan, the Basque more unlike the Andalusian, than the American from any part of the country is to the American from any other. . . . It is rather more difficult to take any assemblage of attributes in any of these European countries and call it the national type than it is to do the like in the United States." The same can be said today notwithstanding America's polyglot immigration or the European Economic Community. Gunnar Myrdal later made Lord Bryce's point in sociological language: "*Most Americans have most variations in common* though they are arranged differently in the sphere of valuations of different individuals and groups and bear different intensity coefficients."

For over a century and a half observers of the United States— the seasoned and scholarly as well as the transient and impressionistic—have written a catalog of American traits and remarked on its coherence. This catalog is, as Clyde Kluckhohn claimed, "based upon stubborn and irreducible facts of repeated observations that have amazing continuity over time." Lately, the forces of instant nationwide communications, constant mobility, a homogenizing popular culture, and the standardization inherent in mass production and a technological culture have steadily reduced the margins of idiosyncratic behavior in the United States.

The foundation of a people's character forms far earlier than their self-consciousness about it. The question of a distinctive American character was moot for the first hundred years and more following the settlements of the early seventeenth century. The early settlers saw themselves as colonists and an extension of British and European empires. Not until the eighteenth century did their nurture and patrimonial stake in the new land, combined with a spatial, commercial, and emotional distance from Europe, evoke the sense of a separate, distinctive society determined to be free. As Robert Frost saw in his poem "The Gift Outright":

> The land was ours before we were the land's.
> She was our land more than a hundred years
> Before we were her people. She was ours
> In Massachusetts, in Virginia,
> But we were England's, still colonials.

There were premonitions of difference from the outset, however, even before the first settlements. As Howard Mumford Jones vividly portrayed in *O Strange New World!* (1964), America inherited a legacy of medieval and Renaissance dreams and romantic visions. "The concept that the New World is the peculiar abode of felicity lingered for centuries in the European imagination and, like the youth of America, is one of its oldest traditions." Goethe's declaration *"Amerika, du hast es besser / Als unser Continent, das Alte"* was a late expression of a well-established sentiment. Over time, the Old World's pastoral visions collided with New World realities of wilderness and frontier. But after the vision of America as Eden came Exotic America, God's New Israel, Republican America, Immigrant America, and the Pax Americana. Each of these encounters of Old and New Worlds, people and environment, has ingrained itself in the American character.

"It is hardly too much to say that the cultural and even the political survival of the United States as we have known it is in jeopardy today."

Immigration Threatens America's Cultural Identity

Dwight D. Murphey

Dwight D. Murphey is professor of business law at Wichita State University in Wichita, Kansas. In the following viewpoint, Murphey argues that many Americans now believe that America does not need a unified culture and that celebrating and encouraging separate ethnic identities is positive. Murphey argues that this attitude, coupled with an immense increase in Third World immigration, is crippling American society, bringing the very culture upon which it was founded under attack.

As you read, consider the following questions:

1. Why does Murphey argue that attacking anything "Eurocentric" is dangerous?
2. What does Murphey think of those who describe America's past actions as immoral? How does he criticize this charge?
3. What is "civilizational suicide" and why is it occurring, according to the author?

Dwight D. Murphey, "Uncontrolled Immigration's Threat to American Identity," *St. Croix Review*, June 1995. Reprinted with permission.

It is hardly too much to say that the cultural and even the political survival of the United States as we have known it is in jeopardy today. For several years Americans have passively allowed an accelerating tide of immigration, legal and illegal, to bring about vast demographic and cultural changes. At some time in the not-too-distant future—if it hasn't happened already—a "tipping point" will be reached beyond which the demographic balance will have been so altered that the "mainstream" of today's Americans will no longer be able to set the tone for our society. This will occur long before the present mainstream loses its majority status.

In their 1994 book *The Immigration Invasion*, Wayne Lutton and John Tanton explore immigration consequences in such areas as health and welfare costs, the labor market, the politics of race, crime, and quality of life. The effects in these areas are extensive and deserve all the attention the authors give them; but it is also important to place the phenomenon in a worldwide perspective. It is a fact of major importance that the Third World influx threatens to swamp not just the United States, but also Europe. A massively swelling world population produces demographic shifts that put into question the long-term existence of a distinctively European and American civilization. World population was only two billion in 1945, but is projected to reach 8.5 billion—centered in the Third World—by the year 2024!

Civilization Under Siege

This is occurring within a critical human context. Since the end of World War II, European and American civilization has been under ideological and moral siege. As the voices of non-European peoples have been amplified the world over, everything "Eurocentric" has come under attack. With notable exceptions, the professional and academic elites in Europe and America, long under the influence of the cultural alienation of the Left, have been anxious to add their voices to this siege. In the United States, for example, a great many educated Americans are more than ready to believe that Americans of past centuries acted immorally in "taking the continent from the Indians" or that the administration of Franklin Delano Roosevelt placed the Japanese-Americans in "concentration camps" during World War II.

It is within this context of demoralized loss of élan that the vast population pressures from the Third World come to bear. Even if Europe's and America's will to exist were at its highest, the vastly exploding world communities would exert a well-nigh irresistible pressure to overflow their national and continental boundaries and to run like a stream into all available spaces, especially into such parts of the world as Europe and the United States that offer affluence and a high quality of life. But this stream confronts no obstacles, no sea walls, when Europe and America have so little moral energy. At least until the election of 1994 in the United States, there was little sign that there was any major force willing to think in terms of having a civilizational prerogative to preserve, much less about how to mobilize a defense against the demographic washing-away that has been occurring.

Rob Rogers reprinted by permission of United Feature Syndicate, Inc.

The American Left, formed out of an alliance between an alienated intellectual culture and whatever disaffected or unassimilated groups it can from time to time cultivate, has long pressed an egalitarian program. Consistently with its amazing adaptability, the theoretical basis for this thrust has passed through a number of phases. At the beginning of the "civil rights movement" it embraced as its own one of the fundamental premises of Western law—equality before the law. From there it went to advocating a system of compensatory preferences. Another leap extended these preferences to embrace not just blacks but women and ethnic minorities that have no history of past mistreatment. Now there is an enormous leap: the championing of the right of non-Americans from all continents to come and share at the egalitarian table.

All of this has been met by an intellectual, moral vacuum

within the mainstream culture. The expression "the silent majority" captures one of the main facts about American society since World War II. At least until the 1994 election, it was clear that the great run of Americans have not been in control of the country's political and ideological direction. Elites have set the agenda.

The American Population

The population of the United States is expanding rapidly from its present 255 million. *Border Watch* reports that "as recently as 1988, the Census Bureau predicted that U.S. population would rise to about 300 million by 2050 and then level off or decline. Now it projects a population of 380 million in 2050 which will continue to rise." The reasons for this increase include not just the number of immigrants, but their much higher birth rate.

Figures from the Census Bureau show a continuing increase in the percentage of the American population composed of minorities. The projection is that 47 percent will be minority by the year 2050. "Non-Hispanic whites," the Population Reference Bureau says, "will decline from 74 percent to 52 percent." Lawrence Auster cites what he considers more realistic calculations by demographer Leon Bouvier that arrive at a 48.9 percent figure.

These projections are startling in themselves. Might we not expect, though, that the volume of immigration will *accelerate* as the population develops ever-larger ethnic minorities? What politician of the future will be able to stand against it? And if that is true, non-Hispanics may be a minority well before 2050.

A news report in early 1993 said that "an estimated 100,000 Asians are illegally entering the United States each year." Columnist Cal Thomas reports that the Haitian population in New York City is estimated at 400,000. Another article tells us that about 300,000 people just stay here each year when their student, visitor, or work visas run out. About the same number cross the border illegally from Mexico. We are told that in California, "white children are now a minority in the public schools." In their book *Thirty Million Texans?* Leon Bouvier and Dudley Poston estimate that in Texas "by 2005 non-Hispanic whites will no longer be the majority."

Effects of the Immigration

There is no doubt that a significant part of the immigration strengthens the American economy. The United States has long been the beneficiary of a "brain drain" of scientific and professional people from throughout the world. This raises, of course, a serious ethical question of whether the United States should be draining intelligence from nations that need it desperately.

Nevertheless, the dangers are palpable. Lawrence Auster refers to what may be the most important question: "What is the impact of immigration on the whole society—on the United States as a *civilization?*" He quotes a Latino author as celebrating the fact that "we're changing the language, the food, the music, the way of being." Auster observes that "American national culture is being supplanted by Third World cultures. We are now experiencing the following phenomena: a 25-foot-high statue of the Aztec god of human sacrifice is being erected in a public square in the Hispanic-majority city of San Jose, California; Santeria, a cult that practices animal sacrifice, is now constitutionally protected under the First Amendment; huge festivals awash in primitive symbols celebrating 'West Indian Day' and 'Hispanic Day' regularly disrupt life in major cities. . . . The Alamo is reconceptualized as a Hispanic monument. The Pearl Harbor memorial is relativized so as not to offend Japanese-Americans."

Concern about national unity and identity is primarily a matter of love and loyalty. It will be a central concern for those who cherish the United States for what it has been. It should be noted, though, that even most of the immigrants have come to the United States because they have valued it for what it is. If that essence is destroyed and we become a Third World nation, their dreams, too, are gone.

The naive assumption that the United States is bound forever to remain a unified country is coming to have less and less foundation. A strong separatist movement has existed in Canada among the French-speaking population of Quebec, and since the collapse of the Soviet Union the world has witnessed a good many ethnic separations. There are today groups demanding a "return" of the entire Southwestern United States to Mexico; and it is very much to the point that *Insight* magazine recently reported that a movement has sprung up in Hawaii for sovereignty as against the United States. Yuji Aida, professor emeritus at the University of Kyoto in Japan, expresses a truism when he says that "it is only a matter of time before U.S. minority groups espouse self-determination in some form. When this happens, the country may become ungovernable."

A Semantic Paralysis

The issue of national identity is among those choked by ideological smog. Love for and loyalty to a civilization that is preeminently European and Caucasian is attacked as "racism." This makes it vital that Americans become clear about what "racism" is. If it is "racism," and hence vicious, to be pro-Caucasian, but colorful and laudatory to wear a "black power" T-shirt or to applaud Hispanics' "appreciation of their heritage," the term ceases to have meaning, and we are left with a raw double standard that is nothing more than an intimidating ploy. No one is being demanded to foreswear allegiance to his kind except Europeans, Euro-Americans, and Caucasians.

The American Immigration Control Foundation recently said that "perhaps the best definition [of racism] is an attitude of superiority and contempt of one racial group for another. This attitude usually shows itself in attempts of the 'superior' group to dominate and oppress its victims." Instead of defining "racism" as "loyalty to one's own kind," and thereby branding as vicious an affinity that people are bound to feel at all times and places, their definition looks to how that loyalty is manifested. Something is racist if it manifests a hostile and oppressive posture towards other peoples. So long as a great many Europeans and Americans of European extraction accept the notion that loyalty to their own heritage constitutes racism, they are on their way to civilizational suicide.

"The Los Angeles riots of 1992 . . . marked the advent of a new, more complex, and more troubling phase in the history of inter-group conflict in America."

Immigrants Unwilling to Assimilate Will Cause Interracial Conflict

Brent A. Nelson

Brent A. Nelson holds a Ph.D. and is the author of *America Balkanized: Immigration's Challenge to Government*, excerpted in the following viewpoint. In it, Nelson argues that recent immigrants are not interested in assimilating into American culture. He contends that this lack of interest will ultimately lead to conflict between Third World immigrants and the European-centered traditions on which the United States was founded.

As you read, consider the following questions:

1. Why does Nelson criticize those who believe that unassimilated immigrants are only a temporary problem?
2. Why are Mexican immigrants particularly hard to assimilate into the United States, according to the author?
3. What is Nelson afraid is happening to the U.S. public education system?

Excerpted from *America Balkanized: Immigration's Challenge to Government* by Brent A. Nelson (Monterey, VA: American Immigration Control Foundation, 1994). Reprinted with permission.

During the 1980s, several observers of political trends in the United States warned that the growing Spanish-speaking population in the Southwest might one day pose a challenge to national unity similar to that presented by the French-speaking population in Canada. The best known among them, Richard D. Lamm, a former governor of Colorado, wrote in 1986 that "I am concerned about the danger of countries in which two language groups clash. I think about the problems caused by Quebec's separatist movement, founded upon the French language. I think about the tensions even within peaceful multilingual countries: the cantonization of Switzerland and the division of Belgium." Writing in 1987, former Senator Eugene McCarthy warned of a "recolonization" which has one manifestation in "the challenge to the status of English in the United States. There has been both a practical and a legal submission to demands that at least some parts of the country should become bilingual or multilingual.". . .

Hispanic Quebec

Noting that the mass media gave little attention to their warnings, skeptics have dismissed [critics] as prophets of doom, haunted by the spectre of a "Hispanic Quebec" which will never become a reality. According to this popular interpretation of the problem, it will remain problematic for only a limited period of time. Millions of immigrants have entered the U.S. in past decades, according to this reassuring argument, and have been more or less readily assimilated into the mainstream of American social and political life.

This optimistic assessment overlooks, however, the transforming impact of a significant change in the origins of the region's population combined with an ongoing failure of the process of assimilation. The demographic shift in the Southwest resulting from an influx of immigrants and differential birthrates among different elements of the population is increasingly evident. The decline of the assimilative powers of American society, while not so evident, can be inferred from the experience of numerous other societies and becomes increasingly apparent within the U.S. itself. Both factors converge to make more and more probable, if not inevitable, the rise of ethnic separatism within the American Southwest and elsewhere.

The demographic factor alone, assuming continued immigration, could transform the Southwest into a "Hispanic Quebec" long before the close of the twenty-first century. According to the rather conservative estimates of demographers Leon F. Bouvier and Cary B. Davis in their *Immigration and the Future Racial Composition of the United States*, Hispanics, over half of whom are or will be Mexican Americans, will comprise 34.1 percent of the total population of the U.S. in 2080, even if the

U.S. limits immigration to two million entrants each year from all areas of the world while birthrates of Hispanics converge with those of non-Hispanics, a possibly unrealistic assumption. Though 34.1 percent is less than a majority of the total population of the U.S., its impact will be overwhelming in the Southwest, where Hispanics will constitute a majority of the population in several states. . . .

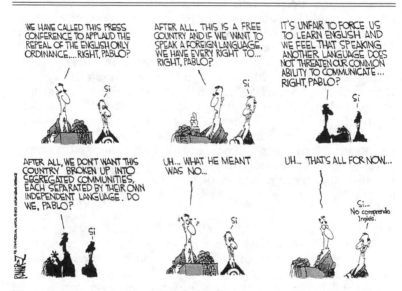

Not all immigrants, of course, will be Hispanics. Bouvier and Davis, on the basis of an annual immigration total of one million, project a striking rise in the percentage of Californians who are "Asian and Other," from 6.6 percent in 1980 to 18.7 percent in 2040. The comparable estimates for Texans are 1.4 and 5.7 percent. The rise in both states of large blocs of non-Hispanic immigrants will further divide the states culturally and politically, enhancing the relative electoral weight of a well-organized and ethnically conscious Hispanic plurality. Hispanic voting blocs of 40 to 50 percent of the electorate, which, in accord with these most conservative demographic estimates, can be projected for these states in 2080, would suffice to control an electoral process in which the remainder of the electorate would be divided among at least two to three major ethnic blocs. . . .

Many Mexican American immigrants live only the proverbial stone's throw away from their nation of birth. Even Mexican

Americans born in the U.S. can realistically regard Mexico as their cultural homeland because millions of them live close enough to the border to allow trips there and back of short duration. This closeness of millions of an ethnic group to their ancestral or native homeland is a unique situation in the immigration history of the U.S. On the basis of geography alone, then, it is patently absurd to claim that Hispanic immigration must follow the pattern of past immigration from Europe.

This geographic closeness to the nation of their ancestors may account more than any other factor for the failure of assimilation reported by James W. Lemare in 1982 in *International Migration Review*. Lemare studied 700 Mexican American children, aged nine through fourteen years, living in El Paso, Texas, all of them children of first through fifth generation immigrants. He found that "Overall, Mexican-American children, regardless of generation, show only limited commitment to the American political community. To be sure, each generation professes a preference for living in the United States, but only the mixed and second generation consider this to be the best country. None of the five cohorts prefers the label 'American' over identification tags more reflective of their national origin. Lastly, no generation exhibits a strong sense of trust in others.". . .

A Lack of Assimilation

"Affirmative ethnicity" . . . will prevail over the traditional ideal of assimilation when those who are to be assimilated begin to outnumber, in ever-greater areas, those who are to bring about the assimilation. Only a subconscious ethnocentrism can account for the belief that an ethnic minority, which the "Anglos" will eventually be in most areas of the Southwest, may in a liberal democracy determine the language, culture and values of an ethnic majority. Such attempts have invariably been undertaken by means of coercive state power and justified by elitist or racist ideologies which are now consciously repudiated by the nation's governing stratum.

Concomitant with this shift of public policy away from "Anglo-conformity" as a strategy of assimilation is a growing rejection within the nation's educational system of what is denounced as "Eurocentrism," an allegedly European bias in the teaching of literature, history, and other subjects. The argument against this supposed "Eurocentrism" has been trenchantly stated, in the following words, by Molefi Asante, chairman of African American studies at Temple University: "We are not living in a Western country. The American project is not yet completed. It is only in the eyes of the Eurocentrists who see it as a Western project, which means to hell with the rest of the people who have yet to create the project." Asante would supplement the "Eurocentric" view with an "Afrocentric and Latinocentric" view of the world. The triumph of this educational philosophy within the nation's public school systems would, obviously, lead to a reinforcement of corporate pluralism [which emphasizes group differences], the precise opposite of assimilation in the commonly received sense of the word.

By 1989, many responsible observers were beginning to admit openly that the Los Angeles area could no longer be understood in terms of older models of assimilation. . . .

Need for Core Values

In the early 1900s the government and the public culture were officially committed to Americanization. When kids came into the American school system they were immediately heaved into the English language, they were educated in English. So the assimilation mechanism was much more rigorous than it is now. So were the citizenship criteria. The assimilative mechanisms that existed in 1900 no longer exist and in fact, if anything, the contrary exists. Public policy seems to be moving toward creating this strange anti-nation of Hispanics. . . . I don't think you can make a free society work unless you have unanimity on certain core values and one of them is the language.

Peter Brimelow, *The San Diego Union-Tribune*, June 4, 1995.

Hitherto unknown intergroup tensions and violence seemed to be becoming the rule, rather than the exception. Building up to an unprecedented vehemence, they exploded into the riots that took place in south central Los Angeles during May 1992. Jack Miles, book editor for the *Los Angeles Times*, contributed a lengthy analysis of the ethnic conflicts involved to the October 1992 issue of the *Atlantic Monthly*. Pointedly entitled "Blacks vs. Browns," Miles's article argues that uncontrolled Hispanic immigration has been even more detrimental than Asian business acumen to the economic interests of African Americans. He believes that this explains why the rioters' fury so frequently found a target in businesses owned by Asians and Hispanics.

The Los Angeles riots of 1992, because they involved mutual antagonisms among three distinct ethnic blocs, marked the advent of a new, more complex, and more troubling phase in the history of inter-group conflict in America. It is perhaps not unjustified to draw a parallel between the destruction wrought upon the Asian merchants of Los Angeles and that suffered in the same year by the Moslems of Bosnia in the name of "ethnic cleansing." When three different groups are polarized in as many different directions, and this polarization erupts into sporadic episodes of violence, then there can be no question of assimilation. Merely keeping the peace must become the focus of all energies.

Throughout the 1980s, the reaction of "Anglos" to this ongoing failure of assimilation was largely limited to attempts to promote a superficial "Anglo-conformity" by demanding legislation to establish English as an "official language." These efforts usually took the form of state legislative acts or referenda aimed to establish English as the state's official language. By the end of 1988, seventeen states had enacted legislation or passed referenda recognizing English as the state's official language. . . .

The new immigration has brought into the United States great numbers of people who do not speak English. . . . They, moreover, are concentrated geographically in particular regions and urban areas. The latter fact is especially salient because in many areas those who are to be assimilated are beginning to outnumber those to whom they are to be assimilated. It would not be remarkable, therefore, if a continued influx of immigrants were to bring about, in some areas, a process of what might be called "reverse assimilation."

Reverse Assimilation

Reverse assimilation seems at first thought to be preposterous only because the conventional concept of assimilation is overly simplistic. It can and does occur when a sufficiently large number of immigrants having one origin move into a limited geographical area. It has occurred in American history in at least one instance involving a foreign-speaking minority, Norwegians in Wisconsin. According to Frank C. Nelson, writing in 1981 in the *Journal of Ethnic Studies*,

> "Resignation to assimilation" was followed by a period of "renewed ethnicity," and lasted from 1870 to 1900. . . . With large numbers of Norwegians coming to America there emerged a significant shift in attitude from the "resignation to assimilation." There developed a new attitude that Norwegians ought "not to be too quick to mimic everything American before we have tested whether it is better than our own." . . . The period between 1870 and 1900 has been called "the Norwegian period." At this time the Norwegian language had been established as the language of the family, church, and neighborhood. . . . Signs of Norwegian culture were increasingly evident in Norwegian settlements.

Reverse assimilation came to a halt among Wisconsin's Norwegians because (1) the influx of new immigrants almost ceased after 1900 and (2) the microdiacritic Norwegians could not be easily distinguished, either by others or by themselves, among the mass of other northern Europeans in the state. As of the mid-1990s, of course, neither of these circumstances applied to slow down, much less halt, the reverse assimilation taking place in Miami and Monterey Park and elsewhere. . . .

The Cubans in Miami and the Asians in Monterey Park have advanced to the stage of communalism. Neither of these groups, regardless of where they live, has produced adherents of the more advanced strategies. . . . The Mexican Americans of the Southwest, however, great in numbers and possessing a different history, are producing spokesmen for the advanced strategies of autonomism [and] separatism.

"This culture is remarkably individualistic and competitive, nourishing a level of group loyalty and social fragmentation that other societies would find intolerable."

Increasing Immigration Will Not Lead to Interracial Conflict

Peter H. Schuck

Peter H. Schuck, a professor of law at Yale Law School, is the author, with Rogers M. Smith, of *Citizenship Without Consent*. In the following viewpoint, Schuck argues that an increasing number of immigrants will not result in unprecedented ethnic competition and conflict. Schuck argues that there is no reason to think that the United States cannot continue to assimilate new immigrants into the country.

As you read, consider the following questions:

1. How do recent immigrants differ from those of the past, according to Schuck?
2. To what event does the author attribute recent immigration trends?
3. How does Schuck address competition between immigrants and blacks? What is his solution?

From "America and the New Immigrant Experience" by Peter H. Schuck, *Los Angeles Times*, May 5, 1991. Reprinted by permission of the author.

Has the melting pot gone the way of Joe DiMaggio and other images of a happier but irretrievably lost America? Some people think a truer metaphor is a laboratory beaker brimming over with explosive, immiscible chemicals in a high-stakes experiment that threatens to go awry. *E pluribus unum*, they fear, is being tragically reversed. Hardly a week goes by without another outbreak of ethnic conflict making the national news. Yet there is ample reason to believe that from many groups we can still forge one politically viable nation.

Ethnic conflict has always been with us, but lately it has become more noticeable, largely because of growth in the number of immigrants, their geographic concentration and their diversity, the politicization of ethnicity, and heightened competition among low-income groups.

In the 1980s we admitted about 8.5 million people, including 2.3 million under the 1986 amnesty law, and the trend was moving upward as the decade ended. This is almost double the total for the 1970s and close to the 8.8 million who came in the first decade of this century when immigration was essentially unrestricted.

Increased Visibility

The new immigrants are especially visible because they are concentrated in a small number of metropolitan areas. About 80% of the legal ones plan to live in six states; 37% plan to live in seven metropolitan areas in California. The undocumented, who depend more on informal job and protection networks, cluster even more than that; 42% of the amnesty applicants plan to live in those seven California communities. In cities like Miami, Houston, Los Angeles and New York, recent immigrants are already important forces in the local economy, culture and political system.

The newcomers are ethnically and linguistically distinct from most of the native population. In 1989 the top 10 source countries for legal (and amnestied) admissions were Mexico, El Salvador, the Philippines, Vietnam, Korea, China, India, the Dominican Republic, Jamaica and Iran. Although many are highly educated, on average they possess fewer skills than either the native population or the immigrants who came during the 1950s.

This remarkable diversity has two major causes: the 1965 amendments to the immigration law and the social chaos caused by the wars in Southeast Asia and Central America. The 1965 changes jettisoned longstanding national-origins quotas, which had favored immigrants from Europe and had permitted little or no legal immigration from Asia, the Pacific, Latin America and Africa.

The Melting Pot Works

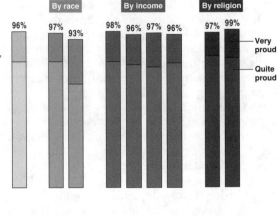

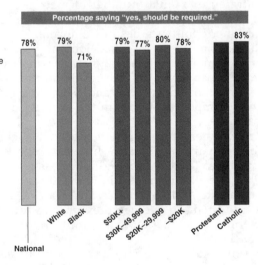

How proud are you to be an American: Very proud, quite proud, not very proud, or not at all proud?

By race: 96% (National), 97% (White), 93% (Black)
By income: 98% ($50K+), 96% ($30K–49,999), 97% ($20K–29,999), 96% (–$20K)
By religion: 97% (Protestant), 99% (Catholic)

Very proud / Quite proud

Which one of these statements best expresses your own point of view?
A. The US is the greatest country in the world, better than all other countries in every possible way.
B. The US is a great country, but so are certain other countries.
C. In many respects, certain other countries are better than the US.

Percentage who chose statement C
9% (National), 9% (White), 9% (Black), 9% ($50K+), 10% ($30K–49,999), 8% ($20K–29,999), 8% (–$20K), 8% (Protestant), 7% (Catholic)

Do you think US school children should be required to pledge allegiance to the flag in all US schools or not?

Percentage saying "yes, should be required."
78% (National), 79% (White), 71% (Black), 79% ($50K+), 77% ($30K–49,999), 80% ($20K–29,999), 78% (–$20K), Protestant, 83% (Catholic)

National — White — Black — $50K+ — $30K–49,999 — $20K–29,999 — –$20K — Protestant — Catholic

Source: Gallup Organization, May 23–26, 1991.

Meanwhile, the stakes in exclusive group identity have been rising. Ethnic politics assumed new significance during the 1970s and '80s—affirmative-action programs in employment, school admissions and public services transformed ethnicity's social meaning. Ethnic self-assertion gained greater political weight through the coercive, symbolic force of law. Under the aegis of the Voting Rights Act, the Justice Department and the courts countenanced, and even required, gerrymandering of legislative districts in pursuit of racially and ethnically defined conceptions of political equality. "Official English" policies were adopted by a number of states, and bilingual education became a fiercely contested public issue.

Group Conflicts

Finally, the continuing decline of central cities and lower-class family structures casts a long, dark shadow over the searing process of group competition. Many blacks and Puerto Ricans mired in decaying ghettos resent the upward mobility of more recently arrived Asians, Cubans and Mexicans, who experience less residential segregation even at similar income levels. Competitive anxieties are driving deep wedges between these groups, as exemplified by their split over employer sanctions on the immigration laws and the redistricting struggle in Los Angeles County.

Ethnic conflicts must be understood in the larger context of our unique political culture. This culture is remarkably individualistic and competitive, nourishing a level of group loyalty and social fragmentation that other societies would find intolerable. Being a Frenchman, Briton or German is more confining and demanding than being an American. Unlike them, we do not subscribe to a common religious or racial heritage; instead, our cultural ideals are inclusionary: They accommodate everyone who will share the commitment to democracy, toleration, mobility and the rule of law.

Assimilation Still Succeeding

U.S. citizenship is easy to acquire, hard to lose and imposes few civic duties. Assimilation, always difficult, is probably easier here than anywhere else: The political culture applauds parochial loyalties; the main pressure to assimilate is economic, not legal, and most Americans celebrate their own immigrant roots.

Without exception, although at distressingly uneven rates, each new group has advanced far beyond its point of origin in the United States. Intermarriage among ethnic and racial groups continues to increase; although black-white intermarriage occurs at a much lower rate, it too has risen dramatically.

All public-opinion evidence indicates that Americans have grown steadily more tolerant of minorities. The political power of the new groups is growing. Upward mobility may take a gen-

139

eration, but for most groups it continues to occur. Latinos born in the United States or who have been here for at least 10 years have already matched the national averages in occupation, education, income and language proficiency. Mexican-origin families are almost as likely to be intact as white ones. A 1988 report by the Civil Rights Commission finds that Asian immigrants generally have higher family and per capita incomes than non-Latino whites, although Vietnamese, Filipino and Indian immigrants still lag behind.

America's performance in integrating ethnic and racial minorities into the mainstream also compares quite favorably with that of other countries, most notably Western Europe. The rise of nativist, often racist movements seeking to bar foreigners is an ugly feature of French, German and British politics, and their support will probably increase as conditions in Eastern Europe deteriorate. Of the significant immigrant-receiving countries, only Canada has arguably done as well as the United States in welcoming immigrants, but it is also much more selective in deciding which ones it will accept.

America's immigrant-welcoming tradition is not merely a thing of the past. We dramatically strengthened this commitment with the Immigration Act of 1990. . . .

Americans evidently recognize that in the increasingly multicultural, interdependent, mobile world of the future, our openness to change and diversity will confer an immense advantage on us—economically, morally, culturally and politically.

Periodical Bibliography

The following articles have been selected to supplement the diverse views presented in this chapter. Addresses are provided for periodicals not indexed in the *Readers' Guide to Periodical Literature*, the *Alternative Press Index*, or the *Social Sciences Index*.

Suzanne Fields	"The Melting Pot Is Cooking a Highly Indigestible Stew," *Insight*, March 14, 1994. Available from 3600 New York Ave. NE, Washington, DC 20002.
Francis Fukuyama	"Immigrants and Family Values," *Commentary*, May 1993.
James A. Johnson	"What Immigrants Want," *Wall Street Journal*, June 20, 1995.
R.K. Lamb	"The Half-Open Door," *Liberty*, February 1993. Available from PO Box 1181, Port Townsend, WA 98368.
Thomas Muller	"The Immigrant Challenge," *Wilson Quarterly*, Autumn 1994.
National Review	"Demystifying Multiculturalism," special issue on immigration, February 21, 1994.
John O'Sullivan	"America's Identity Crisis," *National Review*, November 21, 1994.
Richard Rodriguez	"The New, New World," *Reason*, August/September 1994.
Julian L. Simon	"The Nativists Are Wrong," *Wall Street Journal*, August 4, 1993.
James Thornton	"Multicultural Invasion," *New American*, September 19, 1994.
U.S. News & World Report	"One Nation, One Language?" September 25, 1995.

CHAPTER

4

How Has Affirmative Action Affected Race Relations?

Chapter Preface

Affirmative action is a policy that requires a certain percentage of minorities and women be represented in business, educational institutions, and government offices. Originally part of legislation that came out of the civil rights movement of the 1960s, affirmative action was intended to be a temporary measure to give minorities and women access to jobs and education that they had been denied because of race and gender. Today, affirmative action is controversial because many contend that it is no longer necessary. Whether or not the results are due to affirmative action, many argue that minorities and women have been fully integrated into the workplace and institutions of higher learning. To continue with affirmative action, opponents Paul Craig Roberts and Lawrence M. Stratton argue in *The New Color Line: How Quotas and Privilege Destroy Democracy*, is to ignore these realities. Roberts and Stratton contend that continued quotas will lead to minorities and women becoming privileged classes: "[Quotas] are justified as a new kind of entitlement necessary to indemnify minorities for past wrongdoing and to combat white racism. We are witnessing in the name of 'diversity' the development of a new constitutional right to proportional representation by race and sex in every aspect of life."

Those who support continued affirmative action accuse their opponents of naivete. Racism has not disappeared, these advocates argue, and affirmative action is one of the few assurances minorities have of continued access to jobs and educational opportunities open to white males. As activist Jerry Watts states:

> The United States is a deeply racist country, not only in its enduring historical legacies, but in the ordinary, everyday lack of concern that so many white Americans feel for the plight of poor blacks. . . . Any serious discussion of affirmative action must be situated within this despairing realization of American racial realities. . . . Until white Americans recognize the depth of our racial crisis, our national conversation about affirmative action will be evasive and inadequate.

The authors in the following chapter discuss the cultural, economic, and moral aspects of affirmative action.

"It is government-initiated, government-sponsored, and government-enforced affirmative action that, above all, has placed a curse on race relations in the U.S."

Affirmative Action Is Reverse Discrimination

Irving Kristol

Irving Kristol, a fellow with the American Enterprise Institute, a conservative think tank, co-edits the magazine the *Public Interest* and publishes the *National Interest*. In the following viewpoint, Kristol argues that affirmative action programs have worsened relations between whites and minorities. He argues that because affirmative action places value on race and gender, it sends the erroneous and contradictory message that to correct the wrongs of racism, society must have a program that judges people exclusively according to race.

As you read, consider the following questions:

1. What point does Kristol make about O.J. Simpson?
2. What comparisons does Kristol make between the United States and South Africa?
3. According to the author, how does affirmative action contribute to "the Balkanization of America"?

Irving Kristol, "The Tragic Error of Affirmative Action," *Wall Street Journal*, August 1, 1994. Reprinted with permission of the *Wall Street Journal*, ©1994 Dow Jones & Company, Inc. All rights reserved.

Just who or what is a black American, anyhow? Two recent events have posed this question to me, and in an unexpected way.

First there was (and is) the case of O.J. Simpson. I haven't followed this case closely, but it is clear that it seems to be, among other things, a significant incident in "race relations" in this country. . . .

Now, as a sports fan I have never really thought about the color of O.J. Simpson's skin. But watching him on television, I found myself observing the color of his skin, and deciding that he is not really black at all. Bronze, I should think would be more accurate—so why do we call him "black"? And, it further occurred to me: What if O.J. spoke Spanish instead of English? Would he then be transmuted into a "Hispanic" and no longer be "black"?

The World Cup

The second event was the 1994 World Cup series in soccer. No one mentioned the color of any player's skin, though the surprisingly good Saudi team seemed to be all "black," as were, of course, the Nigerians. Somehow race vanished from our perspective as we watched these games. The Saudis were all and only Saudi, just as the Nigerians were all and only Nigerian. And I realized: Throughout most of the world, national identity trumps racial identity. This is true, even in the U.S., for such groups as the Pakistanis and Indians, who are never defined racially, whatever their skin color.

It's not that, in other mixed-race countries, race and skin color count for nothing. It usually counts for something. And there is always the possibility of discrimination, which is sometimes a reality—occasionally even giving rise to political controversy. But in America, with its liberal traditions, race nevertheless remains a permanent, fixed and deadly problem. How did this come about?

Well, we know how it came about. It was the enduring curse of slavery that instilled a degree of race-consciousness of an extraordinary intensity. Just why this should have happened in the U.S., and not (at least to the same degree) in other countries, scholars are still trying to explain. But happen it did. It is because of slavery that if you are one-quarter black, or even one-eighth black, you are automatically designated as black. In the Old South, if you were merely suspected of having a "touch of the tar brush," you were not properly "white."

This crazy race-consciousness is not replicated in any other country that I know of—except, perhaps, South Africa. And even in South Africa, those of mixed racial ancestry are classified as "coloured," not black. Had we such a classification in the U.S., at least one-quarter to one-third of American "blacks" would overnight become "coloured." Not that it would really matter, of course.

It is to the eternal credit of American liberalism that, after the Civil War, and most especially after World War II, it set out to dismantle all legislation, and the entire set of attitudes, that can properly be called "racist." And much progress has been made. There is no reason to doubt that, in time, more progress would have been steadily made, if it had not been for the Supreme Court's role in school "integration" in the 1950s and the subsequent rise of "affirmative action" in that disastrous decade, the 1960s.

That celebrated Supreme Court decision, *Brown v. Board of Education*, contrary to expectations, turned out to be the prelude to a major step backward in American race relations. The court had the option simply to overturn previous court decisions that legitimated discriminatory legislation by the states. But it ignored this option, which would have opened the way for continuing, gradual progress, and instead decided to rule in such a way as to suggest that the opposite of discrimination was, not non-discrimination, but "integration."

Criticism Interpreted as Racist

It invites attack as a "racist" to point out that "affirmative action" and the "new segregation" have brought on a new divisiveness, especially in the urban areas. And it is creating a backlash, not only among whites but among middle-class blacks who feel that lowered educational and professional standards for them, imposed by "affirmative action," denigrates them and suggests that they were not able to cut the mustard. Increasingly, whites are remarking to each other that blacks constitute some 12 to 13 percent of the population yet seem to be taking up 100 percent of the national attention. And there is a closet industry in pejorative jokes about blacks that never existed before and which are "justified" by a prevailing and blatant black anti-Semitism. . . .

Ironically, the fact may be that, in the long run, those most hurt by "affirmative action" will be its alleged beneficiaries.

Ralph de Toledano, *Conservative Chronicle*, June 14, 1995.

Having decided justly that government at all levels should be color-blind, the courts then went on to insist that schools had to be color-conscious when it came to the student population. This was our first whiff of what later mushroomed into affirmative action. The school busing controversies that followed sharply exacerbated the racism it wished to eradicate. Today, school busing for purposes of racial integration is wildly unpopular among both races, and the courts are in grudging retreat on the issue.

A Curse on Race Relations

But it is government-initiated, government-sponsored, and government-enforced affirmative action that, above all, has placed a curse on race relations in the U.S. This idea was born of a liberalism drunk with success and intoxicated with power, and marked a transformation of liberalism itself—from a Hubert Humphrey–Lyndon Johnson liberalism to a more statist George McGovern–Edward Kennedy liberalism. It is this later liberalism that, with its radical goal of quick racial integration, has given us, among other things, racially gerrymandered congressional districts.

In its origins, affirmative action seemed almost to be a noble idea, elevating blacks even if at some expense to whites. The rectification of economic and societal inequities derived from past injustice was appealing. Moreover, the original idea of such rectification was merely a "reaching out" to those hitherto discriminated against, so that they could compete fairly in the job market. The specter of racial quotas was raised by a few commentators, but since many of them were deemed unfriendly to racial equality in the first place, they were ignored. Today, that specter is a haunting presence in American life and American politics, wreaking its havoc in all sorts of ways.

What happened is that, as a result of administrative decision and judicial intervention, affirmative action has imported racial quotas into American life, and the racist idea has acquired a new lease on life. In all sectors—private, governmental, and not-for-profit—most hiring decisions are shaped by quotas for women and various racial and "ethnic" groups. Government officials, corporate "human relations" executives and university presidents loudly protest that quotas are anathema to them, and that they merely have nonspecific goals in mind. It is also true that these people are lying. Those goals inevitably become numerical—how else can you measure success or failure? And a numerical goal means a quota. Even when the existence of quotas is denied, government regulations stipulate that such-and-such a proportion of such-and-such a group must be hired (or admitted to a university), the proportion mirroring the group's presence in the relevant population source.

Incredibly, though inevitably, our governments at all levels, as well as our major private institutions, have to confront the problem of defining appropriate membership in each quota group. Women are still identifiable in our society, but who, exactly, qualifies as a black? As a Hispanic? As an Asian? The response of the affirmative action establishment has been to institute something akin to the Nuremberg laws in our American democracy.

If you are one-eighth black, you are black. If your parents' native tongue is Spanish, then you are Hispanic—even if you are visibly black or, for the most part, English-speaking. If you look Asian to someone in charge of the counting, that's what you are. Since the rate of intermarriage between native-born Asians and those of European descent is close to 50%, and for Hispanics is about 30%, this whole business is getting very, very complicated. But affirmative action rolls on, showing a remarkable, if frequently absurd, ingenuity in racial and ethnic identification.

And the upshot? The upshot is the Balkanization of America. Racial tensions and ethnic tensions in American life have increased, instead of decreasing. Under the flags of "multicultural-ism" and "diversity" we are moving deliberately and desperately away from being a color-blind or ethnic-blind society to becoming a society that willfully generates racial and ethnic tensions. There are jobs at stake, after all, and political careers to be made, and everyone now wants a piece of that affirmative-action pie.

It took us a century to recover from the curse of slavery. How long will it take us to recover from the tragic error of affirmative action?

"For nearly all our history, affirmative action has been a prerogative of white men."

Discrimination in Favor of Minorities Is Necessary

Eric Foner

Eric Foner is DeWitt Clinton Professor of History at Columbia University. In the following viewpoint, Foner condemns white attacks on affirmative action programs. He argues that racism is invisible to most whites, who benefit from its subtle effects. Since whites have always benefited from society's cultural favoritism, Foner concludes, affirmative action is needed to grant blacks an equal footing.

As you read, consider the following questions:

1. What evidence does Foner offer to support his argument that the United States has never operated on a color-blind basis?
2. What benefits has affirmative action produced, according to the author?
3. Foner concludes by saying that "equal opportunity has never been the American Way." What does he mean by this?

Eric Foner, "Hiring Quotas for White Males Only," *Nation*, June 26, 1995. Reprinted with permission from the *Nation* magazine; © The Nation Company, L.P.

Thirty-two years ago, I graduated from Columbia College. My class of 700 was all-male and virtually all-white. Most of us were young men of ability, yet had we been forced to compete for admission with women and racial minorities, fewer than half of us would have been at Columbia. None of us, to my knowledge, suffered debilitating self-doubt because we were the beneficiaries of affirmative action—that is, favored treatment on the basis of our race and gender.

Affirmative action has emerged as the latest "wedge issue" of American politics. . . . As a historian, I find the current debate dismaying not only because of the crass effort to set Americans against one another for partisan advantage but also because the entire discussion lacks a sense of history.

Opponents of affirmative action, for example, have tried to wrap themselves in the mantle of the civil rights movement, seizing upon the 1963 speech in which Martin Luther King Jr. looked forward to the time when his children would be judged not by the "color of their skin" but by the "content of their character." Rarely mentioned is that King came to be a strong supporter of affirmative action.

In his last book, *Where Do We Go From Here?*, a brooding meditation on America's long history of racism, King acknowledged that "special treatment" for blacks seemed to conflict with the ideal of opportunity based on individual merit. But, he continued, "a society that has done something special *against* the Negro for hundreds of years must now do something special *for* him."

Our country, King realized, has never operated on a color-blind basis. From the beginning of the Republic, membership in American society was defined in racial terms. The first naturalization law, enacted in 1790, restricted citizenship for those emigrating from abroad to "free white persons." Free blacks, even in the North, were barred from juries, public schools, government employment and the militia and regular army. Not until after the Civil War were blacks deemed worthy to be American citizens, while Asians were barred from naturalization until the 1940s.

Standard of Living for Whites Only

White immigrants certainly faced discrimination. But they had access to the political power, jobs and residential neighborhoods denied to blacks. In the nineteenth century, the men among them enjoyed the right to vote even before they were naturalized. Until well into this century, however, the vast majority of black Americans were excluded from the suffrage except for a period immediately after the Civil War. White men, native and immigrant, could find well-paid craft and industrial jobs, while employers and unions limited nonwhites (and women) to unskilled and menial employment. The "American standard of living" was an entitlement of white men alone.

There is no point in dwelling morbidly on past injustices. But this record of unequal treatment cannot be dismissed as "vague or ancient wrongs" with no bearing on the present, as Republican strategist William Kristol recently claimed. Slavery may be gone and legal segregation dismantled, but the effects of past discrimination live on in seniority systems that preserve intact the results of a racially segmented job market, a black unemployment rate double that of whites and pervasive housing segregation.

Reprinted by permission: Tribune Media Services.

Past racism is embedded in the two-tier, racially divided system of social insurance still on the books today. Because key Congressional committees in the 1930s were controlled by Southerners with all-white electorates, they did not allow the supposedly universal entitlement of Social Security to cover the largest categories of black workers—agricultural laborers and domestics. Social Security excluded 80 percent of employed black women, who were forced to depend for a safety net on the much less generous "welfare" system.

The notion that affirmative action stigmatizes its recipients reflects not just belief in advancement according to individual merit but the older idea that the "normal" American is white. There are firemen and black firemen, construction workers and black construction workers: Nonwhites (and women) who obtain such jobs are still widely viewed as interlopers, depriving white men of positions or promotions to which they are historically entitled.

I have yet to meet the white male in whom special favoritism (getting a job, for example, through relatives or an old boys' network, or because of racial discrimination by a union or employer) fostered doubt about his own abilities. In a society where belief in black inferiority is still widespread (witness the success of *The Bell Curve*), many whites and some blacks may question the abilities of beneficiaries of affirmative action. But this social "cost" hardly counterbalances the enormous social benefits affirmative action has produced.

Nonwhites (and even more so, white women) have made deep inroads into the lower middle class and into professions once reserved for white males. Columbia College now admits women and minority students. Would these and other opportunities have opened as widely and as quickly without the pressure of affirmative action programs? American history suggests they would not.

It is certainly true, as critics charge, that affirmative action's benefits have not spread to the poorest members of the black community. The children of Harlem, regrettably, are not in a position to take advantage of the spots Columbia has opened to blacks. But rather than simply ratifying the advantages of already affluent blacks, who traditionally advanced by servicing the segregated black community, affirmative action has helped to create a *new* black middle class, resting on professional and managerial positions within white society.

This new class is much more vulnerable than its white counterpart to the shifting fortunes of the economy and politics. Far more middle-class blacks than whites depend on public employment—positions now threatened by the downsizing of federal, state and municipal governments. The fact that other actions are needed to address the problems of the "underclass" hardly negates the proven value of affirmative action in expanding black access to the middle class and skilled working class.

Rethinking Implementation

There is no harm in rethinking the ways affirmative action is implemented—re-examining, for example, the expansion to numerous other groups of a program originally intended to deal with the legacy of slavery and segregation. In principle, there may well be merit in redefining disadvantage to include poor whites. The present cry for affirmative action based on class

152

rather than race, however, seems as much an evasion as a serious effort to rethink public policy. Efforts to uplift the poor, while indispensable in a just society, are neither a substitute for nor incompatible with programs that address the legacy of the race-based discrimination to which blacks have historically been subjected. Without a robust class politics, moreover, class policies are unlikely to get very far. The . . . Congress may well dismantle affirmative action, but it hardly seems sympathetic to broad "color-blind" programs to assist the poor.

At a time of deindustrialization and stagnant real wages, many whites have come to blame affirmative action for declining economic prospects. Let us not delude ourselves, however, into thinking that eliminating affirmative action will produce a society in which rewards are based on merit. Despite our rhetoric, equal opportunity has never been the American way. For nearly all our history, affirmative action has been a prerogative of white men.

3

VIEWPOINT

"Even if employers do not intend to discriminate, reliance on social contacts to economize on screening costs can systematically exclude qualified members of racial and ethnic groups from employment opportunities."

Affirmative Action Combats Unintentional Racism

Alec R. Levenson and Darrell L. Williams

Alec R. Levenson is a research associate at the Milken Institute for Job and Capital Formation. Darrell L. Williams is an assistant professor of economics at the University of California at Los Angeles. In the following viewpoint, Levenson and Williams argue that an informal social prejudice exists that gives whites an advantage in hiring. Because whites tend to associate with their own racial group, the authors contend, affirmative action programs are necessary to widen the pool of potential candidates.

As you read, consider the following questions:

1. What three realities of the job market do the authors cite as an argument for affirmative action?
2. The authors argue that while affirmative action may be more costly, it has hidden benefits. What are these benefits?
3. What problems can employment discrimination contribute to, according to Levenson and Williams?

Alec R. Levenson and Darrell L. Williams, "An Economic Argument for Affirmative Action Policies in Hiring," *Jobs & Capital*, Summer 1994. Reprinted by permission of the Milken Institute for Job & Capital Formation.

The basic premise underlying U.S. affirmative action policies is that equally qualified people should have the same probability of success in the labor market, regardless of racial or ethnic differences. This is hardly a divisive goal: Both supporters and critics of affirmative action policies frequently pay homage to this ideal. Yet critics of affirmative action hold that if there are no differences in the qualifications and motivation across racial and ethnic groups, then competitive labor markets will ensure the same rates of success in the hiring process. Because many such critics have concluded that there is no longer any racial or ethnic discrimination in this country, they view *all* differences in employment outcomes as a product of differences in the qualifications and/or motivation that different racial and ethnic groups possess.

Inside Information

This argument is flawed because the realities of the job market make it costly for firms to discern the productivity of prospective employees. The cost of distinguishing among prospective employees creates an environment in which an employer is more likely to hire an applicant about whom he has inside information than someone offering only a resume. There are three features of the U.S. labor market that induce such an environment. (1) Informal contacts—friends and family—play a key role in overcoming the information and screening costs inherent in the job match process. (2) Employment decisions are disproportionately made by whites. (3) There is de facto segregation of friends and family along racial and ethnic lines for noneconomic reasons. These three features combine to create a present-day bias toward hiring whites even in the absence of intentional racial or ethnic discrimination. To show this, we now turn to a discussion of each of the contributing factors.

[1] Informal contacts play a key role in the job search process.

Nationwide surveys provide two indications of the importance of informal contacts in hiring. The first measure is based on surveys that consistently show that between 40–60 percent of job seekers use their friends and relatives to find jobs. The 1982 National Longitudinal Survey of Youth (NLSY) yields a comparable 62 percent figure. The second measure takes into account that a number of different types of job-search methods may be used. Roughly one-third of job seekers in the NLSY said that they only used friends and relatives, or that asking friends and relatives "produced the best results."

[2] Employment decisions are disproportionately made by whites.

According to the Current Population Survey (March 1993), 92.6 percent of all managers in the private sector are white and 55.3 percent are white males; compared to 87.1 percent white and 45.6 percent white males for all nonmanagers. The contrast for the subset of managers that actually makes hiring decisions is even sharper: upper-level management has even lower numbers of nonwhites.

[3] There is de facto segregation of friends and family along racial and ethnic lines for noneconomic reasons.

Despite years of attempts at full integration, the reality today is the same as it was at the start of the civil rights movement. Simply put, the vast majority of people spend the vast majority of their time socializing with those of similar racial and ethnic backgrounds. While workplaces and residential neighborhoods are more integrated than they were three decades ago, as a rule people still socialize with their own.

The logic behind our argument is straightforward. It is costly to obtain all the information about a prospective worker that is necessary to evaluate potential productivity. Hence employers rely on more than reservation wages (lowest wage a prospective employee is willing to accept) to select employees. For example, one of the key ingredients an employer might seek for a job is an ability to "succeed at whatever one does." This clearly cannot be accurately measured in an interview and cannot be signaled by a potential applicant in a convincing manner.

One way to screen along this dimension is to contact references. Consider the case of two job applicants: One of whom the employer has never seen before, while the other is a close friend or has been recommended by a reliable family member, friend, or acquaintance. The cost of evaluating the references is much lower when the applicant is known by the prospective employer, or is known by a third party whom the employer trusts. So the profit-maximizing employer hires the friend, passing over the other applicant who is equally well-qualified. This reliance on informal social networks lets a firm economize on the cost of screening prospective employees. The social cost of these individual actions, however, is to exclude on a systematic basis persons not included in the social networks of those making the hiring decisions.

Not all differences in employment among ethnic and racial groups are the result of disparities in social connections. In particular, differences in educational attainment—whether due to discriminatory or nondiscriminatory practices—are an important determinant of differences in employment. It is our contention, however, that information and screening costs play a crucial role in biasing hiring in favor of whites.

Discrimination Persists

Consider the case of African-Americans. The legacy of over two centuries of discrimination is a population of firms with disproportionately low numbers of African-Americans in key positions where employment decisions are made, as well as a disproportionately low number of firms owned by African-Americans. It would be naive to claim that the unintentional discrimination described here is responsible for *all* disparate employment outcomes between blacks and whites. Nonetheless, the discrimination induced by information and screening costs coupled with the dearth of African-American employers implies that the effects of past intentional discrimination can persist long after all malicious behavior has disappeared. Under the conditions outlined here, even in a world where there is equality in educational attainment, the influence of information and screening costs could be a dominant factor in hindering the progress of racial and ethnic minorities.

Not There Yet

As some wise person once said of democracy, affirmative action is a terrible system, except for the others, which have been so much worse.

It is up to all Americans who say they believe in a "colorblind" society to put some time, money and efforts into making that vision a reality. We're not there yet. We have a long way to go.

Clarence Page, *The San Diego Union-Tribune*, February 23, 1995.

If we are really concerned about providing equality of economic opportunity, then we cannot ignore the potential for such discriminatory hiring practices to impede the progress of racial and ethnic groups. Under the conditions outlined here, members of racial and ethnic minorities may end up disproportionately represented in the ranks of the unemployed and in lower-quality jobs in which their skills are not put to the best use. That in and of itself is a problem yielded by a policy of "doing nothing." But the consequences of discrimination are more far-reaching. In particular, knowing that the prospects for employment are lower than they should be, members of the discriminated class have less incentive to invest in their human capital by pursuing educational opportunities, for example. Also, with fewer available market opportunities, there is a greater incentive to resort to crime as a means of generating income. Thus, at the margin, discrimination in hiring may contribute to school dropout rates and crime and the many social ills associated with these phenomena.

As with any public policy, a proper assessment of the effects of affirmative action policies requires an evaluation of the costs and benefits of implementing them compared to the costs of permitting continued employment discrimination. Critics of affirmative action policies typically focus exclusively on the inefficiencies that arise as a consequence of raising firms' costs of hiring. We have explained how the absence of an affirmative action policy to combat employment discrimination has costs as well. Such costs may have to be borne, however, in order to combat employment discrimination, regardless of whether or not discrimination is intentional. The relative magnitude of these costs is an empirical matter, but a comprehensive analysis must include the full array of costs and benefits, including the costs of unemployment and underemployment, and the attendant social consequences.

In conclusion, we have argued for the existence of racial and ethnic discrimination in hiring based on past discrimination and the cost of screening prospective employees. Even if employers do not intend to discriminate, reliance on social contacts to economize on screening costs can systematically exclude *qualified* members of racial and ethnic groups from employment opportunities. This argument is at odds with that of critics of affirmative action who hold that competitive labor markets allocate jobs solely on the basis of the qualifications and motivations of job applicants. Our analysis suggests that this view of labor markets is oversimplified. Competition alone is not sufficient to ensure equal opportunity when it is costly to screen employees. Our analysis further suggests that the emphasis by the courts on proving malicious intent may be misplaced. Regardless of intent, employment discrimination that systematically excludes a large, identifiable segment of the labor market can produce adverse economic consequences beyond merely determining the racial and ethnic distribution of employment; discrimination can contribute to crime and other social problems as well. One thing is clear: Prudent domestic economic policymakers cannot afford to overlook the potential economic consequences of discrimination in order to determine the need for affirmative action policies.

> *"Affirmative action programs make little effort to distinguish among potential beneficiaries on the basis of actual disadvantage, preferring instead to rely on race or ethnicity per se."*

Affirmative Action Aggravates Racial Tension

Linda Chavez

Linda Chavez is president of the Center for Equal Opportunity and the author of *Out of the Barrio*, a book about Hispanics in America. In the following viewpoint, Chavez argues against affirmative action on the basis that it emphasizes race, not disadvantage. In doing so, she maintains, it fails to target minority economic or social disadvantage, which was affirmative action's original intent.

As you read, consider the following questions:

1. Why does Chavez say that affirmative action programs are "not compensatory but presumptive"? What does she contend is wrong with this?
2. Chavez points out several ethnic and religious minority groups that did not receive government aid. What is her point about them?
3. In what ways is affirmative action part of a program to re-racialize America, according to the author?

Excerpted from "The Destruction of Our Heritage" by Linda Chavez, *Crisis*, June 1995. Reprinted with permission of *Crisis*, PO Box 1006, Notre Dame, IN 46556.

The gravamen of the complaint against quotas or other forms of racial or ethnic preferences is that they force both benefactors and beneficiaries to elevate race and ethnicity in importance, which is fundamentally incompatible with reducing racism. It is not possible to argue that race or ethnicity alone entitle individuals to special consideration without also accepting that such characteristics are intrinsically significant. Of course, those who promote preferential affirmative action programs argue that race and ethnicity are important because they are the basis on which individuals have been, and continue to be, discriminated against. Setting employment or college admission quotas, by this reasoning, is simply a way of compensating for the discrimination that blacks, Hispanics, and some other minority groups face on the basis of their skin color.

But most programs that confer special benefits to racial and ethnic minorities make no effort at all to determine whether the individuals who will receive these benefits have ever been victims of discrimination. Indeed, the government regulations that govern federal contractors state explicitly: "Individuals who certify that they are members of named groups (Black Americans, Hispanic Americans, Native Americans, Asian-Pacific Americans, Subcontinental Asian Americans) are to be considered socially and economically disadvantaged."

Such programs are not compensatory but presumptive; they assume that race equals disadvantage. While there are many blacks, Hispanics, and Asians who have been discriminated against on the basis of their race or ethnicity, there are many others who have not; and there are still others for whom the discrimination was either trivial, or even if more serious, had no lasting consequences. Recently, at Indiana University following a debate in which I opposed affirmative action, a group of black and Hispanic students approached me to complain that I was not sensitive enough to the current discrimination they said they faced daily on campus. I asked them to give me some examples. Only two spoke. The first, a young black woman told me that her father was a surgeon who makes over $300,000 a year, but that her economic status doesn't protect her from the prejudice of her teachers. When I asked her to describe how that prejudice manifested itself, she said none of her professors would give above a "B" to any minority student. I pushed her a little further, asking whether that meant that a student who scored a 98 percent on an exam would be given a "B" rather than a deserved "A"—at that point she dropped the issue with a dismissive, "You just don't understand."

A second student, a Mexican American woman, said that she has to deal with discrimination every day, for example when her Spanish teacher expects her to do better than the other students because she is presumed to know Spanish. Actually, I was quite sympathetic with her frustration, since I am aware that most third generation Hispanics speak only English—like third generation Italians, Jews, Germans, and other ethnic groups in the U.S. But, although being presumed to speak your ancestral language may be annoying, it hardly constitutes pernicious discrimination.

In fact, what ethnic or religious minority has not suffered its share of slights and prejudices? Certainly both Jews and Asians have faced significant levels of bigotry at certain points in their history in the United States. Jews were often the victims of private discriminatory actions, and Asians were historically the target of both private and state-sponsored exclusion and bias. The Chinese, for example, were not allowed to become citizens, or own property or enter certain professions, or even to immigrate at all for certain periods of time. Japanese Americans barely fifty years ago had their property confiscated and were forcibly removed from their homes and interned in camps in the west. Nonetheless, despite persistent discrimination, these groups, on average, have excelled in this society, and it is difficult to argue that they are entitled to compensatory, preferential affirmative action on the basis of any current disadvantage.

Too Costly

The single largest obstacle to black advancement remains the lack of technical skills in an age that demands them more than ever before. Any proposal to make affirmative action programs mandatory is one that is fighting a war that is already won. The real tasks of employment law lie in its simplification and in a massive dose of deregulation, not in a new set of restrictions calculated to increase paperwork and reduce output. Affirmative action should be practiced by those firms that choose to do so and shunned by those who find its costs too great. There is no reason to have a costly, coercive, and centralized national solution to a problem on which the views of this nation are so deeply divided.

Richard A. Epstein, *Jobs & Capital*, Summer 1994.

It is true that blacks and, to a lesser degree, Hispanics are far more likely to face present disadvantage, some of it (though a declining share) the result of past discrimination. But, again, many affirmative action programs make little effort to distinguish among potential beneficiaries on the basis of actual disadvantage, preferring instead to rely on race or ethnicity *per se* in awarding benefits. Some of the most prestigious affirmative action slots—such as those at Ivy League universities, Fortune 500 corporations, or Wall Street law firms—go to middle and upper class blacks and Hispanics, who suffer no clear disadvantage compared with their white counterparts. For example, a recent study at the University of California, Berkeley, found that, on average, black, Hispanic and Asian students admitted through affirmative action guidelines come from families whose median income is actually *higher* than the national average. Indeed in 1989, one-third of Asian students, 14 percent of blacks, and 17 percent of Hispanics came from families whose annual income was more than $75,000. Affirmative action recipients are frequently the graduates of elite prep schools, universities and professional schools. Increasingly, advocates of this select type of affirmative action eschew traditional arguments about discrimination or disadvantage, opting to emphasize the presumed benefits of racial and ethnic diversity.

But what does this diversity imply? The current scientific consensus suggests that race or ethnicity is nothing more than a description of broad morphology of skin, hair, and eye color; bone structure; and hair type—hardly the basis for making moral claims or distinctions. If race and ethnicity, stripped of their power to demand retribution, represent nothing more than a common ancestry and similar physical attributes, culture, on the other hand, evinces something more controversial and enduring. Not surprisingly, practitioners of the politics of race have seized on culture as their new weapon. Americans—of all races—have grown tired of affirmative action. Many of those who still support racial preferences, like Yale law professor Stephen Carter, admit that those preferences have been a mixed blessing for the beneficiaries, conferring tangible benefits but often undermining self-confidence. The politics of race requires a new rationale and a new vocabulary. Multiculturalism supplies both.

As I've said, race-conscious policies now permeate not only employment and education but also the courts and even the democratic process itself. Race or ethnicity often determine political representation and establish voting procedures. In addition, the list of groups eligible to benefit continues to grow and now embraces even the most recent immigrants to America, who, by definition, have suffered no past discrimination. As the policies and the beneficiaries expand, so has their rationale.

The compensatory model has given way to one based on culture, which alleviates the necessity of proving past discrimination or present disadvantage. The demand to redress past or present wrongs evolves into the imperative to enhance and preserve culture. America becomes not simply a multi-racial, multi-ethnic society made of individuals of different backgrounds—

some of whom have suffered discrimination because of their color—but a *multicultural* nation. The distinction is an important one, especially in the American context. It implies that Americans differ not only in skin color and origin but in values, mores, customs, temperament, language—all those attributes that endow culture with meaning. Indeed, multiculturalism questions the very concept of an *American* people. Multiculturalism replaces affirmative action as the linchpin in the politics of race—with a much more profound power to shape how all Americans, not just racial and ethnic minorities, think of themselves and conceive the polity. . . .

Competing with White Folks

If affirmative action was so great for me, why am I now questioning the wisdom of its perpetuation? Part of the problem is that the logic used in support of racial preferences escapes me. A few years ago a fuss was made over a Filipino high school student who wasn't accepted by the University of California campus of her choice. Competition was stiff and based on her GPA and SAT scores she wasn't going to make it—unless it was through affirmative action, since members of underrepresented groups had a separate review to help ensure a diverse student body. But Filipino students were no longer underrepresented on that campus and therefore didn't receive special consideration. Surely this should've been cause for celebration, an indication that Filipino Americans were successfully gaining admission to reputable universities. However, the local community was outraged and viewed this development with a jaundiced eye, since the benefits of affirmative action had vanished. Imagine, that poor student having to compete with the rest of the white folks!

José A. Tabuena, *Filipinas*, July 1995.

As one Mexican American freshman summed it up, she was "unaware of the things that have been going on with our people, all the injustices we've suffered, how the world really is. I thought racism didn't exist here, you know, it just comes to light." The researchers went on to note that all "students of color" had difficulty pinpointing exactly what constituted this "subtle form of the new racism." Instead of empirical evidence, the researchers said, "There was much talk of certain facial expressions, or the way people look, and how white students 'take over the class' and speak past you." But if terms like racism and discrimination can be applied to such innocuous behavior, what words do you use to describe the real thing? As George Orwell said in his 1946 essay, "Politics and the English Language," "if

163

thought corrupts language, language can also corrupt thought." By misusing words like racism, we undermine the very legitimacy of the concept.

The re-racialization of American society that is taking place in the name of multiculturalism is not a progressive movement—but a step backward to the America that existed before *Brown V. Board of Education* and the passage of the major civil rights laws of the 1960s. We are at a critical juncture in our history. Even if we are not, as the multiculturalists claim, about to become a majority minority nation; nonetheless, racial and ethnic diversity in our population is increasing. If we allow race and ethnicity to determine public policy, we invite the kind of cleavages that will pit one group against another in ways that cannot be good for the groups themselves or the society in which we all must live. The more diverse we become, the more crucial it is that we commit ourselves to a shared, civic culture. The distinguishing characteristic of American culture has always been its ability to incorporate so many disparate elements into a new whole. While Dr. Russell Kirk was indisputably right that America owes much of its culture to Great Britain—our legal tradition, particularly the concept of the rule of law; our belief in representative government; certainly our language and literature—American assimilation has always entailed some give and take. And American culture itself has been enriched by what individual groups brought to it.

But it is more important that all of us—no matter where we come from or what circumstances brought us or our ancestors here—think of ourselves as Americans if we are to retain the sense that we are one people, not simply a conglomeration of different and competing groups. It is nonsense to think we can do so without being clear about our purposes. . . .

We need to get beyond the point where race or ethnicity are the most important factors in the way we identify ourselves or form our allegiances. The principles and values that unite us remain far more important than our differences in ancestry, a lesson which bears repeating in our schools and universities.

"The American dilemma is still with us, and it imposes upon us a moral obligation to ensure that race is neither a handicap nor an advantage."

Government Must Do More for Minorities Than Affirmative Action

Seymour Martin Lipset

Seymour Martin Lipset is a Wilson Center senior scholar, a Hazel Professor of Public Policy at George Mason University, and a senior fellow at the Hoover Institution. In the following viewpoint, Lipset argues that even though affirmative action programs are criticized on many levels, minority poverty persists. He argues that, instead of pulling back from affirmative action programs, government must broaden its efforts to include job training, education, and further efforts to integrate poor minorities into the economy.

As you read, consider the following questions:

1. Why does the author argue that blacks have a special claim in American society?
2. What proof does Lipset offer to bolster his argument that there is little reverse discrimination with affirmative action?
3. How does the media distort black culture and economic progress, according to Lipset?

Excerpted from "Affirmative Action and the American Creed" by Seymour Martin Lipsett, *Wilson Quarterly*, Winter 1992. Reprinted by permission of the author.

No achievement of 20th-century American politics surpasses the creation of an enduring national consensus on civil rights. This consensus was forged during the past quarter century by a civil-rights movement that compelled Americans finally to confront the wide gap between their treatment of blacks and the egalitarian values of their own cherished national creed.

In recent years, however, the leaders of the civil-rights movement have shifted the focus from the pursuit of equal opportunity to the pursuit of substantive equality through policies of preferential treatment. This has brought matters to a difficult pass, because most Americans, including many blacks, have not shifted with the leaders of the movement. The reason is not hard to find. While the civil-rights movement of the 1960s asked Americans to live up to a single unassailable ideal, today it sets up a conflict between two core American values: egalitarianism and individualism.

Affirmative action was born in 1965 in the spirit of the first civil-rights revolution. Soon thereafter it was transformed into a system of racial preferences, and today affirmative action is rapidly polarizing the politics of race in America. . . .

Reverse Discrimination

Affirmative action is widely seen as reverse discrimination. Many less-affluent whites believe that the number of jobs available for them has declined as a result of preferences for blacks. Two studies undertaken in 1985 and 1987 by Stanley Greenberg of the Analysis Group for the Michigan Democratic Party indicate that negative reaction to affirmative action has played a major role in the defection of white male blue-collar voters from the party. "Much to the surprise and dismay of both Greenberg and his sponsors," one writer noted, "white fury over affirmative action emerged as a top voter concern in both of his reports. Democratic campaign themes such as 'fairness,' 'equity,' and 'justice' were perceived—not without justification—as code words for quotas."

National polls indicate the same concern. Two surveys, one conducted by the University of Michigan's Institute for Social Research in 1986 and the other by NORC in 1990, found large majorities of whites replying that it is "very likely" (28 percent in both) or "somewhat likely" (48 and 42 percent) "that a white person won't get a job or promotion while an equally or less qualified black person gets one instead." Two-fifths of the whites in the 1986 study believed that they or someone in their family would experience job discrimination. A 1991 report on a poll sponsored by the Leadership Conference on Civil Rights concludes that "civil-rights laws are seen by a substantial number of voters as creating unfair advantages, setting up rank or class privilege in the labor market."

"White Americans . . . do not see themselves as racists, or as opponents of equal opportunity and fundamental fairness," observes columnist William Raspberry. "What they oppose are efforts to provide preferential benefits for minorities. . . . How could we expect them to buy a product we [blacks] have spent 400 years trying to have recalled: race-based advantages enshrined in law?"

Ambient Racism

It's a measure of the ambient racism that we find it so hard to believe that affirmative action may actually be doing something right: ensuring that the best guy gets the job, regardless of that guy's race or sex. Eventually, when the occupational hierarchy is so thoroughly integrated that it no longer makes sense for our subconscious minds to invest the notion of competence with a particular skin color or type of genitalia, affirmative action can indeed be cast aside like training wheels.

Barbara Ehrenreich, *Time*, March 13, 1995.

Misperceptions have much to do with the polarization of racial politics. The best research shows, for example, that there is in reality little reverse discrimination in the competition for lower-skill jobs. Recently, Urban Institute researchers sent equally qualified whites and blacks to apply for general labor, service, retail, and clerical positions in Chicago and Washington, D.C. Whites were treated better in job interviews in 20 percent of the cases; blacks were treated better seven percent of the time. Whites were more likely to be hired. One finding is heartening: There was no discrimination in three-quarters of the interview situations. But blacks are still more likely to suffer from racism in working-class job markets than whites are to experience reverse discrimination.

Economic Progress

If whites overestimate the extent of reverse discrimination, whites and blacks alike badly underestimate the extent of black economic progress during the past several decades. The general ignorance of black success is due in part to the reluctance of black leaders to admit it. In opinion polls during the mid-1980s, three-fifths of the black leaders told pollsters that blacks were "going backward," while two-thirds of a national black sample said they were "making progress." (Support for the optimistic view declined somewhat in the latter years of the Reagan era.

In early July 1990, an NBC News–*Wall Street Journal* poll reported that 60 percent of all blacks said that, compared to 10 years ago, blacks in America are "better off," while 29 percent said "worse off.")

The refusal of some black leaders to admit improvement is understandable. The worse things appear, and the greater the gulf seems between themselves and others, the more they can demand. Yet the repeated emphasis on how little progress has been made also helps sustain the argument that government efforts to benefit blacks simply do not work, that there are factors inherent in the black situation that prevent blacks from getting ahead. And many blacks as well as whites tend to swallow that argument. NORC found that during 1985–89, an average of 62 percent of whites and 36 percent of blacks agreed that the reason blacks on average have worse jobs, incomes, and housing than white people is that "most blacks just don't have the motivation or will power to pull themselves out of poverty." An ABC News–*Washington Post* poll in October 1989 found that 60 percent of both whites and blacks agreed with the statement: "If blacks would try harder, they could be just as well off as whites."

Such beliefs feed racist stereotypes and black self-hatred. In early January 1991, NORC released the results of a survey taken in 1990. They indicate that most whites believe that blacks are less intelligent, lazier, more violence-prone, and more inclined to prefer to stay on welfare than whites and several other ethnic groups.

Media Distortions

The damage is compounded by the news media's relentless focus on the social pathologies of the ghettos, which creates the impression that most blacks live wretched existences. Yet social scientists estimate that the underclass, both black and white, is actually fairly small. William Julius Wilson, the social scientist most responsible for focusing attention on the question, now identifies one-sixth of the nation's 30 million blacks as ghetto poor, a term he prefers. (These are people who live in "areas of extreme poverty, that is, those in which 40 percent of the people are poor.") An Urban Institute group arrives at a lower estimate of the underclass: two or three million people in 1980, about two-thirds of them black, one-fifth Hispanic.

Meanwhile the total proportion of blacks living in poverty—many not afflicted by the pathologies of the underclass—has declined radically. While there is a great deal of debate about the definition of poverty, census data indicate that the percentage of blacks living in poverty declined from 55 percent in 1959 to 33.5 percent in 1970. In 1990, a recession year, it was 31.9 percent.

The "invisible man" of the 1990s, to borrow Ralph Ellison's

phrase, is the successful black working- and middle-class suburbanite. Living in stable families outside traditional black areas, the new "invisible man" is removed from the experience of ghetto blacks and largely ignored by whites. The black suburban population grew by 70 percent during the 1970s, fed primarily by an exodus from central cities. During the 1980s the number of black suburbanites swelled from 5.4 million to 8.2 million. Between 1986 and 1990, 73 percent of black population growth occurred in the suburbs.

Not Used Wisely

Affirmative action has done wonderful things for the United States by enlarging opportunity and developing and utilizing a far broader array of the skills available in the American population than in the past. It has not outlived its usefulness. It was never designed to be a program to eliminate poverty. It has not always been used wisely, and some of its permutations do have to be reconsidered, refined or, in some cases, abandoned. It is not a quota program, and those cases where rigid numbers are used (except under a court or administrative order after a specific finding of discrimination) are a bastardization of an otherwise highly beneficial set of public policies.

Roger Wilkins, *The Nation*, March 27, 1995.

Economists James P. Smith and Finis R. Welch, analyzing the changes in the situation of blacks since World War II, concluded in 1986 that "the real story of the last forty years has been the emergence of the black middle class," which "as a group . . . outnumbers the black poor."

The majority of blacks have steady jobs and are either middle class or members of what may be called the yeoman regularly employed working class. They are married or in stable long-term relationships. The income of married blacks is 77 percent that of comparable whites, up from below 60 percent two decades ago. The proportion of blacks who are high school dropouts has fallen, from 31 percent in 1970 to 18 percent in 1988, while that of whites (14 percent) has not changed.

These drastic social and economic changes have led to growing differentiation within the black community. By the early 1980s, a 1989 National Academy of Sciences panel found, black men aged 25 to 34 with at least some college earned 80 to 85 percent as much as their white counterparts. At the other extreme, one-quarter of their black peers had not even finished high school and were thus condemned to lives at the margins of society.

The two largest groups in the black class structure, the authors say, are now "a lower class dominated by female-headed families and a middle class largely composed of families headed by a husband and wife." The problem is that most black adults live in stable family and economic situations, but more black *children* do not. They are the offspring of the large number of black women who are single mothers. The proportion of black children born in female-headed households was 23 percent in 1960, 28 percent in 1969, 45 percent in 1980, and is 62 percent today. Living in such a household frequently guarantees being poor. The poverty rate for black single-parent families with children was 56.3 percent in 1988. That for two-parent black families with children was 12.5 percent.

Children

The popular impression is that an explosion of illegitimacy among blacks is to blame for the growing impoverishment of black children. But Christopher Jencks of Northwestern University calculates that if married black women had borne as many babies in 1987 as they did in 1960, the proportion of black babies born out of wedlock would have risen only from 23 percent to 29 percent during those years. The proportion is much higher because married blacks now have fewer children.

Whatever the causes of childhood poverty, affirmative action is no remedy. Preference policies or quotas are not much help to the illegitimate black ghetto youth who grows up in poverty and receives an inferior education. As William Julius Wilson writes, they are more likely to benefit "minority individuals from the most advantaged families . . . [who are] most qualified for preferred positions—such as higher-paying jobs, college admissions, promotions and so forth. Accordingly, if policies of preferential treatment for such positions are conceived not in terms of the actual disadvantages suffered by individuals but rather in terms of race or ethnic group membership, then these policies will further enhance the opportunities of the more advantaged without addressing the problems of the truly disadvantaged.". . .

To rebuild the national consensus on civil rights and racial justice, affirmative action should be refocused, not discarded. Quotas and special preferences will not help the poorly educated and unskilled secure good jobs. Success in postindustrial society requires a good education. Extending and vastly improving education in the ghettos, establishing very early Head Start programs as well as financial incentives for students, teachers, and successful schools, and expanding apprentice programs, are the directions to be followed. Such programs should be offered to all less-privileged people, regardless of racial and ethnic origins.

The whole society can also learn from the experience of blacks in the military, which has offered blacks career training and a chance for stable employment and upward mobility. That record argues in favor of a large-scale national-service effort. If all American youth are encouraged to volunteer for national service, those with inadequate education and skills can receive job training while they and their peers help rebuild the nation's infrastructure and deliver social services.

Moving away from policies that emphasize special preferences need not—indeed, must not—mean abandoning the nation's commitment to guaranteeing equal opportunity for disadvantaged citizens. The concept of individual rights remains integral to the American Creed, and racial injustice and caste-like divisions blatantly contradict it. The American dilemma is still with us, and it imposes upon us a moral obligation to ensure that race is neither a handicap nor an advantage. Until black Americans are absorbed fully into our nation's economy and society, we should, in Jefferson's words, continue to fear a just God.

"Affirmative action aiming to expand freedom by making inroads on it augmented the trend to social balkanization, increased divisiveness, [and] spread resentment among the disfavored."

Government Should Not Be Responsible for Alleviating Discrimination

Lilian and Oscar Handlin

Oscar Handlin is Carl M. Loeb University Professor at Harvard University. Lilian Handlin has taught history at the Hebrew University. Both are the authors of the four-volume *History of Liberty in America*. In the following viewpoint, the Handlins argue that programs like affirmative action have led to deep dissension and a feeling that government owes minorities equal status in society. They disagree with this premise and conclude by saying the government owes minorities and other disadvantaged groups equal opportunity, not equality of results.

As you read, consider the following questions:

1. How have disadvantaged groups demanding government intervention caused widespread tribalism, according to the authors?
2. Why does state-mandated equality result in a loss of liberty for all, according to the Handlins?
3. How do programs like affirmative action result in conclusions that are the opposite of what America has been founded upon, according to the authors?

Excerpted from "America and Its Discontents" by Lilian and Oscar Handlin, *American Scholar*, vol. 64, no. 3, Summer 1995; ©1995 by Lilian and Oscar Handlin. Used with permission.

Contentment never seemed compatible with the American condition. In the seventeenth as in the twentieth centuries, discontent with a present deemed inadequate set restless people in motion, scrambling to better themselves. Happiness ever pursued, rarely attained, goaded on the aggrieved. Hence, at first view, the petulance infusing public discourse in the 1990s seemed no different from that in any other decade.

Yet the pervasive sense of unhappiness in our country at present is out of accord with a generally benign social context. Now that the Cold War has ended, the United States remains the world's sole superpower. A thriving economy, a steadily expanding employed labor force, and a rising life expectancy should sustain a general sense of well being. Instead, bitter struggles for advantage divide citizens. And laws designed to resolve conflicts only stoke the flames. The Americans with Disabilities Act compels a college to award a football player paralyzed from the waist down an athletic scholarship and to adapt its athletic activities to accommodate the "differently abled." The Equal Employment Opportunity Commission forbids a restaurant to seek "young" waiters lest that discriminate against the elderly. In a Smithsonian television program, the curator of the National Museum of Natural History lauds a New Guinea tribe that ate women who stole bananas as an appropriate model for the United States. Poor brainwashed Americans unable to overcome millennia of ingrained Eurocentric prejudices failed to understand that cannibalism, far from mere repugnant violence, provided the model for a complete, well-functioning criminal justice system. . . .

Multicultural Disunity

Meanwhile, universities formulate Statements on Diversity that affirm "a strong belief in both equal opportunity and affirmative action" for blacks; multicultural councils encourage separate living quarters, ethnic theme halls, and indoctrination workshops; and "classroom climate advisers" seek to counterbalance an environment hostile to women and minorities. The old academic hiring process that reflected the traditional notion of using people's talents regardless of race or national origin is deemed not merely inadequate but manifestly wrong. Correction demanded an expansion of previous limited definitions of equality, excellence, and merit to include other vital though less measurable attributes, such as empathy and identification with students of diverse origins. . . .

Consider such grotesques among the unintended progeny of the Great Society, that prodigious effort to remake the United States in the 1960s, when Depression-generated anxieties had subsided and an expanding economy realigned productive forces to yield previously undreamed of affluence. Abundance then dispelled the specter of want and evoked the vision of a Great Society able to satisfy the wishes of all by fulfilling the promises of Franklin Delano Roosevelt's New Deal and Harry Truman's Fair Deal. . . .

The Great Society aimed to fulfill the expectations of 1944, to guarantee to all a life free of want, to afford everyone liberty, and to end internal divisions by eliminating racial injustice, improving the urban environment, beautifying the countryside, controlling pollution, and advancing education. The programs' architects assumed an underlying social and political consensus on definitions of the common good. Since every deficiency had a social origin, citizens needed only to ask, in the words of President Lyndon B. Johnson, "Where have we gone wrong?" then act to correct the error. All protests by definition became legitimate, each the expression of a righteous cause.

That these visions made individuals merely puppets of forces beyond control bothered the Great Society's planners not at all. They expected to provide for the poor and spread the ability to consume to everyone, without sacrifice by anyone. A vast legislative program aimed, by state action, to guarantee for all life, liberty, and the pursuit of happiness. The Great Society therefore required greater governmental involvement in the management of everyday life and reflected the spreading popularity of a social outlook that asserted the primacy of the public over the private sphere, with the result of bringing ever more areas into the scope of government action. Tightening the limits on citizens' capacity to act narrowed the scope beyond which their freedoms might harm others. Hence the growth of the federal bureaucracy, which swelled from 1,960,000 in 1950 to 2,981,000 by 1970, and the vast increase in intrusive government regulations. . . .

Turning on the United States

Those who concluded that simple government neutrality would not remove the shackles that hampered some people's ability to act now set out to bend the political system to suit their agenda. They thereby put themselves in opposition to the nation's historical development—which bothered them little, since they deemed that past rotten to the core anyway. Textbooks and monographs proved that never in human history had so evil a country as the United States existed. Articles, symposia, conferences, and study groups, subsidized by taxpayer-financed grants, searched high and low for documentable instances of American depravity. And, where the evidence was hard to come by, deconstructed facts and figures were pressed into service to prove their point. However, the activist reformers failed to realize that competing fellow travelers, eager for their share of the pie, would soon enter the contest, all considering life a zero-sum game, in which the benefits of some had to come at the expense of others. In the struggle of each against all, group affiliation improved the chances of success. And if one group could change the rules of that game, so could others.

Social Evils

Entitlements by race, sex, ethnicity and sexual orientation—categories that in no way reflect merit—are at the root of the great social evils in American life. Aside from the obvious unfairness of such entitlements, it is the distorted claims that groups must conjure to gain their benefit that absolutely require racism, sexism, anti-Semitism and all manner of collective animosities. Every such claim is backlit by the hatreds that try to make it singular and urgent.

The reformers of the last few decades have not admitted this. But the means to genuine reform have been here all along—a democracy of individuals that has the discipline never to entitle any group for any reason.

Shelby Steele, *The New York Times*, March 13, 1994.

The superficial success of black tactics attracted imitators who discovered the advantages of minority status and victimhood as a means of expanding their own ability to act. In time, linguistic and ethnic groups, women, the elderly, and the disabled also sought the protection of civil rights legislation. Once the aggrieved had asked government and society to ignore differences of color, gender, religion, and antecedents, to treat everyone alike. Equality they then defined as the condition of lowered barriers, a fundamental component of individual dignity and basic to human liberty. But with equality transformed into a state of uniform outcomes, success pivoted on affiliation rather than on personal achievement, on tribalism rather than individualism. A major component of individual dignity thereupon disappeared. Deliberate misreadings of the Civil Rights Act after 1970 allowed interested parties to exploit Great Society legislation to create ethnic groups where none had existed before.

The proponents of change thereby opted for a separatism that boded ill for the future of American liberty. Instead of working for a level playing field on which all contestants had some chance to win, prominent blacks, and after them other minorities, chose self-segregation, at first as a defensive response to the unwelcoming society around them, soon as a form of self-suffocation. Their bleak outlook premised a liberty tied to color

175

and kin; people could only enlarge their capacity to act among their own kind. And a view originally articulated by a small minority within the civil rights movement, in the decades after 1970, became the self-destructive ethos of all who styled themselves progressives. . . .

Loss of Liberty

Equality mandated by the state entailed a loss of liberty for all. The consequences of discarding tests of competence mattered little when it came to jobs easily learned but mattered a great deal when it came to choosing neurosurgeons or the pilots of 747s. Then, too, the stress on being part of a self-defined entity demanded rigid codes of behavior and allegiance at a time when the dominant cultural values, at the center rather than at margins, stressed individualism, autonomy, and independence. People classified into fixed and artificial groupings defined by presumed ethnic injustices or by tacit admission that only thus could they get a share of American wealth, confronted painful identity problems. Color proved an undependable guide, given the long history of miscegenation and passing. Common language or ancestral nationality provided no help either. Constant comparisons with others reinforced feelings of insecurity, generating further compensatory efforts to make up for shortcomings through group pride. A capacity to act tied to identity would thereafter lend itself to "race norming"—measurement in terms of groupings, not of persons.

Ever more often people treated unequally came to consider themselves underprivileged minorities, denied their full measure of liberty, whatever their genetic or national antecedents. Those who believed their capacity to act circumscribed by external factors sought what they regarded as justifiable redress, available to them not as individuals but as members of a group even if self-defined. Thus the term "Hispanic" enfolded people as diverse as Puerto Ricans and Cubans and Mexicans and Colombians. The trend toward separateness, coupled with the demand for affirmative government action to remedy grievances, paralleled the breakdown of cohesive families and their networks of related associations, which no longer provided a secure emotional framework for daily life. Social pathologies unrelated to tribalist impulses thus fueled the fragmenting of American society. A wide variety of malfunctions—whether broken homes, sexual harassment, or black youth unemployment—legitimized the quest for group identity. All the aggrieved expected government intervention on their behalf and in time acquired political power to secure it. The struggle permanently fixed the self-defined discrete minorities in the American population.

The varied meanings given the word *equality* reflected fundamental disagreements about basic priorities. Whose cry for help would the government answer first, given the restrictions on its resources? Were the needs of white, upper-middle-class and highly educated women really comparable to those of illiterate teenage mothers from the ghetto? And was the political system the forum in which to debate problems that had little to do with the classical definition of democratic government? Efforts to explain disparities that persisted after 1970 occupied the courts and legislatures as well as the legal profession, sociologists, psychologists, economists, and a vast array of other specialists, who transformed the struggles for equal citizenship and equal rights. Many policymakers thereafter ceased to regard equal opportunity as the measure of civil rights and instead depended on outcome as a test.

Redefining Liberty

The impetus to this profound redefinition of the meaning of liberty came not only from the failure of existing programs to offset the effects of past discrimination but also from a clash between perceived needs and political realities. Desegregation, in time, came to require segregation, and integration as a goal yielded to identification by group. One person's gain then meant another's loss. Each expansion of community empowerment and control to help children learn required appropriate role models, a demand plausible when voiced by Brownsville blacks but considered outrageous and proto-fascist when emanating from Irish-Americans in South Boston. To the argument that discrimination against whites was as unconstitutional as discrimination against blacks, Justice Thurgood Marshall replied, "You guys have been practicing discrimination for years. Now it is our turn." The Constitution had referred only to persons, not to groups. But neither its silence nor its color blindness presented an obstacle to the impulse to count by color and to assign places by ethnic identity.

The tactics of controversy soon thrust principle and consistency aside. Subtly, the boundaries of permissible behavior shifted while the ever-more intense sense of forces beyond control alleviated guilt and nurtured feelings of victimization. . . .

Victim Status

After 1970, blacks and their imitators elevated victim status to an art form; insistence on prizes for all replaced the historic understanding of equality as a product of open competition. In the past, a free society assured members neither perfect equality of results nor perfect equality of opportunity. Individuals nevertheless bore responsibility for their own destinies, even though they lacked complete control over them. But after the Great

Society reforms, the failures and their spokesmen lost confidence in the fairness of the course and asserted that the fault lay not in innate inabilities but in some tilt in the track. Once external conditions bore the blame for unequal outcomes, equal results became the true measure of the equality guaranteed by law. Minority demands for remedies shifted from negative to positive government action, from non-discrimination to affirmative preference, encouraged by flabby though fashionable redefinitions of justice, according to which true egalitarianism demanded benevolent rulers to even out differences and impose uniform standards for an utterly homogeneous population, elevating equality over efficiency as a social goal, even if less for everyone resulted. From that point of view, individual rights mattered little, nor did consent of the governed, since the majority would resist the sacrifices entailed. Bolder dreamers modeled the social order on monastic barracks and army camps, examples of total uniformity. In either case, liberty or the capacity to act became irrelevant.

Results of Affirmative Action

Affirmative action aiming to expand freedom by making inroads on it augmented the trend to social balkanization, increased divisiveness, spread resentment among the disfavored, and, by privileging some, left the unprivileged seething. Furthermore, many judicial and administrative rulings violated the core theme of the American government, grounded for centuries on a procedural covenant, entered into for limited purposes. In discarding the shackles of tradition and precedent, citizens lost some of the positive fortifications that in the past had enabled their capacity to act to survive dramatic challenges.

Affirmative action in the 1980s acquired its own identity, independent of the often dubious boons to its beneficiaries. It became embodied in an ideology and also in a growing cadre of functionaries who policed its application to specific cases. Political careers built on a bleak vision of the future and power attained on the basis of outdated perceptions of reality would not readily yield when circumstances changed. The concern with victim and underdog papered over actual disdain for the wider implications of policies that rested on an anti-Americanism, directed against a rotten society ripe for subversion. Crusaders could not bother about cost-or-benefit assessment; guided by a vision of "them versus us," they insisted that morality was all on their side. Few dared acknowledge that blacks rarely gained, except when employed in enforcement. By the 1980s it was clear that the most disadvantaged failed to gain at all, for lethargic whites preferred to lower the bars for occasional underqualified individuals rather than struggle to educate a whole minority so that it could compete.

The aging radicals, still animated by their 1960s enthusiasms, also forgot that the antithesis of liberty was privilege, not inequality. The open society that Americans favored after 1750 held equality of opportunity essential and condemned unjustly derived advantages some enjoyed through brute force, discriminatory laws, or values that arbitrarily favored some over others. In the United States, the state historically had never been the private preserve of the few, exploited on their own behalf, no matter how many tried to make it so. Government always exercised power by the consent of the governed and, representing all citizens, could at least on the face of it never favor some at the expense of others.

The Loss of Responsibility

The advocates of equality of results thus sought to restore to American society a paternalism largely discarded after 1750, although they now wished government to operate not on behalf of the powerful few, but of the supposedly powerless, many whose interest they defined. Hence the assault on all forms of consent that required majority agreement, hard to achieve when the prevailing ideology resisted artificial constraints upon the individual. Although few citizens swallowed it whole, the argument that American freedom was a white monopoly constructed from the beginning on the backs of enslaved blacks encouraged a preference for government by bureaucratic fiat, which obviated the need for popular support. A society in which coercion determined fundamental choices of everyday life left people unfree, even if well educated and fed, as were slaves whose masters cared prudently for their chattels. Most of the electorate, if not some of their chosen leaders, thereupon opted for freedom. . . .

As the civil rights struggle lost relevance, and its participants passed from the scene, a new generation cast a skeptical glance at its history. Since the present left so much to be desired, the motives and slogans of earlier battles lost relevance, their outcome thought to be of questionable value. Hence, Henry Louis Gates, Jr., a prominent academic whose professional career explicated for white America the double voices of black folk (one for their own, a different one for the enemy) movingly re-created his childhood world in a small southern town that insulated blacks against shocks of racism. There life revolved around family and work, and segregation provided black communities an inner cohesiveness since lost. Gone with that world also was an ethic of mutual responsibility in which the better-off cared for those less fortunate with whom they once lived side by side. The hated whites remained distant enough to enable black youngsters to grow up without any sense of inferiority.

179

The difficulties of integration reinforced the attractiveness of such idyllic portrayals. To protect black culture from obliteration by the larger white society, some chose to "cocoon" voluntarily. By 1994, 25 percent of America's blacks lived in the suburbs, often marked off by racial lines, products less of segregation than of voluntary decisions. Ironically, despite the support forced busing had once received from reformers, black intellectuals by then complained that integration meant "some kind of orchestrated effort to mix people together"—precisely what courts in the 1970s had worked overtime to achieve.

More than two centuries earlier, Rousseau had outlined the concomitants of equality of results—enrichment of the state, impoverishment of the people by removal of surpluses through taxation, and destruction of the arts, science, and civilization, which Rousseau regarded as the cause of inequality. In theory, at least, he considered the price worth paying. Most Americans did not, and amidst all the challenges and assaults, they held stubbornly to the the historic concept of equality of opportunity through free competition, which gave them their liberty.

Periodical Bibliography

The following articles have been selected to supplement the diverse views presented in this chapter. Addresses are provided for periodicals not indexed in the *Readers' Guide to Periodical Literature*, the *Alternative Press Index*, or the *Social Sciences Index*.

William M. Adler — "Evening the Score," *Rolling Stone*, August 10, 1995.

Jonathan Alter — "Affirmative Ambivalence," *Newsweek*, March 27, 1995.

Richard A. Epstein — "No Mandatory Affirmative Action Programs," *Jobs & Capital*, Summer 1994.

Nathan Glazer — "Race, Not Class," *Wall Street Journal*, April 5, 1995.

Joe Klein — "Time to Pull the Plug on Affirmative Action?" *Reader's Digest*, June 1995.

Newsweek — "Affirmative Action: Race and Rage," April 3, 1995.

Charles Oliver — "Race and the Numbers Racket," *Reason*, August/September 1995.

Arch Puddington — "Will Affirmative Action Survive?" *Commentary*, October 1995.

Jamin B. Raskin — "Affirmative Action and Racial Reaction," *Z Magazine*, May 1995.

Adolph Reed — "A Polluted Debate," *Village Voice*, August 15, 1995.

Paul Craig Roberts and Lawrence M. Stratton — "Proliferation of Privilege," *National Review*, November 6, 1995.

Tikkun — "Changing the Criteria of Merit: Clinton and Affirmative Action," September/October 1995.

James P. Turner — "The Fairest Cure We Have," *New York Times*, April 16, 1995.

Roger Wilkins — "Racism Has Its Privileges," *Nation*, March 27, 1995.

Don Wycliff — "Affirmative on Affirmative Action," *Commonweal*, May 19, 1995.

How Should Society Treat Interracial Families?

INTERRACIAL
AMERICA

Chapter Preface

Interracial families in the United States are on the increase through marriage, birth, and adoption, although 1990 Census Bureau figures show that interracial marriages still make up only 2 percent of the total. Many people, like Francis Wardle, director of the Center for the Study of Biracial Children, believe that these interracial families embody society's racial ideals: "The ultimate goal should be to do away with all racial categories because they are unscientific and therefore irrelevant, only serving to separate out people." Such optimists argue that interracial families transcend race by unifying people through love, respect, and common humanity.

Arguments about the nature of interracial relationships are even more contentious when it comes to children, whether they are the products of a mixed-race union or adopted into a family not of their race. Anne Hill, director of programs for the National Urban League, contends that "it is the best interests of all children to be raised in families of their same racial origin. . . . African American children raised by white parents will never really be a part of White culture, yet their own heritage and culture have been denied them. That causes tremendous insecurity and confusion." Even when parents are secure in their different races, their children may still have complex identity issues, she concludes. Helen Wong, an American of African and Chinese parents who was interviewed for an article in *A. Magazine*, recalls differences in acceptance between her brother and herself: "He's just a little darker than me, but his hair is a lot straighter. I noticed that when he went to high school, he met a lot of Asian friends and tended to stick with that group more— wanted to be part of them."

In the United States today, interracial families do not represent the elimination of racial differences, prejudices, and stereotypes. Nevertheless, as the following chapter shows, such families are challenging racial divisions in profound ways.

"*To adopt a race-neutral stance and deny the significance of the child's race in family-placement decisions is to negate a very significant part of the child's background.*"

Racial Matching in Adoptions Should Be Encouraged

Ruth G. McRoy

Ruth G. McRoy is a professor in the school of social work at the University of Texas and the coauthor of *Transracial and Inracial Adoptees*. In the following viewpoint, McRoy argues that placing a child in an adoptive family of the same race acknowledges that race is a significant factor in a child's life. She believes that more effort should be placed in finding same-race families for minority children than in encouraging transracial adoption.

As you read, consider the following questions:

1. What role does poverty play in adoption, according to McRoy?
2. What barriers do black families face when they try to adopt black children, according to the author?
3. Why does no one argue that white children should be placed in black families, according to McRoy?

The elimination of race-matching policies is touted as a so-called remedy for the many children of color languishing in foster care since white families would be free to adopt these children.

But let's examine the reasons leading to the growing numbers of children of color in need of permanent homes and the proposed solution: transracial adoption. In 1991, child-protection agencies received reports on an estimated 2.7 million children in need of state intervention. Just under 50 percent were reported as cases of neglect, 25 percent physical abuse, 14 percent sexual abuse and 6 percent emotional abuse. Economic stress, substance abuse and inability to fulfill parenting responsibilities were identified as causes of abuse and neglect. Many of these children were removed from their families and placed in foster care.

Neglect often is correlated with poverty; since minority populations are disproportionately poor, minority children are put disproportionately in out-of-home care or placed for adoption. In 1991, about 429,000 children nationwide were in out-of-home care; by 1992, the number had grown to 450,000. Should this trend continue, there may be as many as 900,000 children in out-of-home care by the year 2000. Although accurate statistics on children needing placements are unavailable, experts estimate that there may be as many as 85,000 children who need adoption services. Children of color are overrepresented in these statistics. In New Jersey, Maryland and Louisiana, more than 50 percent of the children in foster care are African-American. More than half of the children waiting for adoption nationwide are children of color, and this population is increasing rapidly in most states.

Black Children Wait a Long Time

Since in many states the number of African-American children in foster care far exceeds the number of African-American foster families, African-American children often are placed in transracial foster care. Many of these children will remain with white foster families, often separated from their siblings and with limited contact with their parents or extended families, for several years before they either are returned to their families or freed for adoption. The children and families become attached and in a few cases, the foster parents will seek to adopt a child in their care. Unfortunately, it is after these close bonds have formed that agencies then seek to place the child with a same-race adoptive family.

Although the policy of encouraging same-race placement frequently is cited as the reason black children remain in foster care longer than white children, research data reveal that adoption-agency workers may be less active in seeking permanent homes for minority children. Black children enter care at an average age of 7 and spend an average of almost two years in care. They may experience several caseworkers and school changes and generally move at least twice while in care.

When adoption planning is needed for a child of color, many agencies find that they have a short supply of African-American families seeking to adopt. Some assume that black families are not interested in adopting. The fact is that black families generally adopt at much higher rates than whites. According to J. Mason and C.W. Williams, contributors to the 1985 book *Adoption of Children With Special Needs*, the black inracial adoption rate is 18 per 10,000 families, more than four times the rate for whites. The Urban League's 1980 Black Pulse Survey showed that there were 3 million African-American households interested in adopting. With such a pool of potential parents, why are agencies still indicating that they are having difficulty finding black adoptive families?

Privacy Issues

Respect for the privacy and cultural identity of prospective adoptive parents could justify a permissive role for racial preferences in adoption. Strangers have been known to probe adoptive parents, not only about the race or national origins of their children, but also about their personal reasons for electing adoption. For reasons of privacy, whites free of racial hatred might prefer to rule out trans-racial adoption. Even parents who do not plan to pretend that their adopted children are their genetic offspring may reasonably want to avoid the invasive questions and stares of the general public.

Anita Allen, *Reconstruction*, 1992.

The answer lies in the high barriers to prospective minority parents set up by the agencies themselves. According to a 1991 survey by the North American Council on Adoptable Children, barriers to same-race placements include institutional racism, culturally insensitive attitudes of workers, adoption-agency fees, negative perceptions of agencies and their practices, inflexible standards, lack of minority staff and poor recruitment techniques. Other studies have raised the issue of bias linked to the ethnicity of adoption workers and supervisors—more than 75 percent nationwide are white. Little is being done to train current staff in cultural competence or to recruit new minority staff to respond to changing racial demographics and needs of families.

Studies done by the council of the placement patterns of minority children have found that agencies specializing in minority adoption placed 94 percent of black children inracially while agencies without specialized programs in minority adoptions placed 51 percent of black children inracially. Although traditional adoption agencies have been very successful in placing with white adoptive families, many have not adapted their procedures and policies to provide families for the growing numbers of children in care. Clearly, the success of agencies specializing in minorities, such as the Institute for Black Parenting in Los Angeles and Homes for Black Children in Detroit, suggests that African-American families can and do adopt.

Ann Sullivan of the Child Welfare League of America has argued that some agencies perpetuate the myth that African-American families are not available for infants and preschoolers so that such children may be placed with infertile white couples who cannot secure a white infant. Sullivan insists that the majority of African-American school-age children and adolescents can be placed with African-American families. Only after such efforts have failed, she says, should a transracial adoptive family be considered.

Likewise, the positions of several other advocacy groups, including Adoptive Families of America, the North American Council on Adoptable Children and the National Association of Black Social Workers, emphasize the need to give black children an equal opportunity to live in their own families, culture and race, just as white children have the opportunity to live within their own culture and race. However, they do not eliminate transracial adoption as an option if same-race placements cannot be made.

Race Not the Only Factor

Much of the debate about transracial adoption suggests that race is the only factor that adoption agencies consider in selecting adoptive families. But adoption agencies weigh many factors, including the fit or match between the child and family, the stability of the adoptive family, the ability of the family to deal with the child's special needs, marital relationship, parenting skills and the ability to handle issues associated with the adoption.

The practice of matching the race of children with that of prospective parents is not new. For years agencies have taken the position that the more similar the characteristics of the child are to others in his or her environment, the easier the child can be assimilated into the adoptive family. The fit or compatibility is a joint product of the characteristics of the child, the characteristics of the family and the family's social situation. Until the shortage of white infants and young children, most agencies typically followed the principle of race matching, which was thought to be in the best interest of children and families. Race matching of white children and families still is standard practice, as there are only a few reported accounts of a white child being placed with a black family.

Research findings on outcomes of transracial adoptions suggest that most of the children become relative healthy, emotionally stable young adults. But some other findings suggest that the formation of a positive and unambiguous racial identity may be particularly problematic for minority children in white families growing up in a race-conscious society.

Benefits to Same-Race Families

To adopt a race-neutral stance and deny the significance of the child's race in family-placement decisions is to negate a very significant part of the child's background. Transracially adopted children must know more than just their racial background; they must learn to cope with racism, to be in the minority most of the time and to adjust to having very different phenotypic as well as genotypic characteristics from their families.

However, the majority of researchers, like many of the advocacy organizations, have concluded that although same-race placements are preferable, transracial adoption is certainly a far better alternative than remaining in the child-welfare system.

Race and Culture

But one way adoptive and genetic parents alike can derive special meaning from parenting is by repeating culturally significant rituals. Yet some rituals depend on racial characteristics. A black woman's desire to adopt a black daughter may be tied to her wish to perform certain culturally meaningful tasks. She may want to "corn row" braid a little one's thick coarse hair and lotion away her "ash." A child with fine, thin hair and pale skin would not do. Her preference for special moments of virtually race-specific intimacy is not plainly something to stamp out as discriminatory or racist. This example suggests that even if the misguided *de facto* ban on trans-racial adoption . . . were lifted, race could remain a legitimate factor in adoption.

Anita Allen, *Reconstruction*, 1992.

Interestingly, issues of cultural identity are taken for granted through the usual practice of placing white children with white families. Race matching for white children typically is justified by the argument that a great supply of white families is seeking to adopt the very limited supply of available, healthy white infants and young children. Although there are thousands of older white children available for adoption, there is a shortage of families seeking to adopt them, despite an estimated 2 million white couples seeking to adopt. As a result, many white families seek to adopt infants through either intercountry adoptions or transracial adoptions.

Not the Answer

Clearly, there are very serious problems that have led to a half-million children in foster care. The majority of such children are school-age; many are in sibling groups and some have experienced abuse and neglect. Many have been moved several times in care. However, legislation aimed primarily at eliminating barriers to white families adopting black children is not the answer to this problem, since transracial adoptions by whites make up a very small percentage of all adoptions and since the majority of families seeking to adopt transracially are seeking only infants and young children.

America needs to focus its efforts on finding permanent homes for both white and minority children available for adoption and reducing the number of children entering the system as a result of child abuse and neglect. We should work toward family preservation, provide effective and efficient services to children and families once they become part of the system, reduce the barriers to African-American families adopting and develop culturally specific approaches to service delivery. Policies pertaining to the adoption rights of African-American families should be examined with the same vigor as those of the right of white families to adopt black children.

> *"Adoption agencies should clearly be prohibited from exercising any significant preference for same-race families."*

Racial Matching in Adoptions Is Racist and Discriminatory

Elizabeth Bartholet

Elizabeth Bartholet, a professor at Harvard Law School, frequently writes on reproductive issues. In the following viewpoint, she argues that *any* preference given to same-race families in adoption hurts children and is clearly discriminatory. She concludes that adoption decisions should be based on the best interests of the child. Since it is clearly in the interest of the child to be placed in a qualified two-parent home as quickly as possible, she maintains, this is the only criterion that should be used in placement.

As you read, consider the following questions:

1. Why should the courts disallow the types of arguments that racial-matching advocates make, according to Bartholet?
2. Why does the author disagree with even mild preferences for same-race matching?

Excerpted from "Where Do Black Children Belong? The Politics of Race Matching in Adoption" by Elizabeth Bartholet, *Reconstruction*, vol. 1, no. 4, 1992. Reprinted with permission.

There is considerable evidence—and a strong consensus—on the costs to children of delays in adoptive placement and in permanent denial of an adoptive home. Child welfare professionals agree with virtual unanimity that children need the continuity of a permanent home to flourish. There is a significant body of research demonstrating that children do better in adoption than in foster care, and that age at placement in an adoptive family is a central factor in determining just how well adoptees will do in terms of various measures of adjustment. Moreover, to the degree that research studies have attempted to determine whether delay in placement or racial match is a more significant factor in adoptive adjustment, they have found delay to be the key factor. William Feigelman and Arnold Silverman specifically addressed whether race difference and racial isolation in an alien community constitute more potent determinants for a child's adjustment than the discontinuities and hazards associated with delayed placement. In a study involving both black and white children placed with white parents, they found age at time of placement by far the most significant factor in explaining variations in adjustment measures. This and the other available evidence provides a firm basis for believing that the delays in placement and denials of permanent adoptive homes that result from current same-race placement policies are seriously harmful to children.

A Fully Positive Experience

In the context of a society struggling to deal with racial difference, the studies of trans-racial adoptive families are extraordinarily interesting. They do not simply show that black children do well in white adoptive homes. They do not simply show that we put black children at risk by delaying or denying placement while we await black homes. The studies show that black children raised in white homes are comfortable with their blackness and also uniquely comfortable in dealing with whites. In addition, the studies show that trans-racial adoption has an interesting impact on the racial attitudes of the *white* members of these families. The parents tend to describe their lives as significantly changed and enriched by the experience of becoming an interracial family. They describe themselves as having developed a new awareness of racial issues. The white children in transracial adoptive families are described as committed to and protective of their black brothers and sisters. The white as well as the black children are described as unusually free of racial bias, and unusually committed to the vision of a pluralistic world in which one's humanity is more important than one's race.

The studies show parents and children, brothers and sisters, relating to each other in these trans-racial families as if race was no barrier to love and commitment. They show the black adopted children and the white birth children growing up with the sense that race should not be a barrier to their relationships with other people. In a society torn by racial conflict, these studies show human beings transcending racial difference. . . .

Terrible Assumptions

Advocates for racial matching argue that growing up with same-race parents is a benefit of overriding importance to black children. But the claim that a black person, by virtue of his or her race, will necessarily be more capable than a white of parenting a black child is the kind of claim that courts have generally refused to allow as justification for race-conscious action. The near-absolute presumption under our anti-discrimination laws is that race is irrelevant to qualifications. Moreover, the available evidence does not support the claim that same-race placement is beneficial to black children, much less that it outweighs the harm of delayed placement. Ultimately, the argument that racial matching policies are beneficial rather than harmful to the children immediately affected rests on the unsupported assumption that black children will be significantly better off with "their own kind." This is not the kind of assumption that has been permitted under our nation's anti-discrimination laws. More importantly, it is not an assumption that *should* be permitted in a situation where there is evidence that by insisting on a racial match we are doing serious injury to black children.

Blended Homes

I now know how unfair the system can be to both children and prospective parents and how racist our child welfare system can be. It is true that transracial adoption started as a convenience to white adoption agencies and because of the shortage of adoptable white infants, the civil rights climate in the country, and the numbers of black children entering the system. It is also true that our world and our families are changing to include multi-racial, multi-religious, blended and single parent homes.

Janet S. Lifshin, *Interrace*, Spring/Summer 1993.

Although matching policies are inconsistent with the law of the land, many courts have responded to them with either indifference or sympathy. Although courts have generally agreed that race cannot be used by agencies as the sole factor in making placement decisions, a number of judges have ruled that race can be used as a significant and even determinative factor.

Some courts actually require that race be considered. . . .

Judges have come up with little justification for treating the racial issue so differently in the adoption context. Some have relied on unsubstantiated claims that the evidence from the adoption world indicates that black children will necessarily risk serious identity and other problems if they are raised by whites. Some have relied on their own assumptions regarding such problems. Others have expressed what seems to be at the heart of much judicial thinking in this area—the sense that mixing the races in the context of the family is simply not "natural." In one leading case, the majority opinion states: "It is a natural thing for children to be raised by parents of their same ethnic background." The opinion speaks approvingly of traditional matching policies as designed to duplicate the "natural biological environment" so that a child can develop a "normal family relationship."

The sense that same-race relationships are "natural" and "normal" in the intimate context of family is at the heart of the law on trans-racial adoption. But in *Loving v. Virginia*, the Supreme Court rejected similar thinking in striking down Virginia's miscegenation statute. The trial court had reasoned as follows:

> Almighty God created the races white, black, yellow, malay and red, and he placed them on separate continents. And but for the interference with his arrangement there would be no cause for such marriages. The fact that he separated the races shows that he did not intend for the races to mix.

The Supreme Court reversed, holding racial classifications embodied in Virginia's "Racial Integrity Act" unconstitutional, "even assuming an even-handed state purpose to protect the 'integrity' of all races.". . .

Racial Separatism

The issues at the heart of current racial matching policies are the significance of racial difference and the role of racial separatism in dealing with difference. Historically, these policies represent the coming together of white segregationists with black nationalists and the merger of their racial separatist ideologies with "biologism." Adoption professionals have idealized the biological family and structured the adoptive family in its image. They have argued that biological sameness helps to make families work and have therefore promoted the goal of matching adoptive parents with their biological look-alikes. Although adoption professionals surrendered various aspects of their matching philosophy as they struggled to keep up with the realities of the adoption world, they held onto the core idea that racial look-alikes should be placed together. The NABSW's [National Association of Black Social Workers] attack on trans-racial adoption met with relatively ready acceptance from white as well as black social workers, not just because of liberal white guilt, but because it fit with the traditional assumptions of their professional world. The adoption world is part of a larger social context in which there has always been a strong sense that racial differences matter deeply, and a related suspicion about crossing racial lines. Both black nationalists and white segregationists promote separatism, especially in the context of the family, as a way of promoting the power and cultural integrity of their own group. Even those blacks and whites generally committed to integration often see the family as the place to draw the line.

One can recognize the importance of racial and cultural difference without subscribing to separatism. One can celebrate a child's racial identity without insisting that a child born with a particular racial make-up must live within a prescribed racial community. One can understand that there are an endless variety of ways for members of racial groups to define their identities and to define themselves in relationship to various groups. One can believe that people are fully capable of loving those who are not biological and racial likes, but are "other," and that it is important that more learn to do so. One can see the elimination of racial hostilities as more important than the promotion of cultural difference.

From this perspective, which is one I share, trans-racial adoptive families constitute an interesting model of how we might better learn to live with one another in this society. These families can work only if there is both appreciation of racial difference and love that transcends such difference. And the evidence indicates that these families *do* work. Accordingly, I believe that current racial matching policies should be abandoned not simply because they violate the law but because they do serious injury to black children in the interest of promoting an unproductive separatist agenda.

What Role Should Race Play?

Assuming that the powerful matching policies of today were abandoned or outlawed, the question would remain: what role, if any, should race play in the agency placement process? Most critics of today's policies focus their criticism on the degree to which race matching principles dominate the placement process, rather than on the fact that race is allowed to play any role at all. They tend to argue for a rule that would allow race to be used as a factor but not an exclusive factor in decision making, and for limits on the delay to which a child can be subjected while a same-race family is sought.

In my view, adoption agencies should clearly be prohibited from exercising *any significant preference* for same-race families.

No delays in placement—whether for six months or one month—should be tolerated in the interest of ensuring a racial match. Delay harms children because, at the very least, it will cause discontinuity and disruption. And any delay risks further delay.

Accordingly, any preference for same-race placement that involves delay or that otherwise threatens the interest of children in receiving good homes should be viewed as unlawful racial discrimination, inconsistent not simply with traditional limits on affirmative action, but with *any* legitimate concept of affirmative action. The courts and administrators responsible for interpreting and enforcing the law should apply established legal principles to find any such preference in violation of the equal protection clause of the Constitution, Title VI of the Civil Rights Act of 1964, and other applicable anti-discrimination mandates.

Children Need Parents

These children urgently need parents who will love them. What is the virtue of starving a child of love so that, eventually, he may learn about his "cultural heritage"? What does it say about the African-American value system that it would deny a child the love for which he or she so desperately yearns, or that it would deny parents the child they want to nurture? What kind of morality stands defiantly in the way of their well-being? What is there left to say about the misguided attempts of 15th-generation black Americans whose sole mission seems to be to indoctrinate children in pseudo-African traditions and cautionary psychobabble about the hardships of "growing up black in America." Surely this cannot be the reason countless kids are forced to wait for years in foster care.

Darlene Addie Kennedy, *Insight*, June 5, 1995.

The only real question, then, is whether agencies should be allowed to exercise a genuinely mild preference. A mild preference would mean that if an agency had qualified black and white families waiting to adopt, it could take race into account in deciding how to allocate the children waiting for homes. The agency could operate on the principle that all things being essentially equal, it would be better to assign black children to black parents and white children to white parents.

There are some valid arguments in support of a mild preference. There is some reason to think that, all things being equal, same-race placements could serve children's interests. There is, for example, reason to fear that white parents might harbor racial attitudes, on a conscious or subconscious level, which

195

would interfere with their ability to appreciate and celebrate their black child's racial self. One has only to step into the world of adoption to realize how widespread and powerful are the feelings among prospective adopters that race matters as they think about what child they will want to adopt. The adoption world is largely peopled by prospective white parents in search of *white* children. The urgency of their race-conscious quest seems to explain much about that world. But reality is complicated. There is tremendous variation among adoptive parents in their racial attitudes.

Dangers

But there would be real dangers in a rule involving even a mild preference. On a symbolic level, it is problematic for the state to mandate or even tolerate a regime in which social agencies, rather than private individuals, decide what shall be the appropriate racial composition of families. It is similarly problematic for the state to decide what the appropriate racial identity for a child is and how it is best nurtured. The Supreme Court decided some time ago that the state should not be in the business of deciding whether inter-racial marriages are wise. Indeed, we would not want to live in a regime in which social agencies prevented such marriages, or prevented inter-racial couples from producing children. Trans-racial adoption is, of course, different from inter-racial marriage in that it involves minor children, many of whom are unable to express their own desires with respect to the kind of family they would like. But it seems dangerous for the state or its agencies to assert that children should not or would not choose to ignore race if they could exercise choice in the formation of their families, and to conclude that it is presumptively in children's best interest to have a same-race upbringing.

The existence of trans-racial adoptive families in which blacks and whites live in a state of mutual love and commitment, and struggle in this context to understand issues of racial and cultural difference, seems a blessing to be celebrated. The state should not be in the business of discouraging the creation of such families.

"We insist our children are Biracial, normal, and potentially very successful."

Children of Mixed-Race Unions Should Be Raised Biracially

Francis Wardle

Francis Wardle, Ph.D., is the director of the Center for the Study of Biracial Children in Denver, Colorado and the father of four biracial children. In the following viewpoint, Wardle takes issue with the idea that raising his children biracially is a betrayal of blacks. He argues that a mixed-race union is an example for America, and mixed-race children are the epitome of a racist-free society. Mixed-race children are proof that the world can live in harmony, he concludes, and should be raised to identify with both of their parents' races.

As you read, consider the following questions:

1. Why does the author argue that mixed-race couples are receiving a lot of criticism from the black community?
2. Why are blacks who marry whites considered traitors in their community, according to Wardle?
3. Why does the author argue that mixed-race families are fulfilling the goals of the civil rights movement?

Francis Wardle, "Are Biracial Children and Interracial Families a Threat to the Progress of Blacks?" *Interrace*, September/October 1992. Reprinted with permission.

Many people deeply involved in the interracial movement have viewed with concern, and some surprise, the increasing objections of Blacks to our relationships, and to the way we choose to raise our children. Every TV talk show that addresses issues of interracial relationships and families includes "experts" who question our sanity, and our commitment to Black history and social consciousness. Recent issues of *Ebony* and *Essence* have accused healthy multiracial individuals of racial and cultural disloyalty; and adoption publications, such as *Ours*, *Adoptive Child*, and self-help books, either flatly insist adopted Biracial children with part-Black ancestry must be raised as Black, or claim (based on the expertise of Black social workers) the only reason the issue of Biracial identity is even discussed is because White adoptive parents wish to deny their child's Black heritage. And many of us have had personal battles with Blacks over these issues: professionals, talk show call-ins, and journalists,

Why are we suddenly receiving opposition from the Black community?

A Need to Eliminate Race

As the interracial movement nationwide is becoming organized, articulate, and assertive about our rights as parents and individuals, some people in the Black community are moving toward a position of cultural pride, separatism, and a hostility toward the concept of integration. The interracial movement now boasts several national publications, many local newsletters, over 60 local education and affiliation groups, and scholarly annual seminars. We are also becoming militant about the need for a category on forms—school, federal, Census Bureau, Head Start, birth certificates—that accurately reflects the racial, national and ethnic identity of our children; and we insist our children are Biracial, normal, and potentially very successful.

There are also many multiracial adults in this country who believe being forced to choose a single identity has deprived them of much of their birthright. These adults are seeking their true roots; and demanding a formal category that recognizes who they are.

At the same time many leaders, and Blacks in high profile positions, view integration as a failure, and feel the only solution to continued prejudice against Blacks in this country is separatism, Black cultural purity, and unified Black political power. This new militancy is a result of many factors, including recent Supreme Court decisions on affirmative action, the apparent failure of busing to improve educational opportunity for Black youngsters, a rediscovery of Malcom X by today's Black youth, and recent startling data about the high mortality rate and incarceration of Black males.

This increasing move toward Black cultural purism views all Black people in the world as belonging to a single, unified, monolithic cultural group; that the Black race and Black cultural group are synonymous, and that belonging to this group is automatically consigned to anyone with any Black genetic heritage, however small.

Naturally Blacks who outmarry are traitors to this new identity movement, and raising children of these interracial unions as anything but Black is totally unacceptable. Since interracial marriage and Biracial children are the purest form of true integration between the races, these new separatists must find a way to ignore us. This is done by declaring our children Black, and that Black children who marry out of their race are abnormal in some way.

Reconciliation Is Possible

Interracial people, biracial people, non-racial people, *whatever* we call ourselves, are the wave of the future. Our growing numbers are the inevitable result of racial integration. The stubborn impasse America has reached by polarizing along Black-White lines will eventually be overcome by the increasing numbers of people who refuse to align themselves on either side. We are living arguments that a reconciliation is possible, inescapable reminders that humanity shares a common heritage, as well as a common future. Integration is a dirty word these days, but we are by our very natures integrated. Real respect, interaction and love *can* cross racial boundaries, and we can hope to rise above these categories that oppress us. To accept anything otherwise would be to deny who I am.

Tav Nyong'o, *Interrace*, January/February 1994.

Part of the need for insisting on this sense of Black cultural unity and inclusion is for political power. In this society numbers mean action. In sophisticated politics-by-demographics, racial groups can wield significant promises from candidates. The argument goes that all Blacks suffer the same indignities and inequalities; therefore they should unite to change those conditions through political power. Since Biracial children will also face similar hardships, they must then be Black and join the Black political struggle.

There is nothing wrong with cultural pride and an affirmation of one's heritage. In fact this concept is essential to the healthy development of all individuals, and the continued mental health of each of us. This is one reason why interracial families insist on a strong sense of inter-cultural pride and heritage in our children. All groups, subgroups, and families must very conscientiously infuse in their children a sense of pride, respect, and celebration of each child's total history and cultural heritage. Children who don't develop this feeling of belonging to a historical human chain become confused and alienated.

Racism

In supporting and bolstering the pride and sense of belonging of our people, we must never put down, denigrate, or belittle others. This is so easy to do: it is the basis of all prejudices. It is also the basic force that created the concept of the pure Aryan race in Germany. It must be remembered that Hitler came to power at a time when Germans felt betrayed, and the doormat of Europe. He galvanized their attention by redefining their national, racial and cultural pride—primarily at the expense of other peoples—Jews and Gypsies. This is a very human process; that is why it is very dangerous.

In any movement toward cultural purism, separatism, and political unity, individuals always lose. The central concept of movements is to suppress the individual aspirations for the good of the whole. The individual who cannot tow the group line is considered a traitor. Psychologically, however, groups exist to empower individuals, not to limit them. Strong, effective groups should be made up of independent individuals who choose to belong to the group because they believe in its goals, methods, and values. Group membership cannot be forced.

And presenting the Black race and cultural group as a single, unified, world-wide entity is not only inaccurate, but denies the tremendous richness of economic, cultural, linguistic, national, political, social and religious diversity that exists within the world-wide Black community. In an article entitled "Growing Up in Interracial Families," author Paul Spivey points out "I have come to realize that the Black community is not the monolith that racial stereotypes often suggest. Rather, American Blacks encompass a broad range of cultures, customs, physical characteristics and thinking."

In the case of the current movement toward Black cultural purism, interracial families are expected to neatly fit into the overall Black community, or to feel as if we are a threat to Black progress, and thus to feel guilty. This is extremely ironic. We are natural allies to the struggle of Blacks in this country. We know better than anyone who is not Black the reality of being Black today. Our children experience many of the insults and challenges Black children encounter. We have a personal commitment to support Black issues in this country. And we view our children as having the rich cultural heritage of Blacks, as well as the history of struggle and persecution.

We view cultural pride and a knowledge of one's history as a positive concept. Many of the non-Black members in interracial marriages are fascinated and enriched by the culture and history of our Black partners. We consider learning about this culture and history, and exposing our children to it, as very positive for our own growth. To us living in a multicultural society means learning more about each other's cultures and respecting all cultures as important and viable. Thus we cannot understand when our Black partner is accused of being disloyal; we cannot understand how this partner's choice of a non-Black spouse in any way weakens that person's sense of cultural and racial pride. The white member of an interracial marriage does not feel he/she is disloyal to his/her race.

Not the Enemy

We continually wonder at this apparent conflict between high-profile Blacks, and the emerging interracial movement. We are very concerned because we don't believe we are an enemy of Black people; we also know many Blacks—including our spouses—who believe interracial marriage and Biracial children are a very positive affirmation of the ability of people of different racial backgrounds to live together in harmony. Many of my Black friends have also been very articulate about their knowledge that Blacks, not only throughout the world, but also in this country, comprise a rich mosaic of cultural, religious, historical and social groups. They mention the differences of rural vs. urban experiences; generations of college-educated relatives vs. those without college; Blacks with a direct historical line from the Caribbean; those with heritages that include Native American, Hispanic or Asian peoples; and Blacks with vastly different religious backgrounds. They point out Blacks in this country have the same level of subgroups and differences as do Native American tribes and the European Americans. In fact, historically, Blacks have been very open to expand the variability and richness within their communities.

We believe the ultimate result of the Civil Rights movement is to allow Blacks to have all the choices the rest of us have, including the choice to marry whomever they wish, and the right to raise their children as they choose.

As a group interracial families believe they are fulfilling the promise of the Civil Rights movement. And we won't let anyone hold us back—white racists, Black cultural purists or so-called professional experts. We have spent so much energy fighting against white racists that we have no patience left. We will feel good about our choice of a life-long marriage partner; we will raise our Biracial children with a rich sense of the culture, history, and heritage of both parents' families, and we will force society to view us as normal, mature, concerned families. And we believe, as famed Harvard psychiatrist, Dr. Alvin Poussaint, said, "It seems clear that a lot of the myths that a lot of people have about these (Biracial) children, their chances of success, their ability to cope, the capabilities of their parents, are that—myths. All in all they represent a rather successful group in this society."

Borrowing

I am Multiracial—multicultural, even. My parents both are from mixed Black, White and Native American families. As a result, I grew up with a rather ambiguous ethnic/racial self-identity in a world where racial nametags are slapped on according to physical appearance. I have been labeled "Black" because that portion of my ancestry is most obvious and because of society's standards of what each race looks like or is supposed to look like. However, it has been hard accepting that while I am "Black" to the majority, I don't "feel" totally Black. I feel a part of each piece of my ancestral puzzle; this is reflected in my dress and my speech, both of which are as colorful as my ancestry. I don't feel a strong affiliation with *any* one race, so I "borrow" from all of them.

Belinda Paschal, *Interrace*, January/February 1993.

We also want to help in the fight to address conditions for Black Americans: improve schools, address inequalities in employment and law enforcement, seek ways to strengthen the Black family, and reduce the senseless death of Black youth through violence and drugs. We are so aware of the need to improve conditions for so many Blacks in this country that we are very puzzled some high-profile Blacks spend time and energy fighting us.

Insisting on Our Rights

We are not the enemy. But we will insist on our rights. Don't tell us we are disloyal. Don't tell us we are ashamed of the Black heritage of our children. Don't insist we must raise our children to belong to a distinctive (and arbitrary) racial or ethnic category. Don't say that history and society must define who we are and what we want our children to become. And don't force us to choose between supporting Black issues and protecting our right to have a normal relationship and raise our children as we choose.

We cannot allow anyone to attack us. We cannot tolerate high-profile media programs continually portraying us as freaks and fools. We cannot afford to raise our children with an isolated, siege mentality. We must be pro-active. We will be pro-active.

Are we a threat to Blacks and their continual struggle? We don't believe we are. We believe we are strong supporters and advocates. And we know many individual Blacks throughout the country who also support us. Hopefully, they will influence producers, journalists, political leaders, and talk show guests. We belong on the same side. We must unite our energy and commitment to attack our common enemies.

"My mixed-race children were *Black—on their own and at their own peril, on the street, in school, in America."*

Children of Mixed-Race Unions Should Not Be Raised Biracially

Hettie Jones

Hettie Jones is the author of *How I Became Hettie Jones* and *Big Star Fallin' Mama: Five Women in Black Music*. She is also a white woman who married a black man and raised mixed-race children. In the following viewpoint, Jones explains why she believes that children of mixed-race families need to be raised black, and not told they are merely "half" black. She argues that in the eyes of society, her children are black and, even though she may prefer the world to be more accepting, it is not.

As you read, consider the following questions:

1. What anecdotes does the author offer to support her argument that she and her daughters are seen as very different in the eyes of society?
2. Why does the author believe that raising her daughters as blacks did them justice?
3. Jones concludes with an anecdote about her daughter. How does it reinforce her beliefs that she did the right thing?

Hettie Jones, "Mama's White," *Essence*, May 1994. Reprinted with permission.

I'm at a crowded lingerie counter with my teenage daughter. She's looking down at the bras on display, her soft hands spread on the glass, her fingernails like little shells. She's such a peach; I love her to death. But I don't need a bra, I'm only along with the credit card, so I glance up just as the woman on the far side of my daughter also looks up. Noting she's next to a Black person, her expression changes, and she pulls away. Even after years of mothering this child, my rage starts like a chill, then heats. I have to look away to calm down. Will I ever learn—learn to cope like Black people, although I'm White?

I married in 1958. He: a short, fast, funny young African-American. I: a shorter, bold, cheerful little Semite. Within a few years we had two daughters. I learned that racism had to be expected. You'd think by the time I got to that lingerie counter I'd have been used to it.

This was my mother-in-law's phrase: "You'll get used to it." She said it the first time I showed up in a fit—a White man on the train had been glaring at *my baby*. Those, too, were the words she used: "My babies," she'd say, reaching for the children she loved and claimed. My husband's people never felt, as did my own, that I'd shown them a future they couldn't embrace. By now it's been 35 years. My daughters are grown, Black, strong. And I'm still White—but not quite.

Racial Differences

Not quite White isn't Black: I've got this straight. And no way to convert. "No one," said Godfrey Cambridge, "can give you Black lessons." The racial difference between my children and me was apparent. There'd always be someone around to gawk, to blurt out "She's your *mother?*" Or whisper, politely, "Your daughter is . . . isn't she . . . *Black?*" Variations on this theme—hostile or not—have occurred through the years. One of my all-time favorites: An older Black man in an airport terminal, watching our welcome-home hug, said, kindly if ambivalently, "Well, *somebody's* glad to see *somebody*." While behind him, an all-White crowd murmured and tittered, protected by their color and free to turn our private love to public spectacle. The clarity of that moment convinced me—and something about me had been altered. This transformation has stayed with me since. If White remains how I'm seen, what's changed, what I mean by "not quite White," is how I see. It's more than perspective and hard to explain. Some years ago in a story, I came up with this: "The angle is bent, the light refracted, mostly the paranoia is extended." I wrote that after I'd become a single parent, worried about my growing daughters' mental health and physical safety in a world I could see would be harsher to them than to me.

In a recent news account of transracial adoption, White parents told of their shock and dismay at name calling, cold stares, the chill of being ignored. One father asked, "How do you help them through that?"

Helping, it seemed to me, consisted first of not hindering. To call them half-Black didn't suffice. A rabbi once told me, "He who sits on der fence rips der pents." When I was pregnant my husband cautioned, "One-half makes you whole." I encouraged my daughters to set their own terms and establish themselves independent of me. I thought an African-American identity— pride in its vibrancy and the strength to overcome its hardships—could only bring them happiness.

Regretting Classifications

My mother is White. I am Black. This is how I choose to define myself, and this is how America chooses to define me. I have no regrets about my "racial classification" other than to lament, off and on, that classifications exist, period.

Lisa Jones, *Essence*, May 1994.

I also felt it would do them justice. My mixed-race children *were* Black—on their own and at their own peril, on the street, in school, in America, as they looked at American history and into the mirror at the faces they showed to the world, and even when they weren't recognized as Black and for their sanity had to explain themselves.

Of course, it's tough when your mother resembles the villain as well as every Momlike thing you love. In the innocent act of bearing these children, it didn't occur to me that claiming me might sometimes be hard for them. I hadn't envisioned the full range of White *or* Black response—all the way from love and acceptance to anger and mistrust. It was they who bore the brunt. They have all my respect.

Racial difference brought us different experiences, yes, but it didn't make us essentially different; it was something to see, perhaps, but never to feel. It didn't exist when I nursed my daughters and dressed them and hauled them to clinics and school and the dentist. It wasn't the point as I watched them grow and develop. They were just *mine*, beloved companions, my very best girls.

And when they needed backup, that was me. Those were the times that added a bitter taste to my broader vision. In one of my stories from the seventies, a White mother (me) goes to school to defend her Black daughter's use of African fabric in a sewing project. There'd be no one skilled, the home-ec teacher had assumed, to help this Black child cut a print. But facing an angry—unexpectedly *White*—mother, she gives in. Later the mother thinks of her husband's grandmother's fine quilts, a tradition she herself can't offer, and she weeps that sometimes all she can do for her children is *be White.*

Learning the hard way takes a toll. I felt defeated sometimes, and ill-equipped. My mother-in-law was legally that title for only seven years, but all the rest of her life she was Gramma, and my friend. I can still feel her hand on my arm, and her soft, firm, steady voice: "You got to take the bitter with the sweet."

Black Families

That sweet, what Langston Hughes called "the sweet flypaper of life," has made the most difference. In African-American culture, in its splendid music and art and humor, I found a place for my own exuberant nature. I found friends. Women, especially, have held out their hands. Gramma left us a host of caring aunts. When my daughter asks, "Mom, how did you know what to do with our hair?" a flood of memories rush to answer. I see a kitchen, a curling iron in the stove, her aunt and I, at 25, exchanging hair lore. I think of my girlfriend's Afro in the fifties, before that hairstyle had a name, and in the sixties the mohawked musician we knew and our downstairs neighbor's headful of little dreadlocks. African-Americans opened my eyes to a world of possibility. All I ever had to do was take my kids in hand and get there.

Accepting Black generosity, I've had to learn to understand hostility. I've lived through good and bad times, through awkward situations; sometimes I've had to listen to what was hard to hear. In her collection of personal essays, *Pushed Back to Strength: A Black Woman's Journey Home* (Beacon Press, 1993), Spelman professor Gloria Wade-Gayles titles a chapter "The Dilemma of Black Rage and White Friends." The latter, it seems to me, should be the first to understand the former.

I haven't forgotten, either, that walking down the street alone I've got White all over my face. Even with the thumping heart of my anger, without my children I'm anonymously White. In all-White rooms, I'm part of the crowd.

By using this anonymity—the spy detail, I call it—I've learned to cope with what I see. I feel every writer is obliged to bear witness to her time. As Malcolm X suggested Whites do, I take my stories about race to White communities, to confront them with and help them confront their prejudices. But I must also speak to the people who help me deal with my own experience, and most of them are African-American.

Here's a story that starts in my neighborhood five-and-ten. A young Black man—hardly more than a boy—hurries in out of the rain and asks the cashier for a plastic bag. He's clutching some packages, which easily could be books as there are two universities within spitting distance.

"Seventy-five cents," says the cashier.

"Seventy-five cents for a plastic bag?"

"Yes," she barks, and he turns and walks out the door.

"Those people," she says to me. "Always want something for nothing."

"What people?" I ask.

"The . . . homeless," she says.

"That kid wasn't . . ."

"There are jobs in McDonald's and Burger King," she says, cutting me off and reaching past me toward the person next in line.

An Interview with Mom

I've got my pad and pen out, and she's laughing at my efficiency. "Mom, not how, but why did you become Hettie Jones?"

"After the breakup of my marriage, she explains, "people asked me why I didn't change my name, why I didn't, quote, 'go back to the Jews.' There was no going back to something that denied you."

"And why was it important to you that we be Black and not 'biracial'?"

"I was not about to delude you guys into thinking you could be anything different in this country. And, frankly, I didn't think that being anything other than Black would be any more desirable."

Lisa Jones, *Essence*, May 1994.

I leave the store furious, of course. I've handed this woman my money for years. I walk along plotting ways to shame her. Since I'll never, *ever*, get used to this, I think maybe I'm not supposed to. I remember a story I wrote long ago, about a White mother of Black children and a White man she thinks is attractive—until he utters a word that opens between them a chasm as wide as a river, full of her shocked pain and his oblivion. She leaves him thinking, *Nothing, nothing is the same.*

Later when I go to my local Xerox store, I'm down in the dumps. There's a school strike on, and a duo—tall White mother and tall, dark-skinned, neatly dreadlocked daughter—are in the store. We get to talking. "Hangin' with Mom?" I ask the girl, about 10.

"Mom wishes she were in *school*," says the mother. The two of them go eye to eye in happy disagreement. They seem to have equal amounts of spirit and self-regard. They love each other, it's clear. They cheer me right up.

Telling My Daughter

I go home thinking about all this. I call the daughter who happens to be in town to tell her.

"So, Mom," she says, "how do these events connect? What's the point?"

Connect? Point? I hang up wondering. Each encounter reveals something else about race to me; connected, they show the paradox of its relevance and irrelevance—it's at once absolutely important and altogether insignificant. But that's just the way I see it. The point is that tomorrow the little girl will face the cashier. I want my voice among those who defend her—and every other Black person. If all I can do is keep writing, I'll write to come up with the rest of the story, in which the cashier gets her comeuppance in a triumphantly multicultural American future. In the final stages of an evolutionary process, says the scientist Lewis Thomas, predators who have agreed to get along can't get along *without* each other.

Meantime—and there's plenty of meantime—I'm for getting along while we're still as we are, while my daughters and I make our way in the America we've got. We're just three American women these days, leading women's lives. We see one another in the mirror all the time, all our straight and nappy hair, our PMS and sex lives and the circles under our eyes. We've even stuck around long enough to be recognized as family. Recently while shopping, we were spied by a grocer (White) and then by a druggist (Black).

"How did you guess?" we asked.

"You look exactly alike," the grocer said. The answer, although genuine, left out specifics.

The druggist came a bit closer. After some thought, and further inspection, she said, "The *shape* of your face is the same."

As is the shape of our feelings. Since I helped them to be themselves, my daughters have responded in kind. Recently, one of them wrote that she'd never go anyplace, "by way of geography or ideology," where she couldn't bring her mother. I thought of the hands I used to hold on our way to Gramma's, the women's hands extended to me today. The way I reached for them, they reach for me. Flesh of my flesh, and me walking proudly between.

"Interracial couples marry for the same reasons same-race couples marry—love, security, and compatibility."

Interracial Marriage Is Identical to Same-Race Marriage

Candy Mills

In the following viewpoint, Candy Mills attacks several myths about interracial marriage, concluding that interracial couples are not pathological, but merely in love and wanting to spend the rest of their lives together. She argues that people who cannot view this simple fact as a reality are harboring deep prejudices against miscegenation. Mills is the publisher and founding editor of *Interrace* magazine.

As you read, consider the following questions:

1. What is the economic myth about mixed-race couples, according to Mills?
2. Why does Mills believe that those who question mixed-race marriages always view the white partner as the more difficult one to understand?
3. Why does the author argue that it is wrong to generalize about mixed-race couples?

Candy Mills, "Mixed Couples: Popular Myths About Interracial Couples," *Interrace*, May/June 1992. Reprinted with permission.

The increase in the number of interracial couples has not necessarily led to an increase in the acceptance of such unions. Many researchers have reflected this view in their formulation of theories (ulterior motives) as to why two people of different races would desire one another. Most of these theories are speculative at best and unrelated to the true motives of interracially involved persons. . . .

Social and/or Economic Mobility

This is probably the most perpetuated myth about interracial couples—that minorities date and marry Whites to "escape" from their oppressed "situation." It is also believed that this "escape" can lead to higher economic and social status. This may hold true from an economic standpoint if the man is White and the female is, say, Black, due to the fact that Black men earn substantially less, on average, than White men. However, since the vast majority of Black-White interracial relationships and marriages are between Black men and White women (*Black men are nearly three times more likely to intermarry than Black women*), and since White women earn substantially less, on average, than men (Black or White), a Black man–White woman intermarriage is unlikely to result in widening the economic horizons of the Black man.

As for one's social standing, most Black men who marry White women bring their White women back into the Black community to live. In most Black communities today, a Black man with a White woman is generally seen as being "politically incorrect" and in many cases actually lowers the social standing of the Black man. This does not hold true. however, for minority females who marry White men as they (White men) are more inclined to settle their women of color in White communities. This may very well be seen as advancement assuming the minority female is uneducated, poverty-stricken, and/or incapable of making her own way. However, evidence shows that interracially married couples, not unlike same-race couples, generally share similar economic, social and educational backgrounds.

In 1964, A.I. Gordon noted in *Intermarriage: Interfaith, Interracial, Interethnic*, "the White man's suspicion that the Negro is seeking to escape from his own people through interracial marriage is nothing more than the rationalization of prejudice."

Rebellion

Another widely believed "cause" of intermarriage is the White person's need to rebel against his/her family. Although this could be the case where the extended family is against the interracial union, it is clearly not the case where the extended family is supportive. Society, as a whole, is, for the most part, not favorably disposed toward such relationships and in this case the White partner could be seen as rebelling against society. This rebellion is viewed by some as being romantic—"you and me against the world." However, the weakness of this argument lies in the fact that "peer pressure" usually leads persons to conform rather than defy the rules and customs of the greater social order. Thus, people are more likely not to intermarry because they are aware of the "repercussions." And those who do intermarry are generally not concerned with what strangers think of their unions.

Celebrate

To all the couples out there I'd advise them to really look into themselves, search their souls, and think very hard about 'is this true,' what we feel between the two of us? And once you are certain about your feelings do not worry what the world will say. Really! That is what will make your marriage work—that you are so certain that you belong together, that you have a great deal in common, that you are still individuals, and that you are dedicated to certain beliefs and one of which is that all human beings are equal regardless of the color or race that they come in. And above all, believe that love is the bond that binds all of us together. There is nothing to be ashamed of, nothing to apologize for and everything to celebrate in bringing two worlds together.

Mark Mathabane, *Interrace*, June 1992.

Some believe that partners in interracial relationships are self-loathing or resentful of their parents. For this the partner (usually the White partner) must be "treated." A Black person who is involved in an interracial relationship is usually labeled a "traitor" to his/her race. In this case, the White partner is usually seen as the devil, oppressor, rapist (from slave days), and the enemy. Thus, Black persons who "sleep with the enemy" or "dance with the devil" must hate themselves (their "Black culture"). This assumption suggests that Whites possess power over non-White persons by virtue of being born White. In the case where the man is non-White and the woman is White, one cannot so conveniently assume that the White woman is superior over the non-White man. It is clear that, even today, females of any color are considered "inferior" to men in general. After all, the anti-miscegenation laws of yesteryear were established to "protect" White women from men of color (particularly Black men).

It is also useful to note that it is usually the White partner who is considered mentally ill for loving a non-White partner.

Thus, the White partner is believed to be unstable and, in this case, is clearly incapable of oppressing anyone.

Sexual Curiosity, Preoccupation, or Revenge

As played out in Spike Lee's interracial film *Jungle Fever* (1991), it is widely believed that the nature of interracial relationships is primarily sexual. Partners of different races are believed to be preoccupied with the "forbidden fruit." Generally, White women are viewed as the "forbidden fruit"; and Black men as the sexually curious. It is believed that Black men enter into marriage with White women purely to take revenge upon the White man. In cases where the male partners are White, it is non-White females who are then considered forbidden. White men are therefore believed to be just as preoccupied with the sexual aspect of women of color as Black men are supposedly with White women. Not only is this theory racist but sexist as well. In both cases, the female is dehumanized and viewed as a sexual toy to be used and manipulated by men of *any* color.

Exhibitionism

It is believed that celebrity interracial couples parade their marriages for shock value or publicity.

Although these couples are in the public eye, their private lives (i.e., their marriages) are often kept very quiet. Many of these couples refuse to do interviews regarding their interracial unions and fight very hard to not be labeled as an interracial couple. Even today, many people still view interracial relationships adversely, and, as a result, it is more likely that such relationships will be carried on in secrecy.

Prohibitions Based on Racial Groupings

Although anti-miscegenation laws (laws against interracial marriage) no longer exist, the attitude of keeping the races separate from one another still prevails. This separatist view is based on the belief that there are distinct and inherent biological differences between the races. In such an order, Whites are first and Blacks last. This explains why children of interracial unions have been historically given names expressing contamination or scorn, i.e., *half-breeds, mulattos*. Just one drop of "Black blood" is all that is needed to taint the purity of the White Race.

There are three standard races: Caucasoid, Negroid, and Mongoloid. However, there is no scientific definition of race. Due to racial "mixing," since the beginning of mankind, it is almost impossible to distinguish between the characteristics of one "racial" group to the exclusion of all others.

Since the majority of us are made up of percentages of genes from a variety of races, no matter how slight, the classification of peoples as simply Caucasoid, Negroid or Mongoloid is out-dated and racist.

Prohibitions Based on Religious Bias

In 1991 an interracial couple (Black/White man–White woman) made national news when a priest refused to marry the couple because it went against his "religious" beliefs. Often "religious" reasons are cited for prohibitions against interracial unions. An often cited passage is Numbers 12:1—"Then Miriam and Aaron spoke against Moses because of the Ethiopian woman whom he had married; for he had married an Ethiopian woman" (New King James Version). However, it is almost never added that Aaron and Miriam were punished by God for their anti-interracial sentiment. Both were stricken with leprosy for a seven-day period. Aaron and Miriam never again spoke up against Moses and his Ethiopian wife. Passages that clarify who we are free to marry are also rarely cited. 1 Corinthians 7:39 reads "A wife is bound by law as long as her husband lives, but if her husband dies, she is at liberty to be married to whom she wishes, only in the Lord." According to this scripture, a woman is free to marry any man, as long as he is a believer.

Support Interracial Marriage

Let's rejoice over the beautiful children born to interracial marriages and do everything possible to make them fully accepted. Let's recognize the contributions intermarriage can make toward breaking down prejudice. . . . Let's take the lead in defending, protecting, and supporting them in our churches.

Our theology says Christ came to make all things new, where there is "neither Jew nor Greek." Can we see the beauty of Black and White love as easily as we see love within a particular race? Can we equally celebrate the potential of a biracial child, a White child, a Black child? And as Christians, can we begin to lead the way?

Harold Myra, *Christianity Today*, March 7, 1994.

If God intended for the races to "mix," he would have never separated them in the first place, many people believe. This belief is based on the pseudo-scientific notion of race. What is White? What is Black? What is Asian? And in the first place, if God had, indeed, intended for the races to remain separate, as an omnipotent being, God could have seen to it that the "different races" would have remained foreign to one another (not aware of the others' existence in the same way we are not

214

aware or certain of extra-terrestrial life). Why not put Whites on Pluto, Blacks on Mars, and Asians on Saturn?

Of course, there are couples who intermarry who are seeking social and/or economic status, who are rebellious, who are self-hating, and who are sexually curious. However, to theorize and/or generalize that every interracial couple suffers from the above frailties is unfair and unethical from a social science standpoint. And to ascribe these "motives" to specifically inter-racial couples smacks of racism. There are many individuals in-volved in same-race relationships who seek social and/or eco-nomic status (women marrying rich or professional men or vice versa, for example), who are rebellious, who are self-hating, and who are sexually curious, but this is generally viewed as normal behavior. Women who marry rich or professional men of the same race are praised in our society for "marrying well." Isn't it the dream of most little girls to grow up to marry a doctor, a lawyer, a millionaire? However, White women who marry rich Black men, or Black women who marry rich White men, etc., are viewed as being irrational or immoral. To specifically at-tribute such motives as sexual, social and economic fulfillment behind a couple's decision to intermarry is misguided at best and racist at worst.

Interviews with small sample groups of interracial couples or those who seek psychiatric help or marriage counseling, or who are unsuccessful in their relationships, should not serve as the basis for the formulation of theories as to why, in general, peo-ple of different races date and marry. We exist as individuals and thus, should be judged accordingly.

For the most part, interracial couples marry for the same reasons same-race couples marry—love, security, and compati-bility.

> *"Too many black men still fear—and at the same time are so insecure that they need—the thrill that comes with . . . owning . . . the ultimate trophy, the All-American beauty queen, blond and blue-eyed."*

Interracial Marriage Cannot Be Treated Identically to Same-Race Marriage

Jacqueline Adams

Jacqueline Adams is a CBS News correspondent. In the following viewpoint, Adams uses the 1994-1995 murder trial of O.J. Simpson as a launching point to discuss interracial marriage and society's reaction to it. She believes that interracial marriage, for both blacks and whites, has serious racial implications.

As you read, consider the following questions:

1. Why does Adams believe that most of the time blacks are invisible to whites?
2. What types of racial issues does interracial marriage bring out, according to the author?

Months after O.J. Simpson's arrest and the endless public dissection of his family's tragedy, the poll results finally came in. And guess what? Black and white Americans view the case differently.

Surprise, surprise!

Yet the glare bouncing off the O.J. story illuminates wounds I would just as soon ignore, wounds in the hearts of all victims of racism, deep wounds in the psyches of black women and black men.

Most of the time we feel invisible, we middle-class, upwardly mobile, more or less successful African-Americans. Yes, you can pick out a few of us in almost any setting: a posh dinner party, a gathering of corporate vice presidents, even a network newscast. Whites may catch a glimpse of those of us who sing or dance or boast a 2,000-yard career rushing record—those of us who entertain.

But from where I sit, it seems as though white Americans, whether powerful or powerless, truly perceive us only when they're looking down their noses or recoiling in fear or disgust.

It's called racism. It's subtle and omnipresent, and it's driving those poll numbers. It's the reason so many African-Americans doubt that the media would have jumped on the O.J. story with such lip-smacking vigor if O.J. had been accused of murdering his first wife, a black woman; if a white man had been accused of murdering a black woman; or even if a white celebrity had been accused of murdering his wife.

No, the polls reflect a largely unrecognized but very real predicament for blacks who try to live the American dream: a fear that O.J. may be punished, may be put in his place for looking past the face he sees in the mirror every morning, for forgetting the reality of racism, for thinking or acting as if he were white.

The White Wife

I don't want to diminish the horror of the crime. Someone— and perhaps it *was* O.J.—brutally killed the mother of two small children and a young man named Ronald Goldman. Everyone identifies with their pain, especially her pain, both in life and in death. Everyone wants the murderer punished. But Nicole. Nicole. She embodies a little discussed wound in the heart of many African-Americans: the *white wife*.

Many black women feel anger or resentment when they see a "brother" with a white woman. I haven't, largely because I don't have the time or inclination to dictate to others whom they should love. But after the O.J. Simpson story broke, I began to see the twisted, pivotal role racism seems to play in interracial love affairs.

217

The Simpson tragedy has left the black men I talk to hurt, bitter and sad. Too many are whispering, "There but for the grace of God go I." Not because of the violence that was clearly part of the marriage. Not because of the passion. Not because a childhood hero has fallen. But because of the white woman.

Plantation Mentality

I'd thought, or at least hoped, that we'd got over all that. But the plantation mentality lives, even in 1994. Too many black men still fear—and at the same time are so insecure that they need—the thrill that comes with breaking a taboo: showing off—owning, if you will—the ultimate trophy, the All-American beauty queen, blond and blue-eyed.

I didn't realize the depth of this insecurity until I heard two black men, in separate conversations, utter identical reactions. Two men at opposite ends of the corporate organizational chart, two men with widely different educational and geographical backgrounds, and both said "God, if only Nicole hadn't been white! If only O.J. hadn't spent so much money on her!"

Being White Enough

Lisa Bligen, twenty-eight, a black freelance writer in New York City, says she would never date a white man. "They just don't stand out to me," she says, "and besides, my family wouldn't be happy." As for all those black men with white women, "Based on what I've observed over time, it's not like the black men go for the cream of the crop. She doesn't have to be either a Rockefeller or Madonna; being white is enough. On the other hand, when I see a white man with a black woman, it's always a certain kind of black woman—she's just as well dressed, just as important-looking, just as sophisticated-looking as he is. She's someone who made him reach across racial lines."

Elizabeth Stone, *Glamour*, February 1992.

Money! How insensitive! The woman's *dead*, I said. Almost decapitated just yards from her sleeping children. Slavery was abolished more than a century ago. She wasn't property! Living with O.J. for half her life, she certainly earned whatever he gave her, and apparently gave willingly. What could those two very different men be talking about? They were talking about themselves. I learned that each had had a serious relationship with a white woman, a long-haired, All-American beauty queen. Both said they'd truly been in love.

One man threw the relationship away. Interracial couples still

218

draw sidelong glances and raised eyebrows, he said, and he couldn't have dealt with that stigma. He was sure the pressure would have made him snap. What an honest assessment, I thought, and how sad that he felt he had to lose this love because of the prejudice and ignorance of others. Because of racism.

Marriage as Power

The other man married his beauty queen, a showgirl. He said she was his Aladdin's lamp; she gave him the power to do anything, made him better than he was. He reveled in the sidelong glances, all those white boys wondering, Why does he have that white woman? O.J. was like that, he concluded. Nicole had been bought and paid for; she was a woman any man would want but only O.J. could have. This man felt that in his own way, he'd experienced the same thing, and believed that he, like O.J., would decide when it was over—not some court.

Sex. Power. Obsession. These are themes that transcend race, universal themes that have fascinated people for centuries. These were the subjects that I wanted to draw lessons from— hide behind. For me, they were safer than issues of racism and male insecurity. Nicole's trophy value hadn't entered my mind before because I hadn't wanted to see the inner turmoil of men in general and black men in particular. I did not want to acknowledge any man's need for an Aladdin's lamp. I surely did not want to acknowledge the fragility of a whole people's—my people's—psyche. I did not want to see what white people don't want to see—the cost of racism.

I am afraid of how all this will eventually play out. I'm afraid that . . . O.J., the man, . . . [acquitted, will] be transformed from a great crossover football hero to just another nigger. And in the process, all black people will suffer.

On the surface, my fear may seem unrealistic But the tribe mentality is ancient and strong, particularly for a tribe that feels threatened every day, a tribe that becomes visible only when the spotlight of notoriety, the high beam of shame is turned on. Come the O.J. Simpson trial, . . . I'm afraid that racists may find just another rationale for hatred.

Periodical Bibliography

The following articles have been selected to supplement the diverse views presented in this chapter. Addresses are provided for periodicals not indexed in the *Readers' Guide to Periodical Literature*, the *Alternative Press Index*, or the *Social Sciences Index*.

Jose Arcellana — "Special Relations," *Filipinas*, February 1993. Available from 655 Sutter St., Suite 333, San Francisco, CA 94102.

Jody Frost — "Little Teardrops," *Biracial Child*, no. 6, 1995. Available from PO Box 12048, Atlanta, GA 30355.

Allison Joseph — "White Washed: The Effects of Racism on White-Appearing Children of Integrated Marriages," *Interrace*, May/June 1992. Available from PO Box 12048, Atlanta, GA 30355.

Randall Kennedy — "Orphans of Separatism: The Politics of Transracial Adoption," *Current*, October 1994.

Sonya Kimble — "Brothers Speak Frankly: Black Men, White Women," *Today's Black Woman*, October 1995. Available from 210 Route 4 East, Suite 401, Paramus, NJ 07652.

Janet Lifshin — "Should Whites Be Allowed to Adopt Black Children?" *Interrace*, January/February 1993.

Jim Miller — "Adopting the Black Child: Is It for You?" *Biracial Child*, Spring 1994.

Jan Peters — "Sisters Speak Frankly: Black Women, White Men," *Today's Black Woman*, October 1995.

Nina Shokraii — "Adopting Racism," *Reason*, November 1995.

Rita Simon — "Serving the Children's Interest," *Interrace*, August/September 1994.

Elizabeth Stone — "Love and Bigotry," *Glamour*, February 1992.

Francis Wardle — "Are Biracial Children Successful?" *Biracial Child*, Winter 1994.

Utne Reader — "Perspectives: Eight Views on Adoption," November/December 1991.

For Further Discussion

Chapter 1

1. The authors in this chapter are all concerned about America's unique cultural identity and the threats to it. How does each author define America's culture? Compare and contrast what each author believes to be a threat to America's culture. What are the similarities in their perspectives? What are the differences?

2. Russell Kirk claims that America's culture is distinctly British. Many in this chapter would disagree with him, arguing that America is much more multicultural. Using the articles in this chapter, name three ways in which the United States is similar to England. Can you name three ways that the United States is similar to other nations?

3. Virginia I. Postrel argues that American immigrants have always clung to certain traditions and characteristics of their native lands, yet they are still Americans. Do you agree? Why or why not?

Chapter 2

1. Dinesh D'Souza and Andrew Hacker take opposing positions on the issue of race. D'Souza believes that blacks' problems arise from within their own culture, while Hacker believes that racism in society is to blame. In each viewpoint, try to find two supporting arguments that you personally agree with. Why do you agree with them? Is it possible to find valid arguments in both viewpoints?

2. bell hooks and Stephen L. Carter are both prominent black writers, yet they take opposing positions on the need to remain separate from whites. How do hooks's and Carter's opinion of whites differ? How do these differences influence their viewpoints?

3. Although Claud Anderson and Yehudi O. Webster are both arguing about blacks and poverty, their arguments are very dissimilar. Why does Anderson compare blacks to immigrants? What is his point? Why does Webster compare blacks to immigrants? What is his conclusion? Compare and contrast Anderson's and Webster's conclusions about blacks and immigrants. Name one point each makes with which you would also agree.

Chapter 3

1. Examine the graph on page 118 that appears in the Luedtke article. What does it reveal about ethnic and racial attitudes toward hard work? Name several issues about which Americans of different ethnicities and races would agree. What would this prove about immigration, in your opinion?

2. Dwight D. Murphey uses a writing device called scare tactics, or exaggerated language and threats, throughout his viewpoint. Find three examples of his use of scare tactics. How does Murphey's language influence your opinion of his article? Of him?

3. Examine the graph on page 138. What does it reveal about racial and ethnic attitudes toward America? Do you think its findings are accurate? Why or why not? Based on the information in this graph, what would you conclude about immigration?

Chapter 4

1. In general, the authors who support affirmative action in this chapter argue that blacks and other minorities need government help to succeed in the United States. Those who disagree argue that blacks and other minorities no longer need help. What is your opinion—do blacks and minorities need affirmative action? Support your conclusion with facts from the viewpoints in this chapter.

2. Alec R. Levenson and Darrell L. Williams argue that affirmative action is needed because, in American society, employers hire people from their own circle of acquaintances. Do you agree that affirmative action is needed for this reason? Do you think Levenson and Williams are correct when they assert that blacks and whites live mostly within their own racial groups?

3. Linda Chavez argues that affirmative action increases racism by making people believe racism exists and is a problem. She thinks that this focus on race is wrong. Do you agree? Why would Eric Foner, author of viewpoint two in this chapter, disagree with Chavez?

4. What reasons do Lilian and Oscar Handlin give to support their argument that affirmative action has led to a massive lack of responsibility in our society? Do you agree that

people seem to blame the government or others for their personal problems? Why or why not?

Chapter 5

1. Ruth G. McRoy and Elizabeth Bartholet take opposite positions on whether black children should be adopted by white families. In each viewpoint, try to find two supporting arguments with which you agree. Find two with which you disagree.

2. How important do Francis Wardle and Hettie Jones think race is in raising children? On what points about race do they differ?

3. Candy Mills and Jacqueline Adams take opposing positions on the importance of race in interracial marriages. On what points do they disagree? With whom would you agree more? Why?

Organizations to Contact

The editors have compiled the following list of organizations concerned with the issues debated in this book. The descriptions are derived from materials provided by the organizations. All have publications or information available for interested readers. The list was compiled on the date of publication of the present volume; names, addresses, and phone numbers may change. Be aware that many organizations take several weeks or longer to respond to inquiries, so allow as much time as possible.

African Americans for Humanism (AAH)
Box 664
Buffalo, NY 14226
(716) 636-7571

AAH is dedicated to developing humanism in the African-American community through outreach to those who are unchurched and is especially concerned with fighting racism through humanistic education. It publishes the quarterly newsletter *AAH Examiner*.

American Civil Liberties Union (ACLU)
132 W. 43rd St.
New York, NY 10036
(212) 944-9800

The ACLU is a national organization that works to defend Americans' civil rights guaranteed by the U.S. Constitution. The ACLU publishes and distributes policy statements, pamphlets, and the semiannual newsletter *Civil Liberties Alert*.

Anti-Defamation League (ADL)
823 United Nations Plaza
New York, NY 10017
(212) 490-2525

The ADL works to stop the defamation of Jews and to ensure fair treatment for all U.S. citizens. It publishes the periodic *Dimensions* and the quarterly *Facts* magazines.

Association for Multicultural Counseling and Development
c/o American Counseling Association
5999 Stevenson Ave.
Alexandria, VA 22304
(703) 823-9800

This association of professional counselors works to develop programs to improve ethnic and racial empathy and understanding. It publishes the quarterly *Journal of Multicultural Counseling and Development*.

Center for the Applied Study of Prejudice and Ethnoviolence
Stephens Hall Annex
Towson State University
Towson, MD 21204-7097
(410) 838-2435

The center studies responses to violence and intimidation motivated by prejudice. It publishes the quarterly newsletter *Forum* as well as numerous reports.

Center for the Study of Biracial Children
2300 S. Krameria St.
Denver, CO 80222
(303) 692-9008

The center studies biracial children and the unique challenges that face them in a racially conscious society. It publishes papers and studies on these children's success in overcoming prejudice. Call for a list of publications.

Center for the Study of Popular Culture
9911 W. Pico Blvd., Suite 1290
Los Angeles, CA 90035
(800) 752-6562

The center has formed a civil rights project to study and address the effects of affirmative action laws on the nation. The project provides legal assistance to citizens challenging affirmative action and promotes color-blind, equal opportunity for individuals. It publishes and distributes a number of books, including *Liberal Racism*.

Citizens' Commission on Civil Rights (CCCR)
2000 M St. NW, Suite 400
Washington, DC 20036
(202) 659-5565

The CCCR monitors the federal government's enforcement of laws that bar discrimination and promotes equal opportunity for all. It publishes reports on affirmative action and desegregation as well as the book *One Nation Indivisible: The Civil Rights Challenge for the 1990s*.

Hispanic Policy Development Project (HPDP)
1001 Connecticut Ave. NW
Washington, DC 20036
(202) 822-8414

HPDP is a nonprofit organization that encourages analysis of public policies affecting Hispanic youth in the United States, especially in education, employment, and family issues. It publishes a number of books and pamphlets, including *Together Is Better: Building Strong Partnerships Between Schools and Hispanic Parents*.

Interracial Family Alliance
PO Box 16248
Houston, TX 77222
(713) 454-5018

The alliance consists of families that are interracial through marriage, adoption, or biracial birth. Its goals are to strengthen and support the interracial family, to promote acceptance of such families, and to focus on solutions to problems unique to the interracial family. It publishes a newsletter, *Communiqué*.

Interracial Family Circle
PO Box 53290
Washington, DC 20009
(301) 229-7326

This organization seeks to provide a supportive environment for and to affirm the intercultural family as a viable unit. It publishes a monthly newsletter, *Collage*.

Interracial-Intercultural Pride (I-PRIDE)
PO Box 191752
San Francisco, CA 94119-1752
(415) 399-9111

I-PRIDE supports and encourages the well-being and development of children and adults who are of multiethnic and multicultural heritage. It maintains a library and speakers bureau and publishes a monthly newsletter, *I-PRIDE Newsletter*.

Lincoln Institute for Research and Education
2027 Massachusetts Ave. NE
Washington, DC 20036
(202) 223-5110

The institute is a think tank that studies public policy issues affecting the lives of black Americans. It publishes the quarterly *Lincoln Review*.

National Association for the Advancement of Colored People (NAACP)
4805 Mt. Hope Dr.
Baltimore, MD 21215-3297
(410) 358-8900

The NAACP is the oldest and largest civil rights organization in the United States. Its principal objective is to ensure the political, educational, social, and economic equality of minority-group citizens. It publishes a variety of newsletters, books, and pamphlets as well as the monthly magazine *Crisis*.

National Association of Black Social Workers (NABSW)
8436 W. McNichols Rd.
Detroit, MI 48221
(313) 862-6700

NABSW seeks to support, develop, and sponsor programs and projects serving the interests of black communities. It is committed to a policy of same-race adoptions, promoting adoption of black children by black adoptive parents. It publishes the annual *Black Caucus* and occasional position papers.

National Center for Neighborhood Enterprise
1367 Connecticut Ave. NW
Washington, DC 20036
(202) 331-1103

This organization promotes self-sufficiency in low-income communities and the revitalization of urban neighborhoods. It publishes the periodic newsletter *In the News* and *On the Road to Economic Freedom: An Agenda for Black Progress.*

National Coalition to End Racism in America's Child Care System (NCERACCS)
22075 Koths
Taylor, MI 48180
(313) 295-0257

The coalition's goal is to assure that all children requiring placement outside the home, whether through foster care or adoption, are placed in the earliest available home most qualified to meet the child's needs. It believes that in foster care situations, the child should not be moved after initial placement simply to match the child's race or culture. It publishes the quarterly *Children's Voice.*

National Urban League
1111 14th St. NW, 6th Fl.
Washington, DC 20005
(202) 898-1604

A community service agency, the Urban League aims to eliminate institutional racism in the United States. It also provides services for minorities who experience discrimination in employment, housing, welfare, and other areas. It publishes the report *The Price: A Study of the Costs of Racism in America* and the annual *State of Black America.*

Poverty and Race Research Action Council (PRRAC)
1711 Connecticut Ave. NW, Suite 207
Washington, DC 20077-0009
(202) 387-9887

PRRAC is a national organization that promotes research and advocacy on behalf of poor minorities on the issues of race and poverty. It publishes the bimonthly newsletter *Poverty & Race*.

United States Commission on Civil Rights
1121 Vermont Ave. NW
Washington, DC 20425
(202) 376-8177

A fact-finding body, the commission reports directly to Congress and the president on the effectiveness of equal opportunity programs and laws. A catalog of its numerous publications can be obtained from its Publication Management Division.

Bibliography of Books

Claud Anderson   *Black Labor, White Wealth: The Search for Power and Economic Justice.* Edgewood, MD: Duncan & Duncan, 1994.

Derrick A. Bell   *Faces at the Bottom of the Well: The Permanence of Racism.* New York: BasicBooks, 1992.

Richard Bernstein   *Dictatorship of Virtue.* New York: Knopf, 1994.

Peter Brimelow   *Alien Nation: Common Sense About America's Immigration Disaster.* New York: Random House, 1995.

Stephen L. Carter   *Reflections of an Affirmative Action Baby.* New York: BasicBooks, 1991.

Linda Chavez   *Out of the Barrio.* New York: BasicBooks, 1991.

James P. Comer   *Raising Black Children.* New York: Plume, 1992.

Ellis Cose   *A Nation of Strangers: Prejudice, Politics, and the Populating of America.* New York: Morrow, 1992.

Ellis Cose   *The Rage of a Privileged Class.* New York: Harper-Collins, 1993.

Humphrey Dalton, ed.   *Will America Drown? Immigration and the Third World Population Explosion.* New York: Scott Townsend, 1993.

Richard Delgado   *The Rodrigo Chronicles: Conversations About America and Race.* New York: New York University Press, 1995.

Michael Eric Dyson   *Reflecting Black: African-American Cultural Criticism.* Minneapolis: University of Minnesota Press, 1993.

Gerald Early, ed.   *Lure and Loathing: Essays on Race, Identity, and the Ambivalence of Assimilation.* New York: Penguin, 1993.

Audrey Edwards and Craig K. Polite   *Children of the Dream: The Psychology of Black Success.* New York: Doubleday, 1994.

Richard A. Epstein   *Forbidden Grounds: The Case Against Employment Discrimination Laws.* Cambridge, MA: Harvard University Press, 1992.

Gertrude Ezorsky   *Racism and Justice: The Case for Affirmative Action.* Ithaca, NY: Cornell University Press, 1991.

Steven Gregory and Roger Sanjek, eds.   *Race.* New Brunswick, NJ: Rutgers University Press, 1994.

Andrew Hacker	*Two Nations: Black and White, Separate, Hostile, Unequal.* New York: Scribner's, 1992.
bell hooks	*Killing Rage: Ending Racism.* New York: Henry Holt, 1995.
Gerald Horne	*Reversing Discrimination: The Case for Affirmative Action.* New York: International Publishers, 1992.
Robert Hughes	*Culture of Complaint: The Fraying of America.* New York: Oxford University Press, 1993.
Alan L. Keyes	*Masters of the Dream: The Strength and Betrayal of Black America.* New York: Morrow, 1995.
Russell Kirk	*America's British Culture.* New Brunswick, NJ: Transaction, 1993.
Seymour Martin Lipset	*American Exceptionalism: A Double-Edged Sword.* Baltimore: Johns Hopkins University Press, 1996.
Glenn C. Loury	*One by One from the Inside Out: Essays and Reviews on Race and Responsibility in America.* New York: Free Press, 1995.
Wayne Lutton and John Tanton	*The Immigration Invasion.* Petoskey, MI: Social Contract Press, 1994.
Douglas S. Massey and Nancy A. Denton	*American Apartheid: Segregation and the Making of the Underclass.* Cambridge, MA: Harvard University Press, 1993.
Nathan McCall	*Makes Me Wanna Holler: A Young Black Man in America.* New York: Random House, 1994.
John J. Miller	*Strangers at Our Gate: Immigration in the 1990s.* Washington, DC: Center for the New American Community, 1994.
Brent A. Nelson	*America Balkanized: Immigration's Challenge to Government.* Monterey, VA: American Immigration Control Foundation, 1994.
Jan Nederveen Pieterse	*White on Black: Images of Africa and Blacks in Western Popular Culture.* New Haven, CT: Yale University Press, 1992.
David R. Roediger	*Towards the Abolition of Whiteness: Essays on Race, Politics, and Working Class History.* London: Verso, 1994.
David R. Roediger	*The Wages of Whiteness: Race and the Making of the American Working Class.* London: Verso, 1991.
Byron M. Roth	*Prescription for Failure: Race Relations in the Age of Social Science.* New Brunswick, NJ: Transaction, 1994.

Judy Scales-Trent

Notes of a White Black Woman: Race, Color, Community. University Park: Pennsylvania State University Press, 1995.

Arthur Schlesinger

The Disuniting of America. Knoxville, TN: Whittle Direct Books, 1991.

Peter Skerry

Mexican Americans: The Ambivalent Minority. New York: Free Press, 1993.

Paul M. Sniderman and Thomas Piazza

The Scar of Race. Cambridge, MA: Harvard University Press, Belknap Press, 1993.

Thomas Sowell

Race and Culture: A World View. New York: BasicBooks, 1994.

Brent Staples

Parallel Time: Growing Up in Black and White. New York: Pantheon, 1994.

Ronald T. Takaki

A Different Mirror: A History of Multicultural America. Boston: Little, Brown, 1993.

Charles Taylor

Multiculturalism and the Politics of Recognition. Princeton, NJ: Princeton University Press, 1992.

Jared Taylor

Paved with Good Intentions. New York: Carroll & Graf, 1992.

Yehudi O. Webster

The Racialization of America. New York: St. Martin's Press, 1992.

Cornel West

Race Matters. Boston: Beacon Press, 1993.

Steven Yates

Civil Wrongs: What Went Wrong with Affirmative Action. San Francisco: Institute for Contemporary Studies, 1994.

Index

ABC News, 168
Adams, Jacqueline, 216
adoption
    agencies, 185
        idealize biological family, 193
        racism in, 186-87
    racial matching for
        is racist and discriminatory, 190-
            96
        should be encouraged, 184-89
    transracial
        improves racial understanding,
            191, 194, 196
        is preferable to foster care, 188,
            191, 192
*Adoption of Children with Special
    Needs* (Mason & Williams), 186
adoptive families
    high ratio of African American,
        186
    prefer infants, 189, 191
Adoptive Families of America, 187
affirmative action
    aggravates racial tension, 159-64
    combats unintentional racism in
        employment, 154-58
    damages race relations, 146-48
    is divisive, 146, 166, 178-79
    is necessary, 149-53
        because effects of discrimination
            persist, 151, 156-57
        because whites make many
            employment decisions, 155
    is not enough, 165-71
    and quotas, 32, 160
    and reverse discrimination, 144-48,
        166-67
    should be refocused
        for equality of opportunity, not
            preference, 171, 180
        to help the poor, 152-53, 170
Africa, 34, 97
African Americans
    and AIDS, 57, 69
    anger of, 56-58, 79
    are not immigrants, 68, 96, 102
        lack immigrants' advantages, 97,
            98, 99, 101-103, 150
    children. See children; adoption
    come from various backgrounds,
        55, 201
    culture of
        as ennobled sufferers, 91-92

is breaking down 55-56
is mix of ethnic backgrounds, 55,
    201
is undervalued, 43
families, 68, 189, 207
high visibility of, is problematic,
    99-100
    yet so is invisibility of, 168-69,
        217
and Hispanic immigration, 133
history of, 49, 69, 156
    calls for reparation, 100-103
    is unique among minorities, 94,
        95, 96, 151
hold few professional positions,
    155-57
and illegitimacy, 58-59, 170
isolation of, 79
life expectancy of, 69
and persecution complex, 58
politicization of, 74, 79, 199
and politics, 67
and poor self-image, 46-47, 105
and poverty, 107-10, 168
success of, 167-69, 217
in military, 171
see also assimilation; racism
Alger, Horatio, 99
Allen, Anita, 186, 188
American citizenship, 117
    ceremony, 116
    easy to acquire, 139
    intentionality of, 119
American Creed, crisis of, 85-86
American culture
    emphasis on individual rights, 171,
        180
    is ideal, not real, 29
    fragmentation of, 176
    has not fostered equality, 151, 153
    ideological core of, 120
    and immigration, 123-28
    is diverse, 24-30, 120, 164
        yet has own identity, 38, 121-22
    is endangered by ethnic loyalties,
        31-34
        con, 35-39
    is essentially British, 17-23, 164
        con, 117
    is inclusive, 139
    is perceived as depraved, 174-75,
        178
    and race consciousness, 145

232

see also multiculturalism;
  separatism; United States
American Dream, 84-86
Americanism, 122
American Revolution, 110, 117
Americans with Disabilities Act, 173
Amish, 38
Anderson, Claud, 93
Asante, Molefi, 132, 133
Asian Americans, 18, 20, 103, 107
  barred from naturalization until
    1940s, 150
  business success of, 58
  discrimination against, 161
  generally have high income, 140
  have kept ethnic identity, 99, 135
  increasing numbers of, 117-18
  were targeted in L.A. riots, 133
  see also Japanese Americans
assimilation, 37-38, 77
  damages black solidarity, 98
  hampers black success, 72-81
  is failing, 130, 132, 198
    due to outdated Eurocentric
      models, 132-33, 134
  is reserved for nonblack ethnics,
    94, 95
  is rooted in white supremacy, 74,
    75, 76
  is still succeeding, 139-40
  and speaking English, 134, 139
Atlantic Monthly, 133
Auster, Lawrence, 126, 127

Bartholet, Elizabeth, 190
Bell, Derrick, 76, 91-92
Bell Curve, The (Herrnstein & Murray),
  152
Berger, Peter, 92
Bill Cosby Show, 78
Black Rage (Grier and Cobbs), 57
blacks. See African Americans
Bouvier, Leon, 126, 130
Boxill, Bernard, 60
Breitman, George, 80
Brimelow, Peter, 36, 133
Bryce, James, 121

Canada, 33, 127, 130, 140
Carter, Stephen L., 162
Character and Opinion in the United
  States (Santayana), 115
Chavez, Linda, 159
Cherlin, Andrew, 59
Childhood and Society (Erikson), 115
children, 32, 170
  growing numbers in foster care,
    185, 187

mixed-race
  should be reared biracially, 197-
    203
  con, 204-209
  need permanent homes, 191, 194
  need sense of belonging, 200
  older, available for adoption, 189
  see also adoption
Children of the Dream (Polite), 88
Child Welfare League of America,
  187
China, 18, 34
Chinese immigrants, 100
Christianity Today, 214
Chronicle of Higher Education, 29
CIA (Central Intelligence Agency), 98
Cisneros, Sandra, 28, 29
Civil Rights Act, 175, 195
Civil Rights Commission, 140
Civil Rights Leadership Conference,
  166
civil rights movement, 61, 96, 102,
  150
  and interracial families, 201
  now pursues preference, not
    equality, 166, 177, 179
Civil War, 95, 146, 150
Clausen, Christopher, 29
Clinton, Bill, 32
Closing of the American Mind, The
  (Bloom), 25
Cobbs, Price, 57
Columbia College, 150, 152
Columbus, Christopher, 75, 76, 115
Conservative Chronicle, 146
Cubans, 98, 135, 139
Cuddihy, John M., 91
Cultural Bases of Racism and Group
  Oppression (Hodge), 81
Current Population Survey, 155

Dalton, Harlon L., 42
deficiency of black culture, 88-90
deprivation orientation, 90-92
Donahue, Phil, 78
Douglass, Frederick, 62, 79
D'Souza, Dinesh, 54
Du Bois, W.E.B., 56, 62
Dyson, Michael Eric, 69

Eaton, Judith, 84
Edelman, Marian Wright, 55
education, 20, 21, 133
  bilingual, 139
  and ethnic studies, 32
  is Eurocentric, 42-43
  neglects critical thinking, 110
  should be improved in ghettos, 170

should be multicultural, 25, 44, 49-
  50, 75-76, 81
Ehrenreich, Barbara, 167
Eitzen, Stanley, 89
Eliot, T. S., 23
Ellison, Ralph, 62, 168
Elrich, Marc, 45
Elshtain, Jean Bethke, 21
ennobled sufferers, blacks as, 91-92
Epstein, Richard A., 161
Equal Employment Opportunity
  Commission, 173
equality
  varied meanings of, 176-77
Erikson, Erik H., 115
Essence, 198, 206, 208
Eurocentrism, 42-43
  growing rejection of, 18, 19, 20,
  124, 132-23

Fanon, Franz, 48
Farrakhan, Louis, 66
Feagin, Joe, 57
Fishkin, Shelley Fisher, 29, 30
Fitzgerald, F. Scott, 28, 29
Fitzpatrick, Rosemary, 116
Foner, Eric, 149
Freire Paulo, 80
Frost, Robert, 122

Gates, Henry Louis, Jr., 179
Glamour, 218
Glazer, Nathan, 86
Goethe, Johann von, 122
Great Society, the, 173-74, 175, 178
Greenberg, Stanley, 166
Grier, William, 57
guilt, whites', 50, 86, 194

Hacker, Andrew, 64, 96
Hampton, Robert, 60
Handlin, Lilian and Oscar, 172
Harris, William H., 57
Helprin, Mark, 33
Hispanics, 18, 32, 103, 133, 139
  are growing percentage of U.S.
    population, 20, 117, 130-31
  Cuban Americans, 98, 135, 139
  have strong ethnic identity, 99
  include diverse nationalities, 176
  Mexican Americans, 99, 135, 139,
    140, 163
    live near native land, 131-32
    negative stereotypes of, 47-48
    still face disadvantages, 161
    will dominate American
      Southwest, 130-31
Homes for Black Children (Detroit),

187
hooks, bell, 72
Howard University, 87
Hughes, Langston, 46, 207
Hurston, Zora Neale, 65

immigrants
  benefit from affirmative action
    programs, 162
  benefit from black struggle, 96, 97
  Chinese, 100
  Haitian, 126
  have more advantages than blacks,
    97, 98, 99, 150
  shared beliefs of, 118
  various origins of, 18, 20, 117-19,
    137
  see also Asian Americans; Hispanics
immigration
  increases in, 117, 126, 134, 137
  law, 137
    1990 Immigration Act, 140
  may cause interracial conflict, 129-
    35
    con, 136-40
  shapes America's identity, 114-22
  strengthens economy, 126
  threatens American identity, 123-28
  undermines black progress, 95-98,
    101, 102-103
Immigration, Museum of, 116
Immigration Act (1990), 140
Immigration and the Future Racial
  Composition of the United States
  (Bouvier & Davis), 130
Immigration Invasion, The (Lutton &
  Tanton), 124
Insight magazine, 195
Institute for Black Parenting (Los
  Angeles), 187
integration. See assimilation
Intermarriage, Interfaith, Interracial,
  Interethnic (Gordon), 211
Interrace magazine, 192, 199, 202,
  210, 212
interracial marriage, 201
  is identical to same-race marriage,
    210-15
    con, 216-19
  most common among black
    men/white women, 211
  racist assumptions about, 213, 215,
    218
  still frowned on, 205-207, 212

Japanese Americans, 100, 101, 124,
  161
Jefferson, Thomas, 171

Jencks, Christopher, 170
Jews, American, 37, 161
Jim Crow laws, 75, 94, 95
Jobs & Capital, 161
Johnson, Lyndon B., 87, 147, 174
Jones, Hettie, 204
Jones, Howard Mumford, 122
Jones, Lisa, 206, 208
Jordan, June, 56-57
Jungle Fever (movie by Spike Lee), 213

Kennedy, Darlene Addie, 195
King, Martin Luther, Jr., 69, 73, 90, 150
King, Rodney, 48
Kirk, Russell, 17
Kluckhohn, Clyde, 121
Kohn, Hans, 119
Kreyche, Gerald F., 31
Kristol, Irving, 144
Kronus, Sidney, 60

Lacy, Dan, 101
Lamm, Richard D., 130
Lasch, Christopher, 84
Latinos. *See* Hispanics
League of Women Voters, 116
Left, the American, 125
Lemare, James W., 132
Letters from an American Farmer
  (Crevecoeur), 117
Levenson, Alec R., 154
liberalism, 146, 147
liberty, changing nature of, 176-77
Lifshin, Janet S., 192
Lipset, Seymour Martin, 165
Los Angeles riots, 36, 133
Los Angeles Times, 38, 42, 116 119, 133
Loury, Glenn, 59
Luedtke, Luther S., 114
Lure and Loathing (Early, ed.), 97
Lutton, Wayne, 124

Malcolm X, 69, 80, 198, 207
Malveaux, Julianne, 60
Mann, Arthur, 28
Marshall, Thurgood, 78, 177
Martinez, Ruben, 36
Marx, Karl, 19
Mathabane, Mark, 212
McRoy, Ruth G., 184
Mexican Americans. *See under*
  Hispanics
Miles, Jack, 133
Mill, John Stuart, 120
Mills, Candy, 210
Morrison, Toni, 25, 30, 60, 74
Mother Jones magazine, 78
multiculturalism

emphasis on
  is counterproductive, 45-50
  is helpful, 40-44
is divisive, 110, 127, 148, 173
leads to conflict, 34
leads to racial classification, 21
and literary canon, 19, 20, 25-30
supplies new vocabulary, 162
undermines American identity, 163
Murphey, Dwight D., 123
Myra, Harold, 214
Myrdal, Gunnar, 91, 121

NAFTA, (North American Free Trade
  Agreement), 99
Nation magazine, 169
National Academy of Sciences, 169
National Association of Black Social
  Workers, (NABSW), 187, 193
National Longitudinal Survey of
  Youth (NLSY), 155
National Opinion Research Center,
  118
National Park Service, 116
National Review, 36
Native Americans, 18, 33, 50, 75, 76
  migrated from Asia, 96
Navarrett, Ruben, Jr., 38
NBC News, 168
Nelson, Brent A., 129
Nelson, Frank C., 134
Neuman, Elena, 75
Newton, Isaac, 19
New York Times, 175
North American Council on
  Adoptable Children, 186, 187
Notes of a White Black Woman (Scales-
  Trent), 40
Nyong'o, Tav, 199

O.J. Simpson case, 145, 217-19
Orwell, George, 163-64

Page, Clarence, 157
Paschal, Belinda, 202
Pfaff, William, 120
Polite, Craig K., 88
political correctness, 94, 211
Population Reference Bureau, 126
Postrel, Virginia I., 35
Poussaint, Alvin, 55, 202
poverty, 60, 107-109, 168
  and affirmative action, 153

racial classification
  absurdity of, 148, 213-14
  of African Americans
    is by skin color only, 86, 99, 145

235

dangers of, 33
divisive nature of, 206
leads to misleading comparisons,
  105-107, 108
leads to separatism/fragmentation,
  22
overlooks important factors, 106-107
produces negative self-image, 105
Racialization of America, The
  (Webster), 109
racial matching. *See under* adoption
racism, 65, 66, 69
  and adoption agencies, 186-87
  causes black inequality, 64-71
  con, 54-63
  causes economic problems for
    blacks, 93-103
  confused definitions of, 127-28
  does not explain black poverty,
    104-10
  feminist attempts to overcome, 79,
    81
  persistence of, 70-71, 74
  stereotypes of, 46-48, 213
  can be broken, 91
  victims of, 83-92
Rand, Ayn, 86
Raspberry, William, 90, 167
Reagan era, 167
Reason magazine, 35
Reconstruction, 186, 188
Reisman, George, 92
riots, Los Angeles, 36, 133
Robinson, Lillian S., 24
Roosevelt, Franklin Delano, 124, 174

San Diego Union-Tribune, 133, 157
Santayana, George, 115
Scales-Trent, Judy, 40
Schlesinger, Arthur, Jr., 21, 22, 36
school desegregation, 32, 78, 146-47
Schuck, Peter H., 136
Search for a Common Ground, The
  (Thurman), 76
Sennett, Richard, 84, 92
separatism, 127, 130
  and black cultural purism, 198, 199
  chosen by blacks, 180
  dangers of, 200
  encouraged by civil rights
    movement, 175-76
  and ethnic conflict, 33, 34, 130
  influences adoption issues, 193-94
  and interracial marriage, 213
Shakespeare, William, 19, 20, 27, 29
Sikes, Melvin, 57
Sister Outsider (Lorde), 79
Smith, James P., 169
social problems theory, 87-88

South Africa, 34, 73, 78, 145
Southwest (U.S.), 127, 130, 131, 132
Sowell, Thomas, 21, 22
Spivey, Paul, 200
Staples, Robert, 97
Steele, Shelby, 175
Stone, Elizabeth, 218
Sullivan, Ann, 187

Tabuena, Jose A., 163
Tanton, John, 124
Texas Monthly, 28, 29
They Came Before Columbus (Van
  Sertima), 76
Thirty Million Texans? (Bouvier &
  Poston), 126
Thomas, Clarence, 90-91
Thurman, Howard, 76
Time magazine, 27, 167
Toledano, Ralph de, 146
Truman, Harry, 174
Turner, Frederick Jackson, 116
Twain, Mark, 29-30
*Two Nations, Black and White,
  Separate, Hostile, Unequal* (Hacker),
  96

Uncle Toms, 92
United States, 65, 73, 75, 124
  Census Bureau, 115, 126, 198
  Constitution, 119, 120, 177, 195
  expanding population of, 126
  government, 58, 115, 177
  as help to refugees, 97
  historically exercised power by
    consent, 179
  not responsible for alleviating
    discrimination, 172-80
  reparation to Japanese, 101
  should do more for minorities,
    165-71
  history of, needs to be retaught,
    75-76
  is world's sole superpower, 173
  Justice Department, 139
  labor market, 155
  as melting pot, 37, 89, 116, 125,
    137, 138
  is a myth, 26, 98
  Southwest, 127, 130, 131, 132
  State Department, 98
  Supreme Court, 196, 198
  Brown v. Board of Education, 146,
    164
  Loving v. Virginia, 193
University of Chicago statistics, 67
University of Michigan's Institute for
  Social Research, 166
Urban Institute, 167, 168

Urban League, 186

Van den Berghe, Pierre L., 106
victims, of racism, 83-92
Voting Rights Act, 139

Wade-Gayles, Gloria, 207
Walker, Alice, 29
Walljasper, Jay, 26
Wall Street Journal, 33, 168
Walton, Anthony, 55
Wardle, Francis, 197
Washington, Booker T., 61
Washington Post, 168
Webster, Yehudi O., 104, 109
Welch, Finis R., 169
welfare, 84, 86
Weyrich, Paul
white guilt, 50, 194

white liberals
  have betrayed black struggle, 77-78
white supremacy, 73-79
  collective responsibility for, 80
  is more appropriate term than
    racism, 73-74
  unacknowledged by liberals,
    feminists, 79
Whitman, Walt, 120
Wildavsky, Aaron, 83, 86, 87
Wilkins, Roger, 78, 169
Williams, Darrell L., 154
Wilson, August, 65
Wilson, William Julius, 60, 168, 170
Woodward, C. Vann, 84, 86
World Cup, 145
Wortham, Anne, 82

Yale Law School, 136